W9-BUY-204

The Idea of a European Superstate

*

The Idea of a European Superstate

PUBLIC JUSTIFICATION AND
EUROPEAN INTEGRATION

✳

Glyn Morgan

PRINCETON UNIVERSITY PRESS

PRINCETON AND OXFORD

Library of Congress Cataloging-in-Publication Data

Morgan, Glyn, 1958–
The idea of a European superstate : public justification and European
integration / Glyn Morgan.
p. cm.
Includes bibliographical references and index.
ISBN 0-691-12246-6 (cl : alk. paper)
1. European Union. I. Title.
JN30.M676 2005
341.242′2—dc22   2004058687

British Library Cataloging-in-Publication Data is available

This book has been composed in Palatino

Printed on acid-free paper. ∞
pup.princeton.edu

Printed in the United States of America

1 3 5 7 9 10 8 6 4 2

FOR

MY FATHER,

AND IN MEMORY OF

MY MOTHER

*

✳ *Contents* ✳

* Preface *

THIS BOOK considers a variety of justifications for the project of European political integration. I wrote the book to resolve a puzzle. Most of my British nonacademic friends are eurosceptics. Many of them—much like *Daily Mail* and *Daily Telegraph* editorial writers—think that Britain would do well to leave the European Union and form a closer alliance with the United States. Most of my American academic friends approach euroscepticism in much the same way as James Mill is said to have approached Christianity: "with the feelings due not to a mere mental delusion, but to a great moral evil."

The academic literature on the European Union (EU) did not, as I came to discover, offer much guidance in resolving this puzzle. Shelf loads of books exist on every conceivable aspect of the EU. But these books tend, perhaps not surprisingly, to take the EU's existence for granted. Even the normative contributions of European legal and political theorists tend to focus on Europe's current institutional architecture—its alleged democratic deficiencies, for instance—while ignoring the more fundamental justificatory questions raised by an increasingly large and noisy crowd of eurosceptics.

After reflecting on these justificatory questions, I arrived at a conclusion unlikely to appeal to either set of my friends. This book argues that there is much more to be said in favor of a unitary European state—a "European superstate," as those editorial writers would call it—than most people recognize. The more frequently defended alternatives to a European superstate—a Europe of nation-states or some form of postsovereign polity—are, by the same token, much less desirable than commonly believed. Doubtless, this argument will not persuade everyone (or even anyone). Hopefully, my argument will provoke them to produce more convincing justifications for their own preferred alternatives.

While this book takes as its point of departure British eurosceptic criticisms of the EU, the book is directed to a wider audience than those caught up in the quotidian details of the British debate. The question of the justification for European political integration is now an issue for all Europeans. Not only do Europeans—either directly or through their elected representatives—have to take a stance on the constitutional form of the EU. But even when (or if) the current constitutional proposals are ratified by all twenty-five member states, the people of Europe will have to confront some very difficult issues about the scope and character of a future European polity. Ought Europe, for instance, to admit Turkey, Ukraine, and even Russia? How is a European polity to divide responsibilities between the central or federal level of decision making and the national and subnational? How much Europeanwide regulation of the economy is desirable? How much Europeanwide linguistic and cultural uniformity is desirable? It is difficult to address these questions, without arriving first at some settled view of the justification for European political integration.

Even beyond this audience of Europeans, this book takes up a range of topics that ought to be of interest to contemporary political theorists. In recent years, political theorists have started to notice that the sovereign nation-state is neither a ubiquitous fact nor an unalloyed good. We live in an age of increasing cross-boundary flows of people, capital, trade, and ideas. For some observers, the era of the nation-state now lies in the past. Some believe that the European Union provides us with a model of how political units will be organized in the future. There remains, however, one hitch in this story: the United States. One of the arguments of this book is that all talk of the end of sovereignty is premature while the United States, the world's sole superpower, remains a jealous guardian of its own sovereignty. If Europe is to play an effective role in international affairs, it must, in some respects, emulate the United States. A European Union that disperses decision making among twenty-five or more political leaders will always, so I argue, remain weak, ineffectual, and dependent for its security on the United States. There is, in short, more to be said in favor of sovereignty, both internal and external, than many political theorists now like to recognize.

The earliest version of the ideas in this book was worked out in an informal discussion group with Peter Kraus, Andy Moravcsik, and Andrea Sangiovanni at the Minda de Ginsburg Center for European Studies at Harvard University. I am grateful to all three of them for their criticisms, suggestions, and later comments on various versions of the manuscript. Will Phelan and Winn Wasson provided me with some very helpful research assistance. A number of people gave generously of their time to comment on various aspects of my argument. I am especially indebted here to Daniele Archibugi, Richard Bellamy, Lars Erik Cederman, Jeff Friedman, John Gillingham, John Hall, Peter Hall, Hélène Landemore, Melissa Lane, Percy Lehning, Steve Macedo, Jan Werner Müller, Patrizia Nanz, Paul Rosenberg, Nancy Rosenblum, Dennis Thompson, and Richard Tuck. I would also like to thank some anonymous reviewers for providing me with a number of very helpful suggestions for improving the clarity and organization of my argument. Ian Malcolm of Princeton University Press proved to be an extremely savvy and supportive editor.

While writing this book, I received all manner of support from Harvard's Committee on Social Studies and its Government Department. I am especially grateful for the support of my various Chairs, including Seyla Benhabib, Grzegorz Ekiert, Rod Macfarquhar, and Charlie Maier. I would also like to record my gratitude to my political theory colleagues. The multiple perspectives and provocations provided by Sharon Krause, Harvey Mansfield, Pratap Mehta, Russ Muirhead, Nancy Rosenblum, Michael Sandel, Christina Tarnopolsky, Dennis Thompson, and Richard Tuck make for an extremely congenial and lively intellectual atmosphere.

A number of other people deserve a special mention. Istvan Hont, who was visiting from the other Cambridge while I was writing this book, proved an enormously stimulating colleague. Despite the fact that he would yell at me a lot for misunderstanding the point he was trying to make, Istvan taught me a great deal about sovereignty, commerce, the nation-state, and their intellectual histories. While I cannot address all the issues raised by his important work on these topics, I hope to do so in the future. Russ Muirhead listened to most of my arguments many times. He also read various half-baked versions of these chapters and provided me with lots of sound advice. Pratap Mehta gave even more generously. Although he does not drive terribly well, he would happily ferry me to various clubs, bars, and cafés around town. There he would share his vast knowledge of history, the world's religions, comparative politics, political theory, and cricket. Most of what I know, I learnt from him. Finally, I would like to thank Judy Vichniac, who has been my close friend, colleague, and loyal supporter for many years.

I would also like to acknowledge my debts to some of my former teachers. At graduate school at Berkeley, the first two seminar papers I wrote were for Ernie Haas and Ken Waltz. It was with great sadness that I learned that Ernie passed away in November 2002. I had wanted to tell him that I had reached a "Haasian" conclusion through "Waltzian" means. I am sure he would have been most skeptical. I would also like to record my debts to the people at Berkeley who taught me political theory, including Hanna Fenichel Pitkin, Paul Thomas, and Jeremy Waldron. Under their supervision, I wrote a dissertation on political membership, which one day, when I am less bored with the topic, I hope to publish. But until then, I hope they recognize in the present work some of the things that they tried to teach me.

I began writing this book in my father's house in my hometown in Wales. I completed it in my in-laws' house in northern Spain. I wrote a large chunk of the middle sections in California at the homes of Chuck Numbers, Jennifer Schwartz, Corey Brill, and Susan Taylor. I am grateful to them all for putting up with the scattered papers, the half-eaten burritos, and the days-old coffee cups that accompanied me. Margarita Estévez-Abe was, throughout this entire process, her own irreducible self.

The Idea of a European Superstate

*

Introduction

In THE SPRING OF 2001, Mr. Steven Thoburn, a greengrocer from Sunderland in the northeast of England, was convicted in district court of selling one pound of bananas. His conviction, which earned him a criminal record, was a result of a European Union (EU) directive requiring all loose fruit to be sold in kilos and grams. Mr. Thoburn—the "Metric Martyr," as the British tabloids were to call him—argued in his defense that the British Weights and Measures Act of 1985 permitted the sale of goods in both imperial and metric measures. Mr. Thoburn insisted that he would continue to sell his fruit in imperial measures until the British parliament in Westminster introduced a new weights and measures act to replace the old one.

On a point of law, Mr. Thoburn was clearly mistaken. As a member of the EU, Britain, like every other member state, is required to recognize both the "direct effect" and "supremacy" of European law over competing national laws.[1] The district judge who found Mr. Thoburn guilty applied the law correctly.[2] But Thoburn's case raises questions that go beyond the letter of the law. Thoburn and his eurosceptic supporters saw themselves as raising a fundamental question—a philosophical question—concerning the justification of Europe's legal and political authority over its member states. The novelist Frederick Forsyth, one of Thoburn's prominent supporters, has posed this question in the following way: "How, and by whom, do you wish to be governed?"[3]

The nationalist—and many eurosceptics are nationalists—has a ready answer to Forsyth's question. "We wish to be governed by those we trust, those like us, people with whom we share a common nationality." Proponents of European integration—"europhiles," as I will call them—have a more difficult time with the question. Few would want to argue that Europe ought to be governed by "Europeans," because European identity remains relatively thin and insubstantial when compared with most national identities. Furthermore, there is no general agreement about where the boundaries of Europe lie, nor even about what constitutes a European identity. Perhaps a more promising strategy is to focus on the "how" part of the question. "How do you wish to be governed?" Europhiles assume, not unreasonably, that all Europeans want to be governed effectively. Effective government, so they contend, is now no longer possible at the level of the nation-state. This answer, unfortunately, does little to persuade those who believe that the efficacy of a government matters less than its nationality. These eurosceptics (much like Milton's Satan in *Paradise Lost*) would rather govern their own national hell than serve in the new European heaven.[4]

While Mr. Thoburn and his supporters were readying their appeal to the British courts, the European Council meeting at Laeken (December 2001) decided that European integration could proceed no further without a Constitutional Convention to reexamine Europe's existing political architecture.[5] This decision was taken in response to two different challenges. First, the European Union faced the problem of incorporating ten (and possibly thirteen) new members, many of them impoverished, ex-communist countries. Second, the European Union faced a crisis of popularity. Voters in a number of European countries had expressed their dislike for the post-Maastricht EU in a number of embarrassing referendum defeats. Euroscepticism, in short, was showing signs of spreading, much like soccer hooliganism, from England to the Continent. Something had to be done.

The remit of the Constitutional Convention, which was chaired by Valéry Giscard d'Estaing, was both broad and narrow. It was broad in that it sought "to propose a new framework and structures for the European Union."[6] Yet it was narrow in that it neither addressed nor resolved Europe's raison d'être. The eurosceptic challenge to the very idea of a European level of government was thus never confronted. This avoidance strategy was evident in the Constitutional Treaty that emerged from the Convention in June 2003 and was signed (after some modifications) in October 2004. The Preamble—where we might ordinarily expect some account of the reasons why a European polity is desirable—brushed aside basic questions of Europe's existence in favor of vague generalities designed to balance the concerns of those seeking tighter and those seeking looser forms of political integration.[7] Perhaps not surprisingly, neither the Convention nor the Constitutional Treaty managed to put an end to the debate over Europe's political future.[8] If anything, the Convention and the subsequent negotiations over the Constitutional Treaty have exposed new divisions within Europe, including those between larger and smaller states, and between pro- and anti-US states.

It remains to be seen when Europe's national electorates—acting either through their elected representatives or through popular referendums—will ratify the Constitutional Treaty. Even if the treaty is rejected by one or more national electorates, the effort to bring some coherence to Europe's current legal and political institutions is unlikely to disappear. Perhaps there remains some clever institutional solution that will satisfy federalists and antifederalists, big states and small states, US-friendly states and US-allergic states. The assumption of this book, however, is that the European project of political integration is less in need of an institutional than a justificatory fix. Proponents of European political integration need to pay more attention to the fundamental question posed by eurosceptics: What is the justification for European political integration? Unless this question can be answered satisfactorily, there is no good reason for citizens to lend their support to parties, governments, and political leaders who favor European political integration.

This book presents the debate over this justificatory question as a three-sided quarrel between eurosceptics, postsovereignists, and federalists. Eurosceptics alone remain attached to one or another of Europe's nation-states. They seek to maintain (or perhaps return to) a Europe of relatively independent nation-states. Postsovereignists and federalists, in contrast, favor the transfer of political authority away from Europe's nation-states. Both envisage a Europe that distributes political authority among the local, national, and European levels of government. Postsovereignists and federalists disagree, however, about the degrees of centralization, hierarchy, and internal homogeneity desirable in a European polity. Where postsovereignists (also sometimes referred to as "postnationalists") seek a radically new multilevel, decentered polity, European federalists favor something akin to a "United States of Europe." Federalists, in other words, insist that a federal Europe must concentrate the most important political tasks (including defense, foreign policy, and taxation policy) at the European level of government.

These different preferred outcomes—a Europe of many nation-states, a postsovereign polity, and a federal European state—reflect a fundamental disagreement over the facts and values that belong in the debate over European political integration. Different people can and do evaluate European political integration from the perspective of different reference groups. Some evaluate European political integration solely with reference to its impact on their own nation. Others evaluate integration from the perspective of "Europeans" in general. And still others evaluate integration from the perspective of "the world" or humanity writ large. Complicating further the task of justifying European political integration is the fact that people disagree about the criteria of evaluation. Some evaluate European integration on economic grounds. Others eval-

3

uate European integration solely on nationalist grounds. And still others evaluate European integration on democratic grounds. In light of these disagreements, this book places special emphasis on the question of justification. Before I say something more about justification, I want first to clear up certain difficulties with the language and concepts that people employ when discussing European integration.

European Integration: Project, Process, and Product

When talking about European integration, it is helpful to draw a distinction between the project, the process, and the product of integration. The *project of European integration* refers to the efforts of intellectuals, political elites, and popular movements to create some form of European polity. The *process of European integration* refers to the actual step-by-step transformation of Europe's separate-nation states into a more integrated political, legal, and economic system. The *product of European integration* refers to the current outcome of this process, the political institutions, policies, and practices of the European Union itself.

Until Joschka Fischer raised the topic in a controversial speech in June 2000, Europe's political leaders tended to remain silent about the *project* of European integration.[9] Thus the "changes to the Union's basic treaties," as Lenaerts and Desomer have noted, "have been brought about without explicit consideration of the final goal of European integration. Rather, the overall approach of European integration has been one of piece-meal engineering."[10] While this "piece-meal engineering" has proven remarkably successful in constructing a common European market, European integration has reached a stage where its next steps, if taken, would involve the EU taking control of many of the core functions of national governments—including defense, foreign affairs, and personal taxation. This stage of European *political* integration requires, so Fischer and others have argued, something more than "piece-meal engineering." Unfortunately, the terms of the Convention were drawn too narrowly to allow an open-ended debate over the merits of various possible conceptions of the European project.[11]

This book focuses on two different conceptions of the European project: a *federalist project of European integration*; and a *postsovereignist project of European integration*. Conceived as a federalist project, the telos of European integration is to be found in a "United States of Europe." This project spells the disappearance of sovereign nation-states in Europe.

4

Europe's current nation-states would exist only as subordinate units of a federal Europe, much in the same way that the fifty states exist as subordinate units in the United States of America. The most important functions of government (foreign policy, defense, and taxation) would be—and ought to be—in the hands of the federal (or European) level of government. While few proponents of European political integration would admit that this is their goal, many eurosceptics have long feared that European integration is moving ineluctably in this direction.

Conceived as a postsovereignist project, the telos of European integration is to be found not in a European federal state but in a new, complex political entity that distributes political authority among various levels (local, national, and European) depending on the policy issue in question.[12] In a postsovereign Europe, Europe's nation-states would not be sovereign, nor would the political authorities located in Brussels. For postsovereignists, sovereignty is an outmoded concept that does not fit the complex systems of "governance" that would characterize an ideally integrated Europe. Animating the postsovereign project are the principles of subsidiarity, asymmetrical incorporation, and constitutional flexibility.[13] Briefly stated, the principle of subsidiarity requires policy making to take place at that level closest to those affected by that policy. The principle of subsidiarity, in other words, entails a strong presumption in favor of the local and against the federal level of government. The principle of asymmetrical incorporation allows that the local and national communities that make up the constitutive elements of the European polity can have different rights and responsibilities. Some regions, in other words, could be incorporated into the union on different terms than others. The principle of constitutional flexibility allows that the application of the principles of subsidiarity and asymmetrical incorporation must itself remain open to further revision and—favorite word of postsovereignists—"contestation." For the postsovereignists, the European project never reaches a fixed and final destination. The postsovereignist project marks a radical departure from both the "Europe of nation-states" favored by eurosceptics and the "United States of Europe" favored by federalists.

The *process* of European integration is controversial for different reasons than the project of European integration. The actual transformation of postwar European nation-states has proceeded, chrysalis-like, from the European Coal and Steel Community to the European Economic Community to the European Community to now the European Union. Running alongside this process of "deepening," as it is known, "Europe"—which originally consisted of France, Germany, Italy, and the Benelux countries—has added members: Ireland, Denmark, and the United Kingdom in 1973; Greece in 1981; Spain and Portugal in 1986; Austria, Sweden, and Finland in 1995. A decision was taken in 1993 by the European Council to admit, subject to certain qualifying conditions, a large number of central and eastern European states. At Laeken the decision was taken to admit ten countries in 2004 (the three Baltic states, Cyprus, the Czech Republic, Hungary, Malta, Poland, Slovakia, and Slovenia) and to delay the accession of three remaining so-called candidate countries (Bulgaria, Romania, and Turkey). Bulgaria and Romania are expected to join the EU by 2007, but Turkey's accession has not yet been time-tabled. All of which is to say that the process of European integration—a process that involves both the "deepening" and the "widening" of Europe—continues.

It is helpful to distinguish this process of integration from the project of European integration, because they are controversial for somewhat different reasons. It is possible, for instance, to be critical of the process of integration while remaining an ardent proponent of the project (however conceived). In illustration of this point, it is helpful to keep in mind descriptive and normative understandings of the process of European integration. Descriptively, scholars have documented the actual mechanisms and procedures by which postwar Europe has adopted a more integrated economic, legal, and political system.[14] Normatively, people often assess these mechanisms and procedures against some standard of how they *ought* to function. For many critics of the process of European integration, these mechanisms are too elitist, too undemocratic, and insufficiently transparent. The European Convention of 2002–3, which involved a wide variety of different people representing a spectrum of opinions, might be seen as an effort, however inadequate, to overcome some of these criticisms by drawing into the process a wider range of participants.

The current *product* of the process of European integration is the EU itself. From a normative standpoint, it is especially important to distinguish this product—an ever changing political, legal, and economic system—from both the project and the process of European integration. Thus someone who is deeply critical of the current product of European integration—perhaps because of, say, the EU's agricultural policies or because of its structural and cohesion policies—could nonetheless support various conceptions of the project of European integration, including the idea of a federal Europe.[15] Conversely, someone very happy with the current product could conceivably reject the very idea of a project to construct a more politically integrated European polity, whether conceptualized in federal or postsovereignist terms.[16]

To suggest (as I have done at the end of the previous paragraph) that the current product of European integration is distinguishable from both a "federal Europe" and a "postsovereign Europe" does, however, beg an important ontological question concerning the current nature of the EU. If it is not now federal or postsovereign, then what is it? Jacques Delors once described the EU as "un objet politique non-identifié." Many scholars make the same point, albeit less elegantly, through their employment of various neologisms to describe the EU: quasi state, intergovernmental organization, supranational polity, federation, confederation, multilevel system of government, and so forth.[17] Rather than add yet another term to the list, I intend to describe Europe's current political architecture as envisaged by the Constitutional Treaty signed in October 2004.

Europe in the Eyes of Its Constitutional Treaty

The Constitutional Treaty of October 2004 was the product of a lengthy, elaborate European Convention (chaired by Valéry Giscard d'Estaing), which consulted elected representatives from all of Europe's member states, the European parliament, the European Commission, and most shades of European public opinion. The European Convention met from March 2002 to June 2003, when it produced a document (a "draft Constitutional Treaty") that was supposed to be signed by all member states at the end of 2003. This "draft Constitutional Treaty" was not, however, signed, because of a disagreement over the relative voting weights to be accorded to the larger and smaller states. Spain and Poland refused to give up the relatively generous weightings they had earlier secured in the Treaty of Nice (2000). A new Constitutional Treaty, which contained minor modifications of the earlier draft, was later agreed on in June 2004 and was signed in October of that year. This Constitutional Treaty will not take effect until it has been ratified—whether by the approval of national parliaments or in national referendums—by all twenty-five member states. If the process of ratification fails—a distinct possibility—Europe's political leaders will either have to go back to the drawing board to produce a new Constitutional Treaty or muddle through on the basis of preexisting European treaties. Yet even in the event that ratification fails, the Constitutional Treaty will remain for a very long time the point of departure for all future efforts to design an appropriate set of European political institutions.

The Constitutional Treaty of 2004 is (even as constitutions go) a lengthy document (328 pages). The treaty, which is nothing if not complicated, is clearly divided over the nature and future direction of the EU. These features hinder efforts to "sell" the EU to Europe's more skeptical electorates. Furthermore, they make a complete mockery of the initial intention of the European Convention to render the EU more transparent and bring it closer to the ordinary citizen. Leaving aside for the moment the detailed provisions of the Constitutional Treaty, it would be useful to begin by noting the disagreements that emerged during the efforts to produce, sign, and ratify the treaty. At any given time in the future, the product of European political integration will be a function of how these disagreements are resolved.

One disagreement centered on the *division of competences* between local, national, and European levels of government. Here we can draw a distinction between *member-statists*, who wanted to ensure that the most important powers (or "competences") remained in the hands of national-level governments (France, Britain, Spain, and so forth), and *federalists*, who wanted to place those powers in the hands of European-level political institutions.[18]

A second disagreement concerned the *distribution of power* both within and between European-level political institutions. Here we can draw a distinction between *intergovernmentalists*, who wanted to concentrate power in institutions (such as the European Council and the Council of Ministers) that the member states themselves control, and *supranationalists*, who wanted to distribute power to institutions (such as the European parliament and the Commission) that member states as such do not control.[19] A related disagreement between intergovernmentalists and supranationalists concerned the status of national vetoes and majority voting. Intergovernmentalists generally favor national vetoes; supranationalists generally favor majority voting.[20] It is important to recognize here, however, that political leaders might be intergovernmentalists on one issue—as, say, the French are on agricultural policy—while being supranationalists on other issues (the harmonization of taxation policy, for instance).

In addition to these two institutional disagreements, two deep-seated policy disagreements must be mentioned, even if the Convention itself had no remit to discuss policies. One policy disagreement concerned the question of market-constraining regulatory policies. The other policy disagreement concerned Europe's foreign and security policies and, more generally, Europe's relationship with the United States. Disagreements on these topics, even though they were never discussed by the Convention, hovered over many of the discussions concerning the reform of Europe's political institutions.[21] The disagreement over market regulation, for instance, drives much of the aforementioned disagreement over the division of competences between European and national levels of government.[22] A principal reason why British political leaders— even those who, like Tony Blair, are (at least by British standards) relatively well disposed to European integration—cling to member statism and intergovernmentalism is that they fear that any step toward federalism and supranationalism will give rise to a set of market-constraining regulatory policies that will hinder Britain's economic performance.[23] Political elites in France and to a certain extent Germany have the opposite worry. They fear that the EU regulatory regime will limit the capacity of national governments to impose such market-constraining policies as a minimum wage and antitakeover regulations.[24]

The disagreement over Europe's foreign, security, and defense policies remains the greatest unresolved issue in European politics today. The Convention took place against the background of deep divisions within Europe over the legitimacy of military intervention in Iraq.[25] Federalists sought to make foreign, security, and defense policy one of the core competences of the EU. Indeed, supranationalist federalists sought to enable European political institutions to reach decisions in this area on the basis of a majority vote. Given the far-reaching aspirations of these federalists, it is surprising that the changes envisaged by the Constitutional Treaty remain so minor. It is certainly difficult to understand how anyone could interpret the treaty as a victory for those in favor of a "federal superstate."[26] Certainly the document contains some language and provisions designed to appease those seeking a more politically integrated European polity. Thus the Preamble retains some of the earlier language found in the Treaty of Rome that promised "an ever closer union" for Europe. "[W]hile remaining proud of their own national identities and history, the peoples of Europe," as the Preamble puts it, "are determined to transcend their former divisions and, *united ever more closely*, to forge a common destiny" (emphasis added).[27] But these federalist sentiments coexist, as is evident in the quoted passage, with a reaffirmation of Europe's separate nations and peoples. Furthermore, the treaty stipulates that the EU derives its authority from both Europe's citizens and Europe's member states:

> Reflecting the Will of the citizens and States of Europe to build a common future, this Constitution establishes the European Union, on which the Member States confer competences to attain objectives they have in common.[28]

The EU, in other words, is a joint creation of citizens and member states: it is *they* who confer competences on *it*.

Like other constitutions, the Constitutional Treaty defines the role and responsibilities of key political institutions. Here there is little new. For the most part, the Constitutional Treaty merely reaffirms the institutional status quo ante. Briefly described, the European Union will retain its familiar tripartite division of a Council, a Commission and a Parliament.[29] The "Council"—a shorthand term sometimes employed to refer to two rather different institutions, the "European Council" and the "Council of Ministers"—provides Europe's member states with a large measure of control over the outcomes of Europe's political system. The "European Council"—which consists of the presidents or prime ministers of each member state and president of the European Commission—defines the "general political directions and policies" that the EU is to follow. In an important institutional innovation of the Constitutional Treaty, the European Council will in future be chaired by a president, with limited powers, appointed for a period of two and a half years. The other important institutional innovation is the creation of a Union minister of foreign affairs, who will represent the EU internationally.

In addition to the control they exercise through the European Council, member states also control the all-important Council of Ministers, a body made up of ministerial representatives of each member state. Voting in the Council of Ministers proceeds—except in certain crucial areas (such as taxation) where unanimity is still necessary—by a qualified majority vote. The weighting of this vote proved to be the most difficult task in the negotiations over the Constitutional Treaty. The compromise reached involves a procedure whereby a double majority (of both member states and people) is necessary to reach a Council decision. A qualified majority will henceforth require the support of 55 percent of the member states representing 65 percent of the population of the EU. Furthermore, in an effort to check the power of the "big three" (France, Germany, and the United Kingdom), a blocking minority will require a minimum of four member states.

The Constitutional Treaty does little to either expand or diminish the role of the European Commission as Europe's executive and administrative agency. The European Commission now (as before) has a president—who is selected by the European Council and approved by the European parliament—and commissioners drawn from each country.[30] The European Commission is more, however, than a bureaucratic agency: it alone has the right to propose legislation. Given this right of legislation, the European Commission plays a role that in any other democratic political system would be played by a parliamentary or legislative body. The Constitutional Treaty does something (albeit not much) to bolster the power of the European parliament by increasing its authority over the budget and in policy areas (such as agricultural policy) from which it has hitherto been excluded.

It remains to be seen how Europe's political institutions will be modified over the following years. No one knows how these institutions will function when Europe comprises twenty-five (and perhaps eventually twenty-eight or more) member states.[31] It is likely that some further institutional reforms will take place in 2008 when the EU tries to come up with a new budget. There is nothing, it should be noted, exceptional about a political system that remains in a state of flux. The Philadelphia Convention of 1787 certainly did not resolve all disagreements concerning the precise configuration of US political institutions. Both those who favored greater centralization of political authority in the federal government in Washington, D.C., and those who favored "states' rights" continued to press their cause. Even after a Civil War, this disagreement remained—and continues to remain—a central cleavage in US politics. The same is likely to prove true in the case of the European Union.

SOME DIFFICULTIES WITH THE F-WORD

The distinctions drawn above between the project, the process, and the product of European integration are helpful in clarifying one of the most difficult and controversial terms in the debate over European political integration: federalism. In the previous section, federalists were contrasted with member-statists. But a lot more needs to be said about the ambitions of federalists and the nature of a federal Europe. In eurosceptic circles, the term "federalist" is generally employed only as a pejorative. For the eurosceptic, the federalist favors a "European superstate," a "United States of Europe," and the abolition of Europe's independent nation-states.[32] Indeed, for some of the more nationalistically inspired eurosceptics, the term "federalist" describes anyone favoring any form of European political integration. From this fevered perspective, even the defender of the EU status quo—a member-statist and intergovernmentalist who opposes any further European political integration—would nonetheless be branded as a "federalist." So controversial is this term "federalism" in Britain that Tony Blair initially welcomed the Draft Treaty establishing a Constitution for Europe on the grounds that it had ruled out, once and for all, a "federal superstate."[33]

The popular usage of the term "federalist" to suggest someone who favors a centralized state represents a complete transformation of the term as it has been understood in the history of political thought. So marked is the difference between these two usages of the term that it is helpful to distinguish the European federalist who seeks a unitary federal superstate from the genuine *federalist* who seeks a decentralized, multilevel federal polity. (In other words, federalism [unitalicized] as envisaged by eurosceptics is very different from the genuine *federalism* [italicized] that figures in the history of political thought.) Genuine, self-described *federalists* seek the dispersal rather than concentration of power in a centralized political authority. These *federalists* are critical of the sovereignty principle and the modern nation-state, which they seek to replace with a decentralized *federal polity*. In this context, it is well to bear in mind Daniel Elazar's definition of (genuine) *federalism*:

> In the broadest sense, *federalism* involves the linking of individuals, groups, and polities in lasting but limited union in such a way as to provide for the energetic pursuit of common ends while maintaining the respective integrities of all parties. . . . [F]*ederalism* has to do with the constitutional diffusion of power, so that the constituting elements in a federal arrangement share in the processes of common policy-making and administration by right, while the activities of the common government are conducted in such a way as to maintain their respective integrities [emphasis added].[34]

Although Elazar further notes that "a wide variety of political structures can be developed that are consistent with *federal* principles," the form of centralization advocated by alleged proponents of a "European superstate" clearly does not count as an example of such a structure.[35] Indeed, there is a difference, so he argues, not just of degree but of kind between "a unitary state" and "a federal polity."[36] It is worth dwelling on this difference, because it underscores the difference between what I have termed the federal and postsovereign conceptions of the European project.

The precise nature of the difference between a "unitary state" and a *"federal polity"* (the goal of genuine *federalists*) is not easy to describe. One way of capturing the difference is to focus (following Istvan Hont) on the form of "representation" employed by the "unitary state" compared with its alternatives.[37] From this perspective, the modern unitary state has two distinct analytical components. First, the unitary state presupposes the idea of popular sovereignty, which is to say the idea that the people—conceived as free and equal individuals—form the constituting power (*pouvoir constituant*) of that state. Second, the unitary state, once constituted, becomes the representative of the people, who now (qua people) exercise their "sovereignty" only indirectly. Thus, in the modern unitary state, the sovereignty of the people is exercised on their behalf, not directly by themselves. Think, for instance, of the US courts, which prosecute individuals on behalf of "We the People." In providing the people with this "indirect" form of sovereignty, the modern unitary state differs both from earlier participatory republics and from mixed or composite forms of government.[38]

The *federal polity* modifies the form of representation present in the unitary state in an important way. It retains the two aforementioned analytical components but adds a third: the idea that the *federal polity* directly represents a number of constitutive "member states." A *federal polity*, in other words, establishes a double form of representation. It represents citizens conceived as free and equals members of the whole polity; it also represents citizens conceived as members of territorially more limited "member states." In its ideal form—rarely achieved in practice—the relationship between these two levels of representation is one of strict, constitutionally entrenched formal equality rather than (as in the unitary state) a relationship of hierarchy between a central political authority and its subordinate jurisdictions.

Viewed from this perspective, it becomes possible to distinguish the *federal polity* from both the unitary state and the so-called federation, which lack this double form of representation. In the unitary state, representation is one-dimensional and coterminous with the polity as a whole. In a federation—which can be thought of as a loosely knit cooperative arrangement of otherwise independent states—citizens are not represented at the level of the federation as a whole. In this respect, representation is also one-dimensional, but it takes place at the level of each state in the federation. In a federal polity, representation is two-dimensional: citizens are represented at the level of the polity as a whole; they are also represented via their membership of constitutionally defined member states.

The distinctions drawn here between the different forms of representation present in a "unitary state," "*federal polity*," and "federation" allow us to conceptualize more clearly the EU as it is imagined both in its Constitutional Treaty and by those who wish to transform it. In its proposed constitutional form, the EU might appear, at least at first glance, to qualify as a genuine *federal polity*. Its constitutional principles establish the dual form of representation that defines what I have described above as a *federal polity*. Article 1 of the Constitutional Treaty, for instance, acknowledges "the will of the citizens and States of Europe to build a common future." Likewise, the political institutions of the EU represent citizens of the Union as a whole in the European parliament; and they represent the member states in the European Council and Council of Ministers.[39] The representation of the citizens of Europe is further reinforced by a Charter of Fundamental Rights that applies to all individual members of the Union.

Notwithstanding these classic features of a *federal polity*—a two-dimensional form of representation organized at the Union and national levels—the EU (as presently constituted) otherwise falls short. Given the current division of competences between member state and Union levels and the distribution of power among European political institutions themselves, it would be misleading to describe the EU as anything other than a member-state-dominated political arrangement. The two-dimensional form of representation is thus notional rather than actual, because the institutional level defined by the Union is relatively weak. As envisaged by the Constitutional Treaty—and in direct contrast to what many eurosceptics allege to be the case—the member states retain all of the most important competences, including foreign policy and taxation policy.

Having clearly distinguished between two diametrically opposed meanings of the term "federalism," it is possible to summarize the differences between federalists (who seek "a unitary state" in Europe) and *federalists* (who seek a European federal polity). A European federalist seeks a Europe that locates the most important political functions at the

European level of government, even if this requires considerable centralization of power in Brussels. A European *federalist*, in contrast, seeks to disperse power to multiple (different) centers and to the lowest, most decentralized levels possible. While a European federalist could support what I called above the sovereignist project of European integration, a European *federalist* is more likely to favor the postsovereignist project of European political integration.

The final point I wish to make about the concepts and language employed in current debates over European integration concerns the term "United States of Europe"—with its implied analogy to the United States of America—and the term "superstate." Eurosceptics who speak of a "United States of Europe" fear that Europe will come to resemble the United States of America, and that their nation-states will thus be reduced to the (nonsovereign) status of a California or a Texas. The implicit assumption here is that the United States, despite its separation of powers and its distinction between federal and state levels of competence, remains de facto a unitary state rather than what I described above as a *federal polity*.[40] Setting aside the normative judgment that there would be something regrettable about European political institutions coming to resemble those of the United States, the description of the United States as closer to a unitary state than to a *federal polity* is—given the conceptual distinctions adopted here—accurate. The United States of America is certainly closer to a unitary state than to what *federalists* think of as a *federal polity*. True, the US Constitution describes a system of government with a clear division of competences between the state and federal levels. But the federal level is clearly the more important, both constitutionally and in practice. The US Constitution, for instance, more or less excludes states from federal decision making; there is no equivalent in the US Constitution to the European Council or the Council of Ministers. Moreover, the US Constitution gives the federal level of government most of the important "competences," including the right to raise armies, levy taxes, and regulate interstate commerce. Indeed, Article I, Section 8, of the Constitution assigns, as David McKay has noted, "eighteen specific powers to Congress, which, in contemporary eighteenth century terms, amounted to the equivalent of the sort of powers exercised by unitary governments at the time."[41] In addition to the legal competences of the federal level of government, the United States has, over the course of its history, experienced an extensive process of nation building, a process that has, in effect, increased the significance of the federal level at the expense of the state level.[42] In short, when eurosceptics speak fearfully of the EU turning into a "United States of Europe," which is to say adopting the form of government that we see today in the United States of America, their fear is not misplaced. The United States of America *is* closer to a unitary state than to a *federal polity.*

The final conceptual term that I wish to clarify is the term "superstate." The most famous usage of this term comes from Margaret Thatcher's Bruges speech—a speech that forms the manifesto of many British eurosceptics—where she argued, "We have not successfully rolled back the frontiers of the state in Britain, only to see them reimposed at a European level, with a European superstate exercising a new dominance from Brussels."[43] From this perspective, the "superstate" signifies, not only a European level of government with authority over a wide range of important policy issues, but also a European level of government that enacts market-restricting (or in Thatcher's terms "socialist") policies. When eurosceptics complain about the "superstate," it is not always clear whether they are objecting to a federal European state, to market-restricting policies, or to both. In light of this ambiguity, I intend to use the term "superstate" to refer only to a federal European state. Given this usage, it remains an open question whether a federal European state ought to pursue market-restricting or market-expanding policies. It simply confuses the issue to employ (as many eurosceptics do) the term "superstate" to criticize the EU's market-restricting regulatory policies.[44]

I have gone to some trouble to clarify these two contrasting meanings of federalism because this book defends the very federalist project that eurosceptics condemn. This book argues, in short, that the much decried "European superstate" is actually a more justifiable goal than either the so-called Europe of nation-states (favored by eurosceptics) or "the postsovereign form of governance" (favored by Europe's self-described *federalists*).

A DEMOCRATIC STANDARD OF JUSTIFICATION

Descriptions, no matter how detailed, of the desired destination of the European project do nothing to justify that project. Europhiles often overlook this point and discuss European political integration as if the project were self-justifying. Even European political theorists—who might have been expected to place the question of justification at the head of their intellectual agenda—tend to neglect the question of justification, focusing instead on the democratic legitimacy of Europe's political institutions.[45] While this approach has yielded a rich literature devoted to the diagnosis and remedy of the EU's democratic failings, this literature does little to address the more fundamental misgivings of eurosceptics—such as the "Metric Martyr" and his followers—who object to the very idea of a European level of government. To address these misgivings, the question of justification must assume center stage.

The question of justification, as I understand it in this book, is not the same as either the question of legitimacy or the question of popularity. Briefly stated, the question of the justification of European political integration concerns the point or purpose of a European polity.[46] The question of legitimacy, in contrast, concerns the rightful claim of European institutions to issue binding commands. Some people believe that European institutions lack this rightful claim; a subset of these people believe that European institutions lack this rightful claim because these institutions fail to measure up to a minimal standard of democracy. The questions of justification and legitimacy, understood in this way, are clearly different. It is logically possible to think that the European project, process, and product have no good justification but nonetheless to concede that current European political institutions are legitimate. By the same token, it is logically possible to think that Europe's current political institutions lack legitimacy—perhaps because they are deemed insufficiently democratic—but nonetheless to think that the European project to, say, construct a unitary European state has a compelling justification.

The question of the EU's popularity—which fluctuates across countries and over time—stands in a complex relationship to these questions of justification and legitimacy. Clearly, some of this unpopularity can be attributed to the perception that the EU in its current form lacks democratic legitimacy. But it would be a mistake to exaggerate the importance of this concern, not least because the EU's democratic credentials are not obviously any worse than the democratic credentials of Europe's member states.[47] A more important cause of Europe's problems, so I argue in this book, is that proponents of European political integration have failed to provide the European project with a compelling justification. In this respect, Claus Offe gets it right when he notes, "The European public needs a normatively convincing defense of the integration project, and that need grows more pressing as the project moves forward."[48]

Yet while the European project is in need of justificatory arguments ("a normatively convincing defense," in Offe's terms), it is in even greater need of a prior standard of justificatory adequacy. Disagreements over the European project run deep; they extend—as I noted at the start of this chapter—not just to the relevant communities of justification but also to metrics of evaluation. In light of this problem, this book proposes a standard of justification that arguments in support of European political integration must satisfy. The standard of justification defended in this book—I call it a *democratic standard of justification*—holds that any adequate justification for the project of European integration must satisfy three requirements: a requirement of publicity, a requirement of accessibility, and a requirement of sufficiency.

Chapter 1 defends this *democratic standard of justification*. The most important element of this standard of justification, as will become apparent, is the requirement of publicity. This requirement is a feature of all contemporary theories of politics—especially those influenced by the later work of John Rawls—that take seriously the fact that the citizens of modern democratic societies disagree about the merits of substantive (or "comprehensive") ways of life.[49] The requirement of publicity filters out all arguments that presuppose the truth of a substantive way of life. The requirement of publicity would, for example, rule out all efforts to justify the European project on the grounds that it constitutes the fulfillment of God's mission for mankind. The requirement of publicity is not self-justifying, nor is it beyond all disagreement itself. One of the aims of Chapter 1 is to offer some defense both of the concept of public justification and the specific conception of public justification employed in this book.

One of the implications of adopting a standard of justification that includes a requirement of publicity is that any particular justification for the European project will have to appeal to values that all Europeans can accept. This requirement applies with equal force to eurosceptic arguments in support of a Europe of nation-states. Given the current product of European integration, the aim of eurosceptics to return to a Europe of nation-states marks no less of a departure from the institutional status quo in Europe than the project to construct some form of European polity. Given the transformative aspirations of eurosceptics, it is essential that their own arguments satisfy the requirements of a democratic standard of justification.

Chapters 2 and 3 focus on the eurosceptics' challenge to European political integration. Eurosceptics come in a variety of different forms, but principled euroscepticism—which is opposed to the very idea of European political integration—draws its support and much of its strength from nationalism. Chapter 2 situates euroscepticism in the context of sociological, conservative, and liberal forms of nationalism. Chapter 3 examines what I take to be the two most potent and intellectually powerful forms of euroscepticism: the conservative nationalist euroscepticism of Enoch Powell and the liberal nationalist euroscepticism of various contemporary British social democrats. This chapter argues that, whatever their intellectual coherence, these forms of euroscepticism rely on arguments that fail to satisfy a democratic standard of justification.

Chapters 4 and 5 consider arguments that might be advanced in justification of the European project. Broadly stated, the case for European political integration has always appealed to some conception of peace (more broadly understood as "security") and some conception of prosperity (more broadly understood as "welfare"). Chapter 4 examines two influential versions of the welfare argument: the social democratic argument of Jürgen Habermas and the classically liberal argument of Friedrich Hayek. Chapter 5 considers security-based justifications for European political integration. The success of welfare-based and security-based arguments for European political integration turns in large measure on whether it is possible to offer conceptions of, respectively, "welfare" and "security" that can satisfy the requirement imposed by a *democratic standard of justification*. Chapter 5 offers a view of security that does, I think, satisfy this requirement. No individual or state can be "secure," so I argue in this chapter, while vulnerable to uncontrolled, unbalanced, and unrepresentative concentrations of power.

Working with this conception of "security," chapter 6 and 7 argue that the form of political organization most capable of producing security (so defined) is a unitary state. To take security seriously, in short, is to recognize the advantages of a European superstate and the disadvantages of either a "Europe of nation-states" or a "postsovereign Europe." Chapter 6 examines the case for a postsovereign European polity. Many of the arguments put forward in justification of this type of polity fail to meet the requirements of a democratic standard of justification. Such is the failing, so I contend, of arguments that rest on the value of ethnocultural diversity, which—if a value at all—is certainly not a public value. There is, however, a "republican" justification for this type of polity that deserves more careful consideration, because it seems quite compatible with this standard of justification.[50] "Republicans" rightly recognize the importance of security as a form of nondependence. In this respect, the "republican" justification for a postsovereign polity appears to run along the same tracks as my own justification for a European superstate. Where these "republicans" run off the rails is in their failure to meet the challenge posed by the threat of "hegemony"—the concentration of power in the international state system. Whereas proponents of a European superstate are prepared to do what is necessary to balance against hegemonic forms of power, advocates of a "postsovereign polity" tend to hide behind the skirts of a hoped-for multilateral legal order.[51] Indeed, once the international ramifications of the European project are grasped, many of the arguments put forward in favor of a postsovereign Europe appear not only naive but positively dangerous in their disregard for the security of Europe's citizens.

In considering the security dimensions of the choice for and against a European polity, the position adopted in this book draws together the debate over European political integration with the debate over US-European relations. A sad irony of the European Convention was that while its delegates were sitting in a hall discussing how to draw Europeans together, events outside the hall were pulling them apart.[52] The Iraq War of 2003 exposed deep disagreements between European countries over the propriety of the use of military force. Exploiting these disagreements, the American media popularized the idea of a New Europe and an Old Europe, a Europe loyal and a Europe disloyal to the Atlantic Alliance. Since European political integration has historically been animated by a desire to overcome security differences between European countries, these new divisions cannot but be perceived as profoundly troubling. Unfortunately, beyond a rather vague endorsement of a common foreign, security, and defense policy, Europe's Constitutional Treaty has done little to address these problems. A Europe of twenty-five member states, some with venerable and much cherished traditions of neutrality, is unlikely to become a global military power, especially when military action requires the unanimous approval of all twenty-five presidents or prime ministers.

Not all Europeans, it must be noted, are troubled by the fact that Europe lacks the capacity for independent military action. Advocates of a "Europe of nation-states"—most British eurosceptics, for instance—think that Europe's security needs can be taken care of by NATO. Such people are relatively untroubled by the fact that NATO is an alliance that the United States largely dominates. Nor do they worry that the United States seems increasingly able and willing to act in a unilateral fashion. NATO, so British eurosceptics like to think, enables Britain and other European powers to share in the power of "the West" and to influence US actions.[53]

In addition to their membership in NATO, European countries, so some observers contend, should focus their energies on becoming a "civilian power."[54] From this perspective, Europeans ought to let the United States dominate the world militarily. Europe's comparative advantage lies in supplying the world's troubled regions with a police force, humanitarian aid, and the blueprints for reconstruction. Europe, in short, is to play "Robin" to America's "Batman."[55]

Against the idea of Europe as either a subordinate member of an Atlantic Alliance or a mere "civilian power," chapter 7 argues that Europe needs to develop the capacity to take independent military action. This line of argument does not proceed from a crude form of anti-Americanism but from the philosophical account of security developed in chapter 5. Security, as I understand it, requires appropriate safeguards against "hegemony" and "dependence." A "unipolar world"—the world we currently inhabit—is, from this perspective, insecure.

There is nothing terribly controversial in the observation that something needs to be done to address Europe's military imbalance with the United States. In recent years, we have seen efforts to bolster European military spending, to rationalize defense procurement, to create a "Rapid Reaction Force," and even—under French urging—to develop a military structure independent of NATO.[56] Chapters 6 and 7 argue that the effort to equip Europe with an effective foreign, security, and defense policy will, however, prove inadequate while Europe remains anything other than a unitary state. Part of the argument here turns on the claim that a unitary state remains a necessary condition for wielding power effectively. The United States was unable to act effectively on the world stage until it acquired a more centralized, unitary form of government than envisaged by the Founding Fathers. The same point holds true today for Europe.

One of the principal implications of my security-based argument for a unitary European state is that the existing normative debate over European political integration needs to pay a lot more attention to issues typically left in the hands of international relations scholars. The choice between a Europe of nation-states, a unitary European state, and a postsovereign Europe is, in short, a choice that bears on world order.

Political Theory and European Integration

In its emphasis on a security-based justification for the European project, this book shifts the focus of normative inquiry away from the issues of legitimacy that have preoccupied most political theorists who write about European integration. There is now a substantial literature by political theorists devoted to the task of diagnosing and remedying Europe's problems of legitimacy.[57] As a result, we now know a great deal about Europe's alleged "democratic deficit" and the compensatory promise of European citizenship. Unfortunately, we know considerably less about the question that really matters: What is the justification for a European polity? Eurosceptics like the "Metric Martyr" remind us that many people in Europe today do not think that this question has been satisfactorily answered.

In recent years, a number of legal and political theorists have introduced a more differentiated conception of legitimacy that seems better able to address the more fundamental questions raised by eurosceptics about the existence of a European polity.[58] Neil Walker, for instance, draws a distinction between the "performative legitimacy" of the EU, the "regime legitimacy" of the EU, and the "polity legitimacy" of the EU.[59] Performative legitimacy, as he employs the term, refers to "whether the EU has the right priorities and policies and how well it pursues them"; regime legitimacy refers to the institutional framework of the EU; and polity legitimacy—which he acknowledges is of increasing significance—refers to "the overall support for and stability of the polity in question as a self-standing political community."[60]

The notion of "polity legitimacy" represents a significant advance over earlier concepts, because it recognizes the possibility that people evaluate the EU in terms other than the goods it produces and the quality of its institutions. Yet even this notion of "polity legitimacy" does not go far enough. The reason for this is that the EU cannot vindicate its own claims to "polity legitimacy"—its status as "a self-standing political community"—without delegitimating its conceptual rivals: the nation-state and a federal Europe (whether conceived as a unitary European state or a postsovereign polity). All three types of polity—the "EU" (however it is described), the "sovereign nation-state," and a "federal Europe"—cannot coexist in Europe; they are mutually incompatible. Once this point is recognized, political theorists are in a position to conduct an evenhanded inquiry into the relative merits of each. Unfortu-

nately, by focusing exclusively on the legitimacy of the EU, political theorists have tended to foreclose prematurely a debate over the merits of
a "Europe of nation-states" (the preferred option of eurosceptics) or a
"federal Europe" (the preferred option of federalists). This debate, so I
argue in this book, is better conducted in the register of justification than
in the register of legitimacy. Political theorists, in short, ought to examine the justificatory arguments that might be put forward in defense of
these different types of polity. A convincing justificatory argument in
support of any one of these types of polity will go a long way toward its
legitimation and toward the delegitimation of its rivals.

The preoccupation of political theorists with the legitimacy of the EU
goes hand in glove with a similar preoccupation over Europe's alleged
"democratic deficit." Democratic government, as we all know, is better
than its alternatives; democracy is a component of any modern, legitimate political system. But it is not the only component. Chapter 7 argues that a minimal procedural conception of democracy is a necessary
requirement of political institutions, whether they are located at the
local, national, or European levels. Since this requirement can be met
fairly easily, democracy does not provide a reason for preferring a Europe of nation-states to some form of federal Europe. In sum, an adequate political theory of European political integration requires a shift
of attention away from the current preoccupations with Europe's "legitimacy" and its alleged "democratic deficit." To engage fully the central normative issues posed by European political integration (project,
process, and product), political theorists must turn their attention to the
problem of justification.

Justification

THE PROJECT OF European integration (as I have defined it) entails a fundamental transformation of Europe's current intergovernmental political system. In its sovereignist form, this project involves a transition from a Europe of nation-states to a unitary European state—something akin to a "United States of Europe"—a shift in the locus of ultimate political authority from national governments to a European government. In its postsovereignist form, this project involves the creation of a new type of polity that disperses political authority on a policy by policy basis to a variety of bodies located at different jurisdictional levels (local, national, and European). Critics of the project of European integration are correct to think that changes of this magnitude require a robust justification.[1] Europhiles have been surprisingly reluctant to provide such a justification. Some do little more than seek to persuade us that a unitary Europe state would be feasible.[2] Others like to argue that the European Union's current institutional flaws can be remedied only by greater political integration.[3] And still others try to maintain that the EU is already a postsovereign polity that does not need any further fundamental justification.[4] These approaches do nothing, however, to address the normative challenge posed by eurosceptics, a challenge that deserves a more forthright response.

This chapter does not supply a specific justification for the European project. This chapter merely sets the stage by defending a standard of justification that arguments in support of the European project ought to be able to satisfy. This metalevel approach is worth undertaking, because it is not immediately clear what counts as an adequate justification for European political integration. In the absence of a prior account of the types of argument that belong in this context, it is impossible to weigh the very different empirical, conceptual, and moral claims that are brought to bear in arguments over European integration. Consider, for instance, Bruce Ackerman's argument that "there are abundant reasons for *ordinary people* to mobilize for a federal Europe" (emphasis added).[5] Among these abundant reasons, Ackerman lists the following: (1) to avoid nationalist-inspired interstate conflicts, (2) to avoid an impending "environmental crisis" that "cannot be solved within state bounds," (3) to prevent Europe's common market from eroding national welfare states, and (4) to create strong federal institutions to prevent "authoritarian despotisms on more local levels."[6]

Ackerman targets his argument for a federal Europe primarily to "liberals" (or "social democrats," as they would be known in Europe). The creation of a federal Europe forms, so Ackerman contends, the next stage of the "liberal revolution." The obvious difficulty with this approach is that it offers no reason for nonliberals—Europeans who reject the social democratic agenda, in other words—to support the European project. Ackerman simply assumes that Europeans share his own views concerning the protection of the environment and the maintenance of existing forms of the welfare state.[7] He fails to take into consideration the full extent of the disagreement in Europe over environmental and welfare policy. More government intervention to protect the environment and the welfare state will provide a reason for "ordinary people" to mobilize for a federal Europe only if all "ordinary people" in Europe are environmentally conscious social democrats. But they are not. Indeed, to the extent that the European project becomes one of furthering social democratic policies, the greater the likelihood of resistance from more market-oriented (or "classical") liberals.

Perhaps Ackerman is on stronger ground in thinking that all "ordinary people" in Europe would wish to avoid nationalist-inspired conflicts and authoritarian despotism. But here a different problem arises: it is unclear why a federal Europe is necessary to avoid these evils. Postwar Europe—a Europe of nation-states, for the most part—has been relatively peaceful and democratic, so why create a federal Europe now? Any satisfactory justification for the project of European integration needs to answer this question.

This chapter maintains that the case for a federal Europe—whether in its sovereign or postsovereign incarnation—must be built out of arguments that satisfy what might be termed a *democratic standard of justification*. This standard of justification, as I understand it, has three components: a *requirement of publicity*, by which I mean that the arguments for Europe must appeal to reasons that all suitably situated Europeans could accept; a *requirement of accessibility*, by which I mean that the arguments must be intelligible to ordinary Europeans and not just to those with expert skills or specialized knowledge; and a *requirement of sufficiency*, by which I mean that the arguments must show that a federal European polity provides effective and efficient protection for the goods or benefits that purport to justify its existence. I refine and defend these requirements in the remaining sections of this chapter. Before doing so, I want to say something about the practice of justification itself.

The Practice of Justification

In one form or another, the practice of justification forms a central feature of day-to-day politics in all democratic societies.[8] Broadly understood, to justify is "to show or maintain the justice or reasonableness of (an action, claim etc.); to adduce proper grounds for, to defend as right or proper."[9] Justification offers a more acceptable, a more democratic, mode of eliciting support than such alternatives as coercion, trickery, or bribery. To claim that a policy or institution, a law or regime, is justified is to provide people with a reason for them to lend their support. It thus matters a great deal to be able to say that the European project is justified.

Justifying the European project is not, however, exactly the same as justifying a single law or a mere change in policy. The scale of the changes involved in the transformation from a Europe of nation-states to a federal Europe is altogether more substantial, far-reaching and difficult to reverse. This change amounts to a polity change rather than a mere policy change. It thus stands in need of a different type of justification. The idea that there are different types of justification, which apply to different social and political contexts, needs further clarification. To this end, I distinguish the following four types of justification: reconciliatory justification, reformative justification, transvaluative justification, and transformative justification.

RECONCILIATORY JUSTIFICATION

Sometimes political arguments and theoretical treatises try to show that some existing state of affairs—whether a practice, a policy, a law, a regime, or the polity itself—is apt or fitting.[10] This type of justification tries to reveal a hidden or forgotten logic that lies behind the existing state of affairs. Its aim is to show that various practices, policies, institutions, and so forth are as they are for reasons that are both desirable and unavoidable. Typically, this type of justification is employed in the face of proposals for radical change or reform. Reconciliatory justifications seek to stay the twitchy hand of the visionary.

Burke's *Reflections* provides one of the best examples of reconciliatory justification in the history of Western political thought.[11] This text

26

sought inter alia to reconcile the British to their own venerable political institutions. Despite their ostensible irrationalities, these institutions, so Burke tried to show, "fitted" Britain's underlying customs and traditions. They were, he argued, the product of a long and distinctive history; and they contained a wisdom that exceeded the grasp of any single philosopher. Understood in this light, these institutions could be seen as right and proper. In the next chapter, I want to show how reconciliatory justifications play a central role in the efforts of some eurosceptics to defend a "Europe of nation-states." For the moment, however, it is worth recognizing that reconciliatory justifications are not an exclusive preoccupation of conservatives. Rawls's theory of political liberalism contains, as he himself acknowledges, an important reconciliatory dimension: the theory seeks to reconcile us—members of modern democratic societies—to the fact that a modern democratic society cannot, given the unavoidable fact of pluralism, be a community united around a single conception of the good.[12] Jürgen Habermas's democratic theory also contains an important reconciliatory dimension: the theory seeks to persuade us that a modern society cannot, given the unavoidable fact of social complexity, operate with a participatory democratic government.[13]

REFORMATIVE JUSTIFICATION

This type of justification takes place in the context of incremental proposals to reform an existing practice, policy, law, or institution. Much of day-to-day political argument takes place in this contextual space. Justification works here either by showing how the proposed reform would solve a specific problem or by showing how the proposed reform would maximize or protect certain widely accepted goods or benefits. More specifically, reformative justifications (as I understand them) possess three defining features: one, a reform applies to only a limited or circumscribed element of a social or political system; two, a reform can be revisited and overturned; and three, a reform is justified with reference to widely accepted or relatively uncontroversial goods or benefits. The distinctiveness of reformative justifications will emerge when we consider the two following types of justification.

TRANSVALUATIVE JUSTIFICATION

In some contexts, efforts to justify changes in practices, policies, laws, and institutions require an appeal to values that are not widely shared. This is the case for transvaluative justification, which justifies political reforms

27

or changes with reference to normatively defensible if controversial values. Take, for instance, the situation of a liberal egalitarian in a pervasively racist or socially hierarchical society. Such a person could hardly defend what is right and proper through an appeal to widely accepted values. Justification in this case would have to appeal to a different set of values—a set of values that most people in that society would not even perceive as such.[14] It remains an open question what strategy is best employed to defend the values that belong in a transvaluative justification. The history of Western political thought provides us with examples of a variety of different such strategies, including appeals to God, timeless truths, and the preferences of hypothetically situated rational agents.

TRANSFORMATIVE JUSTIFICATION

This type of justification takes place in the context of a wholescale transformation of an existing political or social system. The change here is not incremental and discrete, as in the case of a reform, but radical and systemic. There are at least two different circumstances when a transformative justification seems necessary: (a) regime change and (b) polity change.[15]

(A) Regime changes involve a transformation in the fundamental rules of a political or social system. This type of transformation takes place when a state changes its constitution (as happened, for instance, in the United States in 1787, in France in 1946 and 1962, and in Spain in 1977) or when it transforms its economic system (as happened in many of the former Soviet-bloc countries following the fall of communism). A regime change is fundamentally different from a mere change of government or a change of tax policy. Typically, a transformation of this sort takes place only in the face of a crisis such as a coup or military defeat. But we can identify more peaceful transformational moments in the history of democratic regimes. The constitutional history of the United States serves as an illustrative example. That history contains, as Bruce Ackerman has persuasively argued, a number of extraordinary constitutional transformations that took place at the time of the Reconstruction, the New Deal, and the civil rights movement.[16] The important point to grasp about such regime changes is that they affect the fundamental rules of the game— rules that lie beyond the reach of day-to-day democratic governments. For this reason, they require a different type of justification than that necessary in the case of ordinary reforms.

(B) Polity changes are no less far-reaching than regime changes, but they apply to different features of a political system. Whereas a regime change involves a change in basic rules, a polity change involves a change in the boundaries, membership, and identity of a polity. When a state incorporates another or when one state secedes from another, a polity change takes place. A polity change will often coincide with a regime change—as happened in 1989 in the former Soviet countries—but these two changes are different, and a polity change need not entail a regime change. Consider, for instance, the breakup of Czechoslovakia in 1993. While this breakup, which brought into existence the Czech Republic and Slovakia, involved a polity change, it did not entail a regime change, at least in the sense of a transformation in the nature of the political or economic systems, which remained (roughly) democratic and capitalist in both counties both before and after the breakup.

These four forms of justification—reconciliatory, reformative, transvaluative, and transformative—are not meant to exhaust all the different forms of justification that take place in moral and political life. Nor are they meant to resolve all uncertainty about their own contexts of application. Arguments in moral and political life sometimes take the form of a disagreement about the type of justification needed in a specific situation. But they can also take the form of a disagreement about the actual nature of that situation. Such is the case in arguments over the project, process, and product of European integration. For eurosceptics, the project of European integration represents a fundamental rupture—a transformation—in the political life of their nation and of Europe in general. A transformation of this nature, so they contend, stands in need of a powerful justification. Eurosceptics are not always sure what type of justification would be necessary to legitimate this transformation. For some, a referendum would be necessary to justify the alienation of sovereignty to a supranational authority. For others, this referendum should require a supermajority. For still others, there never can be a justification for the alienation of national sovereignty. Faced with these objections, some proponents of European integration maintain that Europe already constitutes a quasi-federal polity.[17] From this perspective, the justification of any further European integration—including the formation of a unitary sovereign Europe—requires only a reformative rather than a transformative justification. The disagreement here between pro- and anti-Europeans derives, at least in part, from genuine uncertainty about the current nature of the European Union. This uncertainty needs further explanation.

CHAPTER 1

The EU as an Intergovernmental Organization

No one can seriously dispute the fact that the process of European integration has had a profound impact on the domestic and international politics of all European countries. The Treaty of Rome (1957) proclaimed that the aim of this process of integration was to create "an ever closer union . . . among the peoples of Europe." Now, almost fifty years later—following the Single European Act (1986), the Treaty of European Union (1992), the creation of a European Central Bank and a single European currency (2002), and a Constitutional Treaty (2004)—Europeans belong to. . . . what?[18] This ostensibly simple, ontological question provokes considerable scholarly disagreement and political controversy.

Perhaps the least controversial perspective on the nature of the European Union is to describe it as a so-called intergovernmental organization. From this perspective, Europe's member states remain the salient political actors in the EU; they have simply "pooled their sovereignty" over a limited range of policies. In support of this view, "intergovernmentalists" note that the powers that Europe's member states have delegated to the EU remain relatively marginal or inconsequential when compared with the full range of powers exercised by the modern state. Thus, for an "intergovernmentalist" such as Andrew Moravcsik, "the EU plays almost no role . . . in most of the issue-areas about which European voters care most, such as taxation, social welfare provision, defence, high foreign policy, policing, education, cultural policy, human rights, and small business policy."[19] This statement, which was written before the signing of the Constitutional Treaty, would have to be modified in light of that treaty, but only marginally. Even under the new Constitutional Treaty, member states will retain most of the core competences mentioned by Moravcsik, and the EU will continue to be governed by political institutions that allow member states a great deal of direct or indirect control. For this reason, it is only a slight exaggeration to describe the EU, as Moravcsik does, as

a limited international institution to coordinate national regulation of trade in goods and services, and the resulting flow of economic factors. Its substantive scope and institutional prerogatives are limited accordingly. The EU constitutional order is not only barely a federal state; it is barely recognizable as a state at all. To term it a "superstate" is absurd.[20]

30

It is important to recognize, however, that even if we accept the "intergovernmentalist" view that the EU is not now a "superstate," nothing follows about the normative desirability of such a state. It is, in short, quite possible to hold the view that the EU is currently an intergovernmental organization and is likely to remain so but also to believe on normative grounds that it ought to be transformed into a superstate. Descriptive, predictive, and normative judgments need not, in other words, coincide. No less important, if the EU in its present form *is* an intergovernmental organization, then a federal Europe—whether in its sovereignist or postsovereignist incarnations—would constitute a radical change. For this reason, the sovereignist and postsovereignist project of European political integration thus requires what I called above a transformative rather than a reformative justification.

In calling for a transformative justification for the European project, I am advancing a line of argument most commonly advanced by eurosceptics, who complain that the European process of integration has proceeded—and continues to proceed—without appropriate acknowledgement of the far-reaching changes involved. But the argument advanced here in support of a transformative justification applies in equal measure to the eurosceptic project of a Europe of nation-states. In other words, the goal of at least some eurosceptics to abolish the EU is no less far-reaching than the project of at least some European federalists to establish a "superstate." If the arguments of these federalists must meet strict justificatory standards, because their goals are so transformative, then the arguments of eurosceptics must meet strict justificatory standards too. I consider the difficulties facing eurosceptics in the next chapter. In the remaining sections of this chapter, I describe and defend a standard of justification that arguments in support of the European project must satisfy.

Justification and European Integration

Justification plays a central role in contemporary political theory partly for sociological reasons and partly for normative reasons.[21] From a sociological point of view, the emphasis on justification represents an effort to find a basis of agreement among people who share different conceptions of the good. The idea of basing the social bond on a thick collective ethos—a religion, say, or a life of civic engagement—is, from this perspective, obsolete. If modern democratic societies are to forge unity out of diversity, they must look elsewhere for a common basis of agreement. The hope is that, notwithstanding the fact of moral and cultural diversity, the members of a modern society can agree on basic justificatory procedures.

From a normative point of view, basic justificatory procedures must also be fair. A normative theory of justification supplies a conception of fairness partly through a specification of these procedures and partly through a specification of the participants in these procedures. Normatively, it is not actual agreement that matters but the hypothetical agreement of suitably situated persons. In a modern liberal society, a suitably situated person rightfully thinks of himself or herself as a free and equal citizen. A fair justificatory procedure yields outcomes acceptable to such a person.

In their efforts to specify a fair justificatory procedure, political theorists variously provide more and less detailed specifications of procedures and participants. With this point in mind, it would be helpful to distinguish between what might be termed *filtering* and *funneling* approaches to fair justificatory procedures. In the filtering approach, a fair justificatory procedure restricts very few types of arguments or claims. It does not seek to produce a single fair outcome but merely to get rid of the most unfair outcomes. In contrast to this filtering approach to justification, the funneling approach filters out a wide range of arguments and "funnels" those remaining in such a way that they yield if not a single determinate outcome then a very limited range of outcomes.

Most contemporary political theories of justification employ a mixture of filtering and funneling devices. Stuart Hampshire's procedural theory of justice represents perhaps the purest example of the filtering approach.[22] For Hampshire—who values very highly moral and cultural pluralism—a fair justificatory procedure is so nonrestrictive that it could conceivably yield outcomes unacceptable to a free and equal citizen. No liberal theory of justification could be this permissive. Some liberal theorists are, however, closer to the filtering end of the spectrum than others. Jürgen Habermas's discourse theory, for example, is far less restrictive and thus allows for a greater range of outcomes than does John Rawls's political liberalism.[23]

The value of the distinction between filtering and funneling approaches to justification will become more apparent below. Suffice it here to say that the current debate over European political integration is desperately in need of a standard of adequacy that arguments in support of the European project must meet. This standard of adequacy will filter out irrelevant considerations, unfair considerations, and considerations insufficient to the task of justifying the far-reaching transformations envisaged by European federalists. With these aims in mind, I intend in the remainder of this chapter to defend what I term a *democratic standard of justification*. This standard of justification imposes three requirements on arguments seeking to justify the European project: a *requirement of publicity*, a *requirement of accessibility*, and a *requirement of sufficiency*.

The Requirement of Publicity

A very crude justification for the project of European integration might take the form of the claim that a federal Europe would be extremely beneficial to a particular segment of European society, such as, say, "Irish pig farmers," "Brussels real estate owners," "Italians," or—to mention a more impersonal segment of European society—"Europe's multinational corporations." Such justifications can be described as sectarian justifications. They identify a particular group that will benefit from European integration. It is possible, but unlikely, that the European project can proceed through a multiplicity of sectarian justifications. If enough powerful groups within Europe have a self-serving interest in establishing a federal Europe, then a federal Europe will likely emerge. The problem with sectarian justifications for European integration is that they do not appeal more broadly to Europeans in general. The opposite of a sectarian justification might thus be termed a general justification. On the face of it, the European project needs a general justification, which is to say a justification that appeals to all Europeans.

Earlier, when describing the role of justification in contemporary political theory, I noted that justification has a sociological and a normative dimension. The search for a general justification for European integration corresponds to the sociological dimension. The search for what might be termed a public justification corresponds to the normative dimension of justification. Most political theorists care more about public justification than general justification. A public justification seeks to identify a standpoint from which political institutions can be justified to the people who must live under and operate these institutions. In an ideal world, the political institutions that can be publicly justified would coincide with the political institutions that currently exist. But the aim of a public justification is as much transformative as reconciliatory. It seeks to identify a standpoint for identifying the institutions that *ought* to exist.

John Rawls's political theory provides the most influential modern example of a theory of public justification.[24] In his *Theory of Justice*, Rawls famously posits a hypothetical choice situation (an "original position") that defines the standpoint from which we can justify to each other our basic political institutions. The hypothetical choice situation aims to capture the essential features of the modern individual and contemporary society. Indeed, the hypothetical choice situation owes its justificatory power solely to the fact that it has *filtered out* everything but these essential features.[25] The critical task that confronts anyone seeking to employ a public justification is the selection of these essential features. Ideally, these features ought to capture the fundamental values of our current way of life. Thus, for Rawls, "the conditions embodied in the description of the original position are ones that we do in fact accept. Or, if we do not, then perhaps we can be persuaded to do so by philosophical reflection."[26] Rawls's own theory of justice captures the essential features of the person and society in terms of a highly moralized conception of the person. Rather than follow Rawls's own account of the person, it suffices here to define the essential features of the person and society in terms of certain basic values that lie at the center of our current way of life. These basic values—which I intend to call *public values*—form the essential presuppositions of our form of social cooperation. These public values can be specified, *at least provisionally*, to include the moral equality of all individuals, personal security, personal and political liberty, and material prosperity.[27] A public justification is a justification that an individual who embraced these public values *could accept*. Such an individual I call (for reasons of brevity) a *bare citizen*.

The account provided here of public justification remains abstract and incomplete. A lot more needs to be said about both the content and the status of these public values. But before I say more about these values, I want to clarify the conditional nature of public justifications. A public justification does not provide a universal apodictic justification that all people everywhere must—on pain of contradiction or disqualification as a rational agent—accept.[28] A public justification seeks only to justify political principles or institutions from the perspective of a hypothetical choice situation designed to capture the essential features of our situation. Thus someone *could accept* these principles and institutions if they adopted the standpoint of what I termed above the *bare citizen*.

Whether anyone actually does accept these principles and institutions will turn on a number of further considerations. Here it would be helpful to distinguish a number of different ways that political principles and institutions can be related to the public values that define the bedrock commitments of the bare citizen. First, there are some justificatory arguments that the bare citizen is logically compelled to accept given the prior commitment to any or all of the public values. Thus it might be argued that the bare citizen is logically compelled to accept some form of democratic government given a prior commitment to personal and political liberty. Second, there are some justificatory arguments that the bare citizen could accept given the truth of certain empirical claims connecting various states of the world to these public values. Thus it might be argued that the bare citizen ought reasonably to accept some form of market economy given a prior commitment to material prosperity and knowing what we now know about the functioning of nonmarket economies. And third, there are some justificatory arguments that the bare citizen could not—either logically or reasonably—accept. Thus the bare citizen could not accept slavery, feudalism, or the disenfranchisement of Welshmen.

If there is a good case to be made for the European project of political integration, it must be made out of justificatory arguments that the bare citizen is either logically or reasonably required to accept. The idea of a public justification—the requirement of publicity, in short—is designed to clarify these two types of justificatory argument. It is also designed to filter out justificatory arguments—and, by extension, political principles and institutions—that contradict or deny one or more of the public values that define the commitments of a bare citizen. Thus the requirement of publicity will filter out arguments, whether for or against European political integration, that deny the importance of equality, personal and political liberty, and other public values that define our form of social cooperation.

It must now be fairly obvious that the requirement of publicity rests on a set of public values that are alleged to lie at the very core of contemporary European societies. Arriving at a list of these public values is a somewhat more contentious process than some political philosophers like to acknowledge. But (following Rawls again) we can begin by positing certain public values as fixed points of agreement—equality, liberty, security, and so forth—from which we can develop a provisional account of public justification. The content of these public values must, however, remain open on due reflection to modification—whether by

subtraction or addition.[29] Anyone who invokes a standard of public justification in Europe today must further be prepared to explain why the
bare citizen embraces personal and political liberty but not, say, Christianity, environmentalism, or ethnocultural nationalism. This challenge
is especially germane in the context of the debate over a European Constitution, because some political leaders have sought to include in the
constitutional Preamble a commitment to Europe's Christian heritage.
Others have sought to justify European political institutions on the basis
of a distinctive European form of social democratic solidarity. In later
chapters, I will argue that the requirement of publicity filters out these
more substantial (or "comprehensive") conceptions of the good. At this
stage, however, I want to consider a further range of arguments that a
democratic standard of justification will exclude.

The Requirement of Accessibility

The requirement of accessibility filters out a certain class of complex justificatory argument that cannot be grasped by people who lack training
or expertise. The intuitive idea behind this requirement is that citizens
ought to be able to participate on equal terms in any debate involving a
constitutional transformation. In taking this approach, I follow Christopher Bertram, who captures nicely the grounds for rejecting a certain
type of complex argument:

> [I]f someone is committed to a certain sort of ideal of democratic com-
> munity . . . then they ought to reject as basic constitutional principles
> to govern that community principles that are fully comprehensible
> only to those with specialized knowledge. Moreover, there will be a
> strong presumption against principles which, though transparent in
> themselves, require for their justification arguments available only to
> those with specialized knowledge.[30]

Bertram himself leaves the ideal of democratic community "largely un-
defended," but it is not difficult to understand why this ideal has a certain appeal in contemporary European society. Rather than speaking
here of a "democratic community," it would be better employ the term a
"democratic society," which can be understood in the Tocquevillean
sense of a society of moral, legal, and social equals. A democratic society
is, in this sense, the achievement of an age that has freed itself from an
aristocratic social order. In the first half of the nineteenth century, Tocque-

ville had to leave Europe and travel to America in order to witness a democratic society in operation. Now European societies are, for the most part, democratic. Europeans rightfully think of themselves as social equals, regardless of differences in wealth, birth, or educational achievement. Democratic societies, however, remain a fragile achievement. They exist today in a socioeconomic environment of increasing disparities of income and wealth. These disparities are partly a function of, and partly coincident with, the emergence of new elites made up of people whose knowledge-intensive skills are essential for the maintenance of a technologically advanced economy. A democratic society is no longer, as in Tocqueville's day, vulnerable to hereditary aristocracy. But it is vulnerable to this new elite. A democratic society must insist, in the face of technological and scientific experts, that the basic political and institutional rules of society be understandable to ordinary citizens equipped with the knowledge that can be acquired from, say, completing a high school education and watching the news.[31]

To insist that justifying arguments meet some standard of accessibility is especially important in the case of the project of European integration. That project involves a fundamental transformation in the political structure of postwar Europe; it envisages the replacement of nation-states with a federal entity (whether a unitary state or a postsovereign polity). Such a transformation must be justified in terms that the ordinary citizen of Europe can grasp. Many of the arguments employed in the justification of European integration simply fail this test. Certainly, this is the case with many of the economic and political-economic arguments used to justify European integration. No ordinary citizen can be expected to understand Hecksher-Olin trade theory, Mundell's theory of currency, or the notion of optimum bargaining strategies under conditions of asymmetrical interdependence. Insofar as the European project depends on arguments as complex as these, the European project will fail to satisfy the requirement of accessibility.

Like the other requirements defended here, there is room for reasonable disagreement about the level of complexity that is permitted by the requirement of accessibility. There is no unambiguous boundary that divides the acceptably difficult from the unacceptably complex. Yet if people argue about the location of this boundary, they are at least arguing about something important. Members of a democratic society ought to insist that, on matters of great constitutional importance, arguments be conducted in terms that they can comprehend. This does not mean, however, that all policy decisions, all laws enacted, have to draw on arguments that meet the requirement of accessibility. To insist on such a requirement would condemn all democratic societies to the poverty of a preindustrial era. The requirement of accessibility applies only to the justification of a fundamental constitutional transformation. This point begs the further question of what constitutes a fundamental constitutional transformation. For some eurosceptics, the Single European Act and the Treaty of European Union count as constitutional transformations. From their perspective, the requirement of accessibility ought to apply in all cases that involve a transfer of sovereignty away from the nation-state. Again it would be naive to believe that a bright-line boundary separates "an incremental reform" from "a constitutional transformation." But disagreement over this issue is not unhealthy. The premise of such a disagreement is that a fundamental transformation in a political institutional structure requires an extraordinary justification. When people demand that arguments in support of any such transformation meet the test of accessibility, they are acting in the right democratic spirit.

It might well be the case that all cognitively valid arguments can be presented in a way that would allow them to pass through the filter imposed by a requirement of accessibility. If this is indeed true, the requirement of accessibility applies to the manner in which arguments are presented rather than to any substantive class of arguments. It is, however, a possibility that some cognitively valid arguments simply cannot be presented in a way comprehensible to the citizen of ordinary knowledge and average intelligence. If this is the case, a strict adherence to the requirement of accessibility will force Europeans to accept a political-institutional structure that is less than optimal. If we value a democratic society, however, we should be willing to put up with this cost.

The Requirement of Sufficiency

The requirements of publicity and accessibility function primarily as filters of arguments in support of the European project. Thus the publicity requirement filters out what might be termed inappropriate arguments, and the accessibility requirement filters out excessively complex arguments. The requirement of sufficiency plays a similar role. It filters out arguments that are empirically false or weak.

Many arguments in support of European political integration do little more than show that a politically integrated Europe is consistent with some specific political value, such as democracy or citizenship or peace or prosperity. Mere consistence is, however, inadequate. If Europe is to undergo the wrenching transformations entailed by the sovereignist and postsovereignist conceptions of the European project, then Europe needs a stronger justification.

It is difficult, in the abstract, to describe the necessary degree of strength that arguments for European integration must possess. To gain more precision, I want to draw a distinction between a weak justification for European integration, a strong justification for European integration, and a specific justification for European integration. A specific justification, as we shall see, occupies a position in between a weak justification and a strong justification.

An argument yields a weak justification for a policy, law, or institutional arrangement when it appeals to values, interests, or normative principles that are merely *consistent* with—which is to say, not contradicted, nor ruled out, by—that policy, law, or institutional arrangement. Thus it might be said that liberty as a value yields only a weak justification for jury trials. This point follows from the fact that some liberal democratic states have jury trials, while others, without obvious damage to their status as liberal democratic states, do not. An argument yields a strong justification for a policy, law, or institutional arrangement when it appeals to values, interests, or normative principles that *require*—which is to say, could not be present in the absence of—that policy, law, or institutional arrangement. Thus it might be said that liberty as a value provides a strong justification for the rule of law. In states that lack the rule of law—in states characterized by arbitrary government, in other words—political liberty does not exist. An argument yields a specific justification for a policy, law, or institutional arrangement when it appeals to values, interests, or normative principles that are *effectively* and *efficiently* protected by that policy, law, or institutional arrangement.

The terms introduced here—weak justification, strong justification, and specific justification—help to clarify the debate over European integration in a number of useful ways. They permit us, for instance, to identify the inadequacy of purely weak justifications. Political philosophers are particularly culpable here. They spend tremendous intellectual energy on the task of showing that a federal Europe could, given the right mixture of institutions, also be a democratic Europe. They rarely notice that this argument, even if it were valid, provides only a weak justification for the construction of a federal Europe.[32] Democracy is, on the face of it, already effectively and efficiently protected at the national level. While it may be desirable to democratize Europe's existing political institutions, democracy does not provide a specific justification for those institutions.

In making the condition of sufficiency a component of the justification for European integration, a burden is placed on proponents of the European project to specify how that project is connected to its justifying values or principles. In the account offered here of the requirement of sufficiency, this effort requires an argument, first, about the *efficacy* of the European project and, second, about the *efficiency* of the European project. The European project may offer *effective* protection for its justifying values—securing peace in Europe, for instance—yet fail to provide *efficient* protection. Effective protection is a matter of matching means to ends. Efficient protection is a matter of selecting the least costly means.

Arguments put forward in support of the European project will be *ineffective* when they are based on factually incorrect evidence or bogus causal claims. Chapter 4 below argues that this problem afflicts much of the literature that attempts to justify European political integration on the grounds that it provides a solution to the alleged problems posed by globalization. Thus even if we were to allow that, say, capital flight and competition from low-wage economies constitute "problems," the federalist conception of the European project does not, so I argue, provide an effective solution. In this respect, the globalization argument for the European project fails the requirement of sufficiency.

Arguments put forward in support of the European project will be *inefficient* when they propose effective but unnecessarily costly solutions to purported problems. Removing one's teeth to solve the problem of toothache may be effective, but it is hardly efficient. In the case of arguments over European political integration, the problem of inefficient solutions arises most frequently in the case of arguments concerning the relationship between the European project and Europe's success in achieving peace since 1945. There are a number of problems with this line of argument, some of which have to do with efficacy and some with efficiency considerations. Let us assume, for the sake of argument, that the European project offers an effective solution to the problems of insecurity in Europe. This still leaves open the issue of efficiency. A eurosceptic might contend that there are less "costly" ways of ensuring peace in Europe than the construction of a federal Europe. A Europe of nation-states allied with the United States in NATO, so this eurosceptic might further argue, provides effective security without requiring Europeans to give up anything so valuable as their national sovereignty. This eurosceptic argument makes it clear that the idea of providing efficient protection for a justifying value entails something akin to seeking a Pareto optimal form of protection. An effective protection of any justifying value is efficient when it does not require the sacrifice of anything of comparable value.

The account of effective and efficient protection provided here does not resolve all ambiguities concerning the application of these terms. It is far from clear, for instance, how people are to arrive at conclusions concerning the sacrifice of comparable values. To a certain extent, some of these ambiguities will be resolved when the requirement of sufficiency is used in conjunction with the requirements of publicity and accessibility. Thus it follows from the requirement of publicity, for instance, that not all values are indeed comparable. But even allowing for the gains to precision that will come from these other requirements, people will continue to disagree about the nature of effective and efficient protection. The important point to recognize here, however, is that when they disagree about the application of these terms, they are at least disagreeing about the right things. Even if the requirement of sufficiency does nothing more than focus these disagreements, it furthers the cause of intelligent debate.

A DEMOCRATIC STANDARD OF JUSTIFICATION

This chapter has defended a conception of justification suitable for discussing and evaluating the project of European integration. The basic conceptual premise of the discussion is that the project of European integration involves a transformation of Europe's existing political system. Eurosceptics are correct to challenge proponents of this project to provide some justification for such a transformation. Actual political debates over the European project suffer from a lack of any agreement on—or even minimal understanding of—the type of arguments that are relevant in thinking about this issue. Political philosophers have an important role to play here in identifying and defending a conception of justification suitable for evaluating such a transformation. The conception of justification defended here contains three basic requirements: a requirement of publicity, a requirement of accessibility, and a requirement of sufficiency.

41

In the following chapters, I intend to evaluate a variety of different arguments—both for and against the project of European integration—against the benchmark defined by this conception of justification. Before doing so, it would be useful to consider first a number of objections that might be raised to the approach adopted here. The most obvious objection concerns my account of the project of European integration itself. The project of European integration as defined here involves either the construction of a unitary European state (the *sovereignist project of European integration*) or the establishment of a new type of federal polity that locates the functions of governance at a number of different jurisdictional levels (the *postsovereignist project of European integration*). Critics might object that this characterization of the European project lacks all credibility. Even the most ardent defenders of European political integration do not envisage a unitary European state. For many observers, the true project of European integration is simply to ensure that Europe acquires some political institutions—ideally democratic political institutions—that can hold in check the extensive form of economic integration that has already occurred.[33]

Against this objection, two different responses are available. One response, which I do not wish to pursue here, would be to retrieve from the historical record the federalist statements, actions, and ambitions of Europe's leading politicians and administrators.[34] It is conceivable—although I do not wish to press the point—that federalist ideas and ambitions have played a much more significant causal role than is generally acknowledged.[35] The other response—that taken here—is to allow that even if federalism were nothing more than "a bogeyman"—as Alan Milward describes it—it is a bogeyman with the power to frighten a lot of people in Europe today.[36] For this reason alone, it is worthy of philosophical scrutiny. Viewed up close, a bogeymen can lose his power. That was true of the Wizard of Oz. Perhaps that will be true here too.

A second objection to the argument of this chapter concerns the account given here of a transformative justification. I have argued that the European project entails a fundamental transformation in a regime or polity. Such a transformation requires, so I argued, a particularly stringent form of justification. It might of course be objected that the European project, even when defined as entailing a form of federalism, does not involve any great transformation, because the European Union—in its present institutional shape and with its present legal-political competences—is already a quasi-federal entity. This being the case, a federal Europe does not need to meet the requirements of a transformative justification; it needs to satisfy only the lower standard of a reformative justification.

Again I have two responses to this criticism. First, I think that the view of the current EU as a quasi-federal political entity is inaccurate. The EU is still run largely by, and in the interests of, national governments. The "intergovernmentalists" are, in this respect, correct. Yet even if I were wrong about this, it would be a mistake to think that we can dispense with a transformative justification. Most Europeans are familiar with the nation-state as a mode of political organization. If the new Europe—whether a unitary state or some form of postsovereign entity—is to achieve some popular legitimacy, it will be because people comprehend its raison d'être. By demanding that arguments in support of the new Europe pass a standard of transformative justification, we can be more confident in our support for this new political entity (however it is best described).

A third objection to the argument of this chapter concerns the tripartite standard of justification I have defended here. The three requirements (publicity, accessibility, and sufficiency) will strike some critics as too permissive and others as too restrictive. My standard of justification might be construed as too permissive because my account of the commitments of the so-called bare citizen fails to incorporate public values (such as social justice) that are features of all modern European societies. Alternatively, my standard might be construed as too restrictive because it excludes arguments that are necessary to justify the European project. Thus anyone who believes that the European project requires a commitment to comprehensive conceptions of cosmopolitan citizenship might find my standard of justification too restrictive.

In the abstract, it is difficult to say much in response to these criticisms. In the following three chapters, I draw on this standard of justification to evaluate some specific arguments that have been made both for and against the European project. Suffice it here to say that the tripartite standard of justification defended in this chapter rests on a spare democratic ideal. I take it as axiomatic—and thus do not provide any defense for the claim—that European society is deeply and irreversibly democratic. While some contemporary political philosophers like to build into the idea of democracy all manner of controversial substantive commitments, I assume that, beyond a set of minimal commitments to security, equality, liberty, and material affluence, the members of a democratic society can reasonably disagree about such issues as the place of religion in public life, the morality of abortion or euthanasia, and the appropriate levels and types of social protection.[37]

A fourth (and, for the moment, final) objection to the argument of this chapter focuses on the effort to identify a justification for the European project that people in Europe *could accept* rather than a justification that no one could "reasonably reject."[38] Yet while it makes sense to conceptualize urgent moral claims—do not murder, steal from the poor, and so forth—in terms of requirements that *no one* could reasonably reject, political arguments are different. In politics, it is enough that we identify a common perspective that "we," the members of a particular society at a particular time, could, given a commitment to certain basic public values, accept. Indeed, the force of a justification that no one could "reasonably reject" seems out of place—even undesirable—in the messy, contingent world of politics, whatever might be the case in the world of morality.

Nationalism

Fifty years ago—roughly at the time when the current process of European integration got going—very few people in European intellectual and scholarly circles had anything very favorable to say about nationalism. Conservatives disliked it because of its revolutionary potential to undermine existing state boundaries; socialists saw it as a threat to the international solidarity of workers; and liberals condemned it as a regressive form of collectivism.[1] In its formative postwar stages, the European project benefited from this animus toward nationalism. Overcoming nationalism and integrating Europe were widely seen as desirable and complementary goals.[2]

Nationalism is far more intellectually respectable today than in the early postwar period. This respectability does not, to be sure, extend to all forms of nationalism, which remains an extremely variegated, multifaceted phenomenon. Few intellectuals and scholars would defend those nationalisms that take xenophobic or chauvinistic forms. But more moderate forms of nationalism—such as the notion that the modern state ought to protect and promote a common national culture—are now widely defended.[3] Part of nationalism's new respectability derives from a sociological observation: most successful modern democratic states possess a common national culture (which is not to deny the existence in those states of distinctive minority cultures). Some sociological theorists of nationalism—including, most influentially, Ernest Gellner—have argued that that the overlap between "state" and "nation" is not a contingent but an inescapable feature of the modern world. If this sociological thesis is correct, then the case for a multinational European federal polity—and a fortiori a unitary European superstate—is simply a nonstarter. To gauge the plausibility of this sociological thesis, it is worth considering in more detail the factors that have led people to conclude that the nation-state remains the only viable type of polity in the world today.

Some consideration of the potency of nationalism is especially important in the case of European integration, because nationalism—in the form of an ideology rather than a set of social processes—forms a central strand of the worldview of the eurosceptic. The next chapter considers the eurosceptics' defense of the nation-state. But it would be useful first to understand the social and historical context in which these arguments over the nation-state take place.

MODERNITY AND NATIONALISM

Since the term "nationalism" is now used, in both common and scholarly parlance, in so many different ways, it would be helpful to distinguish a number of the more common usages of the term. Broadly stated, it is possible to identify at least seven major uses of the term "nationalism": (1) nationalism as a social, economic, and/or political process that forms and sustains a modern nation-state; (2) nationalism as a principle of political legitimacy; (3) nationalism as an ideology or movement of national self-determination; (4) nationalism as an expression of loyalty or solidarity toward one's nation; (5) nationalism as an ideology or movement of (national) cultural preservation or renewal; (6) nationalism as an ideology or movement focused on the purity of "the nation" understood in ethnic terms; (7) nationalism as an aggressive and militaristic form of xenophobia.

Most contemporary social theorists are primarily concerned with nationalism in the first two senses—(1) nationalism as nation-state formation and (2) nationalism as a principle of political legitimacy—rather than with the various ideological manifestations of nationalism. The intellectual point of departure for most social theorists of nationalism is a commonplace historical observation: political units in the medieval and early modern periods contained many different cultural communities; political units in the modern period contain—or it is widely believed that they ought to contain—a common cultural community. Thus even though most advanced industrial states contain numerous different cultural minorities, many of them comprising relatively recent immigrants, most governments see their mission as assimilating these minorities. The creation of a shared public culture—a national culture—that is taught in schools is now thought to be an essential requirement of a stable and prosperous polity. Why? What has changed to make the state a national culture–creating entity?

The most sustained and influential attempt to answer these questions is found in the writings of Ernest Gellner. Gellner himself, it should be noted, is no ideological nationalist. He has little favorable to say about nationalist doctrines, which he thinks contain a great deal of false consciousness and historical error.[4] He nonetheless contends that nationalism—which he defines as a principle of political legitimacy requiring states to represent culturally defined nations—is an inevitable consequence of industrialization.[5] While premodern polities once contained multiple different locally segmented subcultures, the modern polity, so Gellner argues, requires a common public culture. Such a culture, he argues, is the precondition for any successful modern industrial society. The modern state must, as a consequence, either transform its local, segmented subcultures into a common public culture—a "national" culture, in other words—or lose out to neighboring states that have pulled off this transformation. Put differently, the modern state must, as a condition of its own legitimacy, represent a culturally defined nation (or "nation-state").

The notion that nationalism (understood in Gellner's sense of the term) is "modern" now forms something of a scholarly consensus.[6] Disagreement persists, however, on the question of what features of the modern world give rise to the "one (cultural) nation, one state" principle. Few scholars follow Gellner in stressing the role played by industrialization.[7] Other factors that have drawn attention include the rise of popular sovereignty, the appearance of print capitalism, and the concurrent emergence of the centralized bureaucratic state and the international state system. The merits of these competing explanations need not, for the moment, concern us.[8] What matters is the more general point: nationalism—the process by which sovereign territorial states and nations coincide—is widely believed to be a central feature of modernity. If this thesis is correct, it bears directly on arguments for and against European political integration.

Faced with the claim that the nation-state is a necessary feature of the modern world, the proponent of European political integration would appear to confront a limited number of not very congenial options. One option would be to accept Gellner's claim about the indispensability of the nation-state but to deny that this claim possesses any normative significance. This option would, however, reduce European political integration to a mere utopian aspiration, a worthy and desirable goal but impossible to achieve in the modern world that we now inhabit. A second option would be to reject the claim that the nation-state is a necessary feature of the modern world. We live now, so it might then be argued, in a postmodern and thus "postnationalist" world, a world where the nation-state is an anachronism.[9] A third option would be to accept much of the sociological thesis concerning the indispensability of the nation-state but to argue that a Europeanwide "nation-state" remains a feasible and desirable goal. In this light, it is possible to imagine, as Margaret Canavan puts it,

> that living within the framework of common institutions will create among the population of the EU a new European identity. But if that were to happen, and the new political structure were indeed to be able to act as a single unit in critical situations, this would imply not that the European Union had superseded the nation-state but that it had turned into a nation-state on a grander scale.[10]

An obvious objection to this third option is that nationalism sustains existing nation-states rather than the creation of a nation-state on any "grander scale." The next section of this chapter offers an account of nationalism that is consistent with the idea that nationalism could, under certain circumstances, operate on a European-wide level.

HOBBES, NATIONALISM, AND POLITICAL LEGITIMACY

Despite an emphasis on nationalism as a principle of political legitimacy, Gellner and other sociological theorists of nationalism rarely consider in any detail those alternative conceptions of political legitimacy that nationalism is supposed to have discredited and made irrelevant. Yet unless one identifies these alternatives, which are numerous, it is difficult to assess claims about the inevitability of nationalism as a principle of political legitimacy and the indispensability of the type of polity—the "nation-state"—that this principle legitimates. In an effort to gain a clearer sense of the distinctiveness of nationalism as a principle of political legitimacy, it would be useful to consider at least one nonnationalist conception of political legitimacy. I take as my example Hobbes's theory of indirect sovereignty, which can be understood as an approach to political legitimacy that the modern nationalist world has rejected.

Hobbes's political writings provide an account of the form that popular sovereignty ought to assume in a world that needs effective, impersonal, and absolute rule. Popular sovereignty itself is not a modern idea. Direct popular government by leading citizens was a feature of the Athenian polis, the Roman republic, and a number of the medieval Italian city-states.[11] Each instance of direct popular government inspired its propagandists and its detractors, whose writings were later read and criticized by scholars across Europe and America. Thomas Hobbes is one of the most important of these later critics. While Hobbes is widely acknowledged as the chief intellectual proponent of a new form of sovereign political authority, his political writings are no less important for the battery of arguments they contain against various alternative conceptions of legitimate political authority, including divine right of kings, mixed government, direct popular government, and—if we choose to read him anachronistically (and why not?)—nationalism.

Hobbes worked out a theory of political legitimacy that reconciled what all other political thinkers had considered irreconcilable: popular sovereignty, on the one hand, and effective, impersonal, and absolute rule, on the other.[12] Hobbes achieved this goal through the devices of "representation" and "indirect sovereignty." "A multitude of men," as Hobbes put it, "are made one person when they are by one man, or one person, represented. . . . For it is the unity of the represener, not the unity of the represented, that maketh the person one."[13] For Hobbes, individuals—conceived in their natural state as free and equal—form the constituting force of a sovereign political authority, which, once constituted, does not permit them to play any direct role in the exercise of that political authority: hence, "indirect sovereignty."[14] To allow citizens a role in the running of the polity—direct participatory government, in other words—is, for Hobbes, a recipe for disorder. In Hobbes's alternative conception of indirect sovereignty, the people are represented by the sovereign. They remain the authors of the sovereign's actions, even though they themselves do not directly participate in the decisions that the sovereign takes.

Hobbes often used the term "nation" in his political writings, and it is not difficult to discern a number of apparent similarities between his account of indirect popular sovereignty and the later emergence of the modern nation-state. Two similarities in particular stand out. First, Hobbes's emphasis on the role of representation in providing unity means that there are no limits to the territory or to the size of the population that the sovereign can represent.[15] Second, Hobbes's sovereign is personified as an "Artificial Man" (*Leviathan*) or a "Civil Person" (*De Cive*) that represents individuals. These individuals—as the famous frontispiece of *Leviathan* shows—possess a commonality defined solely by their relationship to political power. In this respect, the Hobbesian "Artificial Man" or "Civil Person" bears some similarities to what later theorists of nationalism describe as "a civic nation"—a people defined exclusively by their common and equal relationship to political power.[16]

Notwithstanding these two similarities, the dissimilarities between Hobbes's account of indirect popular sovereignty and the nationalist principle of political legitimacy are even more striking and revealing. Four differences stand out. First, Hobbes makes it clear that the state represents individuals rather than a preexisting corporate body. He constantly reminds his readers that the constituting force of the sovereign state is a multitude of individuals. Prior to the formation of the Sovereign, this multitude is nothing but an agglomeration of individuals.[17] Were the state to dissolve, it would not leave an antecedent nation, people, or prepolitical community; it would leave only these individuals.[18] Second, the Hobbesian Sovereign remains supremely indifferent to the cultural and ethnic characteristics of the individuals it represents. For Hobbes, a state is legitimate simply when it satisfies the conditions of statehood: effective, impersonal, and absolute rule. A third difference is that even if the Hobbesian Sovereign appears to have been created by "a civic (or political) nation"—a body of "citizens" whose political identity is defined exclusively in relationship to political power—this "civic nation" essentially disappears in the act of creating (or authorizing) the Sovereign. Once created, the Hobbesian Sovereign does not need to mobilize "citizens" or to encourage them to think of themselves as anything other than the passive recipients of its—and by extension their own—commands.

For present purposes, the merits of the Hobbesian theory of political legitimacy are less important than the suggestion—contained in Gellner's sociological accounts of nationalism—that this nonnationalist conception of legitimacy is no longer viable. Gellner's objection, in other words, is sociological rather than normative. He claims that something in the modern world has changed. For one reason or another, a state that merely supplies effective, impersonal, and absolute rule will be judged illegitimate unless it can plausibly claim to represent "a culturally defined nation." This point yields a fourth—and perhaps the most important—difference between the Hobbesian theory of political legitimacy and the modern nationalist theory of political legitimacy. In the modern world, most states that have successfully accomplished the Hobbesian task of securing peace and order have done so by first creating and then mobilizing "a culturally defined nation." Modern sociological theories of nationalism seek to explain why the mobilization of nationality is now the route to Hobbesian security whereas in the recent past it was not.[19]

Sociologists have offered a number of different explanations for the centrality of nation-states and nationalism. Gellner, as we have seen, emphasizes the role of industrialization. The difficulty with this argument, however, is that it seeks to identify a materialist explanation for what, in essence, is an ideal phenomenon: a particular conception of political legitimacy. A more plausible explanation of the shift that took place roughly between the seventeenth century (when legitimate political authorities did not need to represent a culturally defined nation) and today (when they do) is to be found in those processes that are commonly lumped together under the term "democratization." Broadly stated, "democratization" has three distinct components: (1) the idea of popular sovereignty, (2) the universal franchise, and (3) an egalitarian (or "Tocquevillean") society. These three components are not only analytically but also historically distinct, in the sense that they can and do appear in different societies at different periods. Thus the idea of popular sovereignty, which emerged in northwestern European societies in the twelfth and thirteenth centuries, entails neither a universal franchise nor the abolition of a society of ranks and orders.

It is crucial to distinguish these three components of democratization in order to comprehend the bearing of popular sovereignty on nationalism. The medieval notion of a regnum as the monarch's property, bestowed on him by God, simply could not accommodate a nationalist principle of political legitimacy. Yet the idea that the state represents the *populus*, the essential point of the doctrine of popular sovereignty, does not—as the brief discussion of Hobbes's political theory has hopefully now made clear—entail the additional idea that a legitimate state must represent "a culturally defined nation." Hobbes himself rejects the idea of a culturally defined nation in favor of a body of individuals who are united solely in virtue of their common membership in the state. In this respect, Istvan Hont is quite correct to observe that for Hobbes (and for those thinkers he directly influenced) there is no distinction between "nation" and "state"; the term "nation-state" is, from this perspective, a tautology. But this observation serves only to underscore the extent to which Hobbes and his epigones differed from modern theorists of nationalism. For these later nationalists, a legitimate state must represent a culturally defined nation, a claim that makes sense only insofar as it is possible to distinguish "nation" and "state." A political theory that does not recognize a distinction between these two terms—nation (which always has a cultural dimension) and state—cannot be recognized as a form of nationalism.

Viewed as a principle that demands some form of congruence between nation and state, nationalism is less directly related to popular sovereignty than it is to two more recent phenomena: the universal franchise and the emergence of (or at least the demand for) social equality. It was only when the middle and lower classes demanded political and social equality that Europe's social and political elites felt the need to create a *nation*—a community of fate that shares a common, distinctive, public culture. The French Revolution is a decisive event in the history of nationalism, not because it marks the emergence of popular sovereignty, but because it marks the emergence in Europe of a polity whose members were encouraged to think of themselves as political and social equals. This is not to say, however, that the French nation-state emerged simultaneously with the French Revolution. It took a long time for the sense of nationhood to triumph over the sectoral divisions of region, religion, class, and ethnicity.[20] The French nation-state, in other words, required an extensive form of state- and elite-led "nation building." In the absence of the state's efforts to create a common public culture, the French state would simply have lacked the unity, cohesion, and animating loyalties necessary to survive the process of democratization.

While it would be a mistake to think that the process that France underwent to become a nation-state can be generalized to all other nation-states, certain features of the French example are generalizable to other cases, and these features allow us to formulate an answer to the question posed at the start of this discussion: Why does nationalism become the dominant mode of legitimating states in the modern era? The Hobbesian doctrine of indirect sovereignty, so we have argued, represents a path not taken. The Hobbesian state, while premised on the idea of popular sovereignty, does not seek to legitimate itself as the representative of an antecedent culturally distinctive nation. In the Hobbesian state, the nation is nothing but a body of individuals under a common state. The principal reason why the modern state requires a shared common public culture is that the modern state needs to engender a deeper sense of loyalty and attachment. To this end, the modern nation-state serves as the representative and guardian of a unique set of practices, customs and traditions. When successful the modern nation-state can thereby transform itself from an impersonal apparatus of law and command into an object of attachment and reverence.

NATIONALISM AND THE APPEAL OF NATIONAL CULTURE

Any explanation of nationalism that emphasizes its macrosociological causes remains vulnerable to the criticism that it simply begs the question of why people care about their common national culture, especially since that culture is invariably a product of myth and artifice. Gellner is one of many sociologists to emphasize the constructed nature of national cultures. He thus explains the appeal of a common public culture in terms of its importance to the individual who wishes to flourish in a modern industrial society. Mastery, through formal education, of this common public culture is the precondition for later occupational success. Such a reductive explanation of the appeal of a national culture does little, however, to explain the fact that people often embrace minority cultures when they would benefit economically from assimilation into the dominant national culture; nor does it explain the ability of national cultures to elicit strong forms of romantic identification and attachment.

A more plausible general explanation of the appeal of national cultures is that people prefer the familiar to the alien. Indeed, people have a tremendous capacity to become attached to, and feel nostalgia for, even the most dysfunctional familiar culture. The modern nation-state legitimates itself, at least in part, by creating a familiar way of life that it then protects. In doing so, the state can appeal to customs and practices that evoke memories associated with one's early childhood. The familiarity of a national culture is, however, not always sufficient to hold people's loyalties, for sometimes people assimilate to new cultures. They leave their villages for cities; they acquire new languages; and they abandon the customs and practices of their parents and ancestors. From the perspective of individuals, the story of the formation of a national culture is less a bookish survey of the impersonal macrosociological changes brought about by popular sovereignty, the universal franchise, and a social equality. It is more palpably a story about choices made by parents and ancestors who, at certain critical junctures, decided that they would forsake old ways of life and embrace the new.

Once enough people have chosen to embrace a new culture, those left behind in the village (or backwater) may find that their traditional way of life can no longer sustain itself. The choices that some people make voluntarily will force others to adapt. Thus, when the more upwardly mobile youth of a particular region decide to move away to work, those left behind will often find that they have no choice but to adapt or follow. This complex pattern of voluntary assimilation and less than voluntary adaptation led in the eighteenth and nineteenth centuries to the formation of core national cultures in Europe's territorial states. In some cases, national minorities successfully resisted the formation of a single national culture. Typically, these national minorities survived because they occupied some niche in the global economy that enabled them to resist the pressure to assimilate. The Welsh, to select a wholly random example, survived as a national minority only because the Welsh economy was sufficiently vibrant at the turn of the last century to allow a Welsh-speaking rural peasantry to form a Welsh-speaking urban proletariat. Wales survived as a distinctive national minority not because it possessed a separate language (that was true of many minorities that subsequently disappeared), nor because the Welsh possessed a venerable history as a self-governing people (they did not), but because of choices—primarily economic choices—that particular individuals and families made in the last century.[21]

The claim made earlier about the tendency of people to prefer the familiar is not incompatible with the observation that people also often choose, with various degrees of willingness, to assimilate to new cultures. The factors that lead people to choose one option rather than the other require further empirical investigation. It is important, however, to recognize that people can and do make different choices when presented with the option of assimilation, because many scholars of nationalism seem to think that they will always choose to preserve the more local and personal culture and reject the option of assimilation.[22] If this were true, nation-states would never have emerged in the first place.

For some theorists of nationalism, the emphasis on national cultures as constructed and chosen misconstrues the unchosen, ethnic character of these national cultures. This ethnosymbolist approach to nationalism is important, if only because it leads to the conclusion that nationalism cannot operate on a grander scale than Europe's current nation-state. Viewed as a set of sociological propositions—rather than a normative defense of the nation-state—the ethnosymbolist approach can be summarized in terms of the following four claims. First, modern nation-states derive at least part of their legitimacy from preexisting ethnic communities. Second, ethnic communities are constituted by myths of descent and shared memories embodied in various cultural symbols, customs, and values. Third, the content of these cultural symbols limits the extent to which latter-day nationalists can construct a modern national identity. Fourth, the individual members of a modern nation-state care about such things as myths of descent and shared memories.

Viewed as a sociological theory, the ethnosymbolist approach to nationalism is difficult to assess. None of its four claims is easy to test empirically, not least because the conceptual terms employed by the theory—ethnic community, myths of descent, shared memories, and so forth—are all but impossible to measure. In the absence of any empirical support, ethnosymbolism relies heavily on the claim that individuals care about myths of descent and shared memories—a claim that ethnosymbolists share with many ardent nationalists. It is worth noting, however, that if this claim were true, it would be difficult to explain the process of European nation-state formation. Most of the major European nation-states have been constructed out of preexisting local, sectoral communities each with its own distinctive customs, myths, and memories. People who once thought of themselves in terms of a class or region now think of themselves as members of a nation. Once we allow that a process of nation building has succeeded in the past, it is difficult to sustain the claim that a process of nation building is an impossibility on a grander European scale. Typically, those who hold this impossibility thesis really want to say that there is something undesirable about the idea of Europe itself as a " nation-state." In the present debate over European political integration, the most politically important versions of the impossibility and undesirability arguments about nation building on the broadest European scale are to be found in the writings of conservative and social democratic nationalists. These two different forms of ideological nationalism, which I will examine in the next chapter, draw on the sociological theory of nationalism to support their claim that an all-comprehensive European "nation-state" is neither possible nor desirable.

✳ CHAPTER 3 ✳

Euroscepticism

Euroscepticism in its broadest sense refers to a political doctrine or movement motivated by hostility to European political integration. The distinctions drawn earlier (in the introduction) between different dimensions of European political integration permit us to distinguish three somewhat different targets of the eurosceptics' hostility. One target is the *product* of European integration—the EU itself. Eurosceptics variously complain that the EU is (among other things) wasteful, unnecessary, unaccountable, corrupt, protectionist, antidemocratic, and—worst of all—foreign.[1] Another target is the *process* of integration. Eurosceptics complain that this process is undemocratic, secretive, bureaucratic, and "deceptive" (in the sense that ostensibly minor reforms frequently yield far-reaching, irreversible changes).[2] Still another target of eurosceptics is the *project* of European political integration. Eurosceptics (particularly in Britain) are constantly in fear of the EU turning into some form of federal entity (whether a unitary European "superstate" or a postsovereign polity).

This chapter is primarily concerned with those forms of euroscepticism directed against the federalists' project of European integration. While the euroscepticism directed against the process and the current product can be addressed through various reforms, project-focused euroscepticism suggests that no matter how transparent the process, no matter what institutional tinkering with the product, a more politically unified Europe is flatly undesirable. Since the argument of this book suggests otherwise, project-focused euroscepticism deserves a closer look.

The most potent forms of project-focused euroscepticism draw support from both the sociological and ideological dimensions of nationalism. From a sociological standpoint, nationalism can be understood as a set of processes—some ideational, some material—that lead the boundaries of nations and the boundaries of states to coincide.[3] Many social scientists believe that nationalism (so defined) is a central feature of the modern world. Eurosceptics can draw support from this sociological thesis, because it suggests that the idea of a European multinational polity—or indeed any type of polity designed to overcome or replace the nation-state—is an impossibility in the modern world and that those who think otherwise can be dismissed as utopian fantasists.

The sociological thesis concerning the ineluctability of the nation-state in the modern world presents europhiles with three options: one, to reject the thesis; two, to argue that it does not matter (the European project is meant to be utopian); and three, to accept it. The third of these options would appear, on the face of it, to concede the argument in favor of Europe's current nation-states and against the European project. But it is at least conceivable that the European project represents a further stage in the development of the nation-state. From this perspective, the spread of English as the European lingua franca, the emergence of a common transnational youth culture, the convergence of business practices, and—most important of all— widespread adoption of European constitutional practices (and perhaps even a Constitution) can be seen as steps along the road to a European nation-state. Yet any suggestion that nationalism conceived as a sociological process might support the European project immediately runs into another dimension of nationalism: ideological nationalism.[4]

From an ideological point of view, nationalism comes in a variety of different forms, the two most important of which—at least as they bear on euroscepticism—are *conservative nationalism* and *social democratic nationalism*. Conservative nationalists reject the European project because it threatens their nation's identity, which they interpret (or "imagine") in terms of traditions, historical memories, and past-oriented narratives. Conservative nationalists fear that the European project entails the end of hundreds (perhaps even thousands) of years of their nation's distinctive history. Social democratic nationalists also fear the European project. But whereas conservative nationalists conceptualize the nation in terms of its distinctive historical identity, social democratic nationalists conceptualize the nation as a shared public culture that sustains a solidaristic form of political membership. Social democratic nationalists contend that a European polity will not be able to maintain the level of social welfare protection that Europe's nation-states have achieved in the postwar era.

In evaluating the challenge posed by these nationalist-inspired versions of euroscepticism, I draw on the democratic standard of justification defended in chapter 1. According to this standard of justification, arguments in support of political transformations—whether involving a change of regime or a change in the polity itself—must meet requirements of publicity, accessibility, and sufficiency. Euroscepticism does not, on the face of it, call for a transformative project of its own; it merely seeks to block the transformation sought by europhiles. Yet insofar as eurosceptics reject the "intergovernmentalist" status quo in favor of a Europe of independent nation-states, then eurosceptics *are* committed to a transformative project. To seek to withdraw from the European Union is to pursue a goal no less far-reaching than that envisaged by any federalist. Many conservative nationalists are quite open about their desire for withdrawal. Social democratic nationalists tend to be more reticent. But the implied goals of social democratic and conservative nationalism are the same: a Europe of relatively independent nation-states. A multinational European polity represents a repudiation of the national values that they both (albeit for different reasons) hold dear. Given the transformative implications of the conservative and social democratic nationalist positions on Europe, the arguments in support of those positions must satisfy a strict standard of justification.

Conservative Euroscepticism

It is not difficult to understand why conservatives would be opposed to the project of European political integration. Conservativism, which is as much a social philosophy as a political doctrine, is generally opposed to all forms of radical social and political change. For the conservative, political authority is immanent in venerable institutions, which have shown their ability, as the saying goes, "to stand the test of time." Venerable political institutions embody tried and tested methods of government; they embody a practical wisdom that exceeds that of any theory, rational plan, or political philosophy deduced from first principles. The effort to build new political institutions—as a grand project—is more likely, so the conservative fears, to end in failure.[5]

The reluctance of conservatives to envisage radical social change explains, however, only part of their antipathy toward European political integration. A more important source of the objection to European political integration comes from the conservatives' commitment to the preservation of their distinctive national identity. Given the fact that national identity takes different forms in different nations, there are as many different versions of conservative euroscepticism as there are nations in Europe. Rather than discuss all of these, I intend to focus here on the British version of conservative euroscepticism. This version of euroscepticism is especially worth considering because, in its most extreme form, it supports not just disengagement from the project of European political integration but disengagement from the European Union as such.[6] Conservative euroscepticism, in short, calls for a fundamental change in Britain's relationship with Europe. While conservatives tend to minimize the extent of these changes, their uiltimate aspiration is no less far-reaching, no less disruptive of the intergovernmental status quo than that sought by federalist proponents of European political integration. Thus if a "federal Europe" must meet a stringent democratic standard of justification, the same holds true for the conservative demand for a "Europe of independent nation-states."

Conservative euroscepticism is often expressed in the form of critiques of the EU's institutional and policy failings. These critiques might suggest that were the EU to reform itself—to pursue sounder policies through better institutions—the conservatives would be less critical of European political integration. It is important to recognize, however, that many conservatives base their euroscepticism not on contingent but on principled grounds. The principle that informs their euroscepticism is nationalism. In amplification of this point, I want to consider the arguments against European political integration put forward by Enoch Powell, who was not only one of the most influential postwar British conservative intellectuals but who located his opposition to European political integration in a defense of British national identity.

Powell's opposition to Britain's membership in Europe was formulated in a number of books, articles, and parliamentary speeches that he produced from the late 1960s until his death in 1998. In contrast to many of his conservative colleagues, Powell saw Europe primarily as a political rather than an economic arrangement. Indeed, Powell was prescient in predicting that the European Economic Community would evolve into some form of political union. He thought that the debate over Britain's entry into the Common Market ought to take the form of a debate over the desirability of abolishing British national sovereignty. The decision to enter the Common Market was, as he put it, "one of those final decisions, to be or not to be, [which] must be entrusted to whole peoples."[7] For Powell, it was unthinkable that a government would decide to enter the Common Market without first gaining the consent of a preponderance of the people in a plebiscite. In the absence of the fullhearted consent of the people to the abolition of their own national sovereignty, it was wrong, Powell argued, to take even the first steps toward membership in a Common Market.

At one level, Powell's case against membership in any European economic and political arrangements simply turned on the perfectly accurate assessment that a preponderance of the British people were opposed to the abolition of their own national sovereignty. But there was more to his euroscepticism than an assessment of what the British people currently wanted. For Powell, full-hearted consent was politically significant, because it represented an expression of a national will. Self-government, he argued, was impossible unless it was the government of a distinctive nation with a unique and separate history. Europe was not—nor would it ever be—a distinctive nation. European self-government was thus an impossibility. To pretend otherwise was to mislead voters about the prospects for self-government in a politically unified and integrated Europe.

Powell's defense of national sovereignty and self-government remains the most nuanced and intelligent statement of British conservative euroscepticism. It is thus worth considering his argument in some detail. Powell's starting point—as with all nationalists—is "the nation," which he defines wholly in political terms. "The essence of a nation," Powell argues, "is that it accepts a single sovereignty, it accepts a single system . . . [and] that every part of it thinks that the whole is more important than the parts."[8] In the absence of a nation whose members are willing to accept "a single sovereignty," no genuine form of self-government, so Powell argues, is possible. For in the absence of the necessary degree of "acceptance"—a key term in his political vocabulary—the commands of government will be seen as the commands not of "us" but of some alien political authority.

Powell recognizes that his usage of the term "nation" is idiosyncratic. Not all cultural, religious, or ethnic communities are "nations" in his strict sense of the term, because not all of these communities are willing to accept rule by a single, unitary sovereign. For Powell, an essential condition of a genuine self-governing nation is "political homogeneity." In a politically homogeneous nation such as Britain, the electorate is "capable of perceiving the totality of the nation in such a way as to submit to the will of the totality." Powell—in a very controversial speech that ended his ministerial career—maintained that large-scale immigration jeopardized "the survival of political homogeneity."[9] In his published reflections he applies the same type of reasoning to membership in the European Union. Europe, he argues, lacks any common political homogeneity. People identify first and foremost with their nation rather than with "Europe." As long as this condition prevails, the conditions for European self-government will be absent.

Given the weight that Powell's argument places on the current sentiments and attachments of people, it might be thought that his argument
provides only a contingent (rather than a principled) objection to European political integration. Certainly, a lot for him turns on the presence
or absence of an intersubjective "commonality of introspection," which
he understands as the essential defining feature of a nation.[10] Presumably, if this form of intersubjectivity and, more generally, the condition
of "acceptance" were present at the European level, then Powell could
have no objection to European political institutions. But there remains a
further, more conservative, dimension of Powell's conception of nationality. Powell writes not as a sociologist but as a nationalist—and,
more especially, a conservative nationalist—who is deeply attached to
his own particular nation. Like other nationalists, Powell perceives this
nation—"England" or "Britain" (Powell like many conservative nationalists tends to treat these terms as synonyms)—in terms of unique
and distinctive traits.[11] Thus, just as many Welsh nationalists see the
Welsh language as the unique and distinctive feature of the Welsh nation, so Powell identifies a unique and distinctive feature of England
(Britain): its parliament. This part of his argument is worth quoting in
full:

> It is a fact that the British parliament and its paramount authority oc-
> cupies a position in relation to the British nation which no other elected
> assembly in Europe possesses. Take parliament out of the history of
> England [sic] and that history itself becomes meaningless. . . . the
> British [sic] nation could not imagine itself except with and through its
> parliament.[12]

Powell goes on to say that the distinctive feature of Britain's parliament is that it has enjoyed "a thousand year" history of sovereignty.[13]
Were it to lose sovereignty, it would no longer be recognizable as a symbol of national identity. Britain's thousand-year uninterrupted history
as a nation would thus come to an end. The nationalist-inspired arguments that Powell advances against European political integration are
anything but idiosyncratic and exceptional. While distinctive in their
logical clarity, Powell's arguments now form the stock-in-trade of most
conservative British eurosceptics. Westminster parliamentary sovereignty constitutes, so these conservatives maintain, *the* distinctive symbol of British national identity. Any transfer of sovereignty to Brussels
thus signals the death of Britain.[14]

Britain and Europe have, in many ways, moved on since Powell first warned of the dangers posed by European integration. Westminster parliamentary sovereignty, the symbol of Britain's national identity, has changed in recent years in at least four different ways. First, many legislative powers (or "competences" to use the jargon of the EU)—including all aspects of trade policy—have, as Powell feared, been transferred to European political institutions. Second, Scotland and Wales now have their own parliaments, which possess (at least in the case of Scotland) both revenue-raising and legislative competences. Third, Britain has now incorporated the European Convention on Human Rights into UK law, a fact that has profound (if uncertain) implications for parliamentary sovereignty. And fourth, parliaments in most advanced industrial societies—including Britain—have lost power to nonmajoritarian institutions (including the executive, the judiciary, a central bank, and many other specialized regulatory agencies). The parliament in Westminster, in short, is much less central to the political life of Britain than it was forty years ago.[15]

Yet notwithstanding these important changes, some of what Powell has to say in opposition to European political integration remains valid. Powell is, I think, quite correct to note that many of the arguments put forward by proponents of European political integration are plausible only if Europe were to form a superstate.[16] Powell rightly notices the advantages of sovereignty, but he draws—wrongly in my view—the conclusion that sovereignty must forever be located at the level of Europe's current nation-states. For Powell and his contemporary eurosceptic followers, it is imperative for Britain to withdraw from all European political institutions. The European project must, from this perspective, be rejected in favor of an independent, sovereign Britain. Given the existing political status quo in Europe today, this proposal, which would bring to an end any involvement in the EU, is radical and transformative. It thus stands in need of a justification that satisfies the requirements of publicity, accessibility, and sufficiency.

The publicity requirement poses the greatest difficulty for the conservative nationalism that forms the basis of Powell's euroscepticism. This publicity requirement is designed to filter out justificatory arguments—and, by extension, political principles and institutions—that contradict or diminish one or more of the public values that define the commitments of what I called in chapter 2 the "bare citizen." These public values are drawn from an understanding of the form of social cooperation present in European societies today.[17]

At one level, Powell's conservative nationalism does not pose any problem for the requirement of publicity. His argument turns on the importance of what he terms "political homogeneity," which could conceivably be interpreted (even if Powell himself does not) in ways that are consistent with the basic equality and liberty of all British citizens. Yet Powell does more than just appeal to the importance of "political homogeneity": he also offers an account of the nature of political homogeneity. It is at this level that Powell's argument becomes problematic. For Powell, the "political homogeneity" of Britain is inseparable from Britain's distinctive historical identity. Powell conceptualizes this identity in terms of a thousand-year history as a parliamentary nation. The Westminster parliament thus becomes, for Powell, an inextinguishable symbol of Britain's identity. The loss of parliamentary sovereignty—which he sees as an inevitable consequence of European integration—thus extinguishes Britain's identity. Furthermore, since the identity of the nation is fixed historically, Powell is skeptical of the ability of the nation to incorporate new ethnic and religious minorities. These minorities, he believes, cannot have the same relationship to the nation "as the rest."

Insofar as the justificatory force of Powell's argument turns on this account of national identity, then Powell's argument—and, by extension, the conservative eurosceptics' argument for withdrawal from the EU—does not meet the requirement of publicity. Bluntly stated, the conservative conception of nationality is not itself a "public value"; nor is it linked, by any further chain of logical or empirical arguments, to any "public value." A public justification is designed to rule out those moral and political arguments that appeal to conceptions of value that not all citizens have a good reason to accept. While a case could conceivably be made that national unity or solidarity is a "public value"—although even this claim is, as we shall see in the next section, controversial—there is no reason why all citizens in Britain have a good reason to accept Powell's description of British national identity. Fortunately, Powell's appeal to British national identity is so obviously partisan, sectarian, and exclusionary it is unnecessary in this case to go over again the philosophical basis of a public justification. In some respects, Powell himself gives the game away in his equivocations between "Britain" and "England." His writings and speeches tend to treat these as synonyms, but they are clearly not. It makes very little historical sense to speak of England's one-thousand-year history as a self-governing parliamentary nation; it does not even make sense as a "myth" to speak of Britain in this way. The reason why is obvious. Prior to the Act of Union of 1707, Britain, in any political sense of the term, simply did not exist.[18] Westminster parliamentary sovereignty means very different things to people in England, Wales, Scotland, and Northern Ireland. To members of those countries who seek regional self-government or more, the Westminster parliament is of little value at all. Powell's arguments about "political homogeneity" are even more problematic for members of the immigrant ethnic minorities that he believed would never be accepted by the British/English nation. These minorities certainly have no reason to accept Powell's description of their own political community. Indeed, this conservative conception of the nation makes it all but impossible for nonwhite English people to think of themselves as full and equal members.

Powell's arguments are not by any means atypical of the conservative nationalist strain of euroscepticism. Many contemporary conservative eurosceptics advance similar arguments. The "nation," from this perspective, has a determinate identity that it takes from its own unique past. Not all forms of ideological nationalism are, however, conservative. There is another important strain of nationalism that sustains a somewhat different form of euroscepticism: social democratic nationalism.

SOCIAL DEMOCRATIC EUROSCEPTICISM

The social democratic form of nationalism is very different from the conservative form and, not surprisingly, it generates its own particular type of euroscepticism. Bluntly stated, social democratic eurosceptics fear that the project of European political integration will lead to the demise of the European *Sozialstaat* and the return of a classical liberal *Rechtstaat*. In other words, social democrats fear that while a politically integrated Europe may prove capable of protecting basic liberties and the rule of law (the achievement of the *Rechtstaat*), it will not prove capable of sustaining a socialized market, a redistributive welfare state, and progressive taxation policies (the achievement of the *Sozialstaat*). Going forward with European integration, in short, entails moving backward to a Europe without social justice.

Social democratic euroscepticism rests on a very different conception of nationalism than conservative euroscepticism. Indeed, the nationalist dimension of social democratic euroscepticism might not seem immediately apparent. Unlike conservative nationalists, social democratic nationalists—or "liberal nationalists," as they are also called—do not think of the nation as something that is intrinsically valuable. Social democratic nationalists are not necessarily enamored of national cultures, particular traditions, or venerable institutions. Social democratic nationalists think of nations primarily as bounded communities of solidarity. Social democratic nationalists, in short, value nations primarily for what they do rather than what they are.

The social democrats' instrumentalist approach to nations is very different from the conservative nationalism of Enoch Powell and his followers. Powell was concerned with the loss of national identity, not merely because he valued "political homogeneity," but because he valued England and its parliamentary sovereignty (which he saw as its quintessential symbol). Social democrats, in contrast, tend to see their own nation as a solidaristic community that secures social justice. Logically, a nation can achieve this goal only insofar as it becomes an object of affection and loyalty. But social democratic nationalists have themselves little to say about their own personal affection and loyalty for their own particular nation. They value the nation impersonally and dispassionately, as if they were embarrassed to express any particular affections for their nation. Not surprisingly, most social democratic nationalists are academics. In exploring the form of euroscepticism generated by social democratic nationalism, I intend to take as my examples some recent writings by David Miller and Claus Offe.

Before turning to the arguments of Miller and Offe, it would be useful to bear in mind a distinction between what might be termed the *horizontal solidarity* of members of a common polity and the *vertical loyalty* that they have for the polity and its basic institutions. In its simplest form, social democratic nationalism contains three claims: (1) any modern polity worthy of *vertical loyalty* must be a *Sozialstaat*; (2) vertical loyalty presupposes a certain level of *horizontal solidarity*; and (3) horizontal solidarity presupposes a common public culture, a shared language, a distinctive set of traditions, or some other "objective" nation-defining characteristics. Social democratic nationalists interpret and defend these claims in different ways. They differ, most importantly, in their account of the "objective" characteristics necessary to form a nation.

It is not difficult to understand why social democratic nationalists would be skeptical of the project of European political integration. This project seeks to create a unitary state or federal polity that would, at least in the short term, lack many of the "objective" characteristics that we normally think of as essential to any nation, including a shared language, history, and common culture. The social democratic eurosceptic fears that in the absence of any sense of common nationality, there could be no European *Sozialstaat*. Claus Offe, for instance, argues that a sense of solidarity presupposes a sense of geographical boundedness. A sense of belonging to a bounded community contributes, so he argues, to the trust and solidarity needed for a *Sozialstaat*. Trust and solidarity evaporate as borders erode. "[B]orderless systems," as Offe puts it, "become breeding grounds for postmodern and neoliberal tendencies."[19] European political integration, in short, fosters tendencies detrimental to the *Sozialstaat*.

Social democratic eurosceptics are generally more reticent than conservative eurosceptics in specifying the political arrangements they would favor in place of a politically integrated Europe. Some clearly have nothing more in mind than preserving the current "intergovernmental" arrangements. But others share the conservative eurosceptics' ambitions of creating a Europe of independent nation-states. Insofar as social democratic eurosceptics envisage a transformative project, they face the same justificatory requirements as those facing conservative eurosceptics and European federalists.

The *Sozialstaat*, the basic aim of social democratic nationalists, runs into immediate difficulties from the requirement of publicity. These difficulties form the central topic of the next chapter, where I discuss the arguments of those (including, most influentially, Jürgen Habermas) who believe that the *Sozialstaat* can now be defended only at the European level. For present purposes, I intend to assume that the social democratic argument for an independent nation-state can satisfy both the requirements of publicity and accessibility. This leaves the requirement of sufficiency. In order to satisfy this requirement, social democratic eurosceptics need to be able to show that the *Sozialstaat* actually does require an independent nation-state. It is not enough to show that the *Sozialstaat* and nation-state are, for instance, mutually compatible with one another. Nor does it suffice to point out that some *Sozialstaaten* are also nation-states. The requirement of sufficiency seeks to weed out weak arguments, empirical falsehoods, and bogus causal claims. It requires that projected political arrangements—whether an independent nation-state or some form of federal Europe—plausibly provide *effective* and *efficient* protection for their justifying values (in this case, some form of egalitarian, redistributive social citizenship).

The most sophisticated contemporary argument in support of the claim that social democracy requires a nation-state is to be found in the writings of David Miller.[20] Since Miller also claims that European political integration jeopardizes the achievement of national *Sozialstaaten*, his argument deserves careful consideration.[21] By "nation-state," Miller means "a political institution exercising most of the powers and rights that we traditionally associate with sovereignty over a group of people who share a common national identity."[22] And by "national identity" or "nationality," he means "a community constituted by mutual belief, extended in history, active in character, connected with a particular territory, and thought to be marked off from other communities by its members' distinct traits."[23] For Miller, any satisfactory form of political membership must be able to generate sufficient *horizontal solidarity* among citizens to sustain redistributive welfare programs and a deliberative (or participatory) form of democracy. "Nationality . . . ," in short,

> is the appropriate form of solidarity for societies that are mobile . . . and egalitarian. . . . [I]t provides the wherewithal for a common culture against whose background people can make more individual decisions about how to lead their lives; it provides the setting in which ideas of social justice can be pursued, particularly ideas that require us to treat our individual talents as to some degree a common asset . . . and it helps to foster the mutual understanding and trust that makes democratic citizenship possible.[24]

Miller's argument in support of nation-states relies on certain assumptions concerning the motivational force of group loyalties. "[W]hen I see my own welfare as bound up with the community to which I belong," he notes, "contributing to it is also a form of goal fulfillment."[25] In other words, people are more likely to act benevolently toward members of their group than toward outsiders. Members of a nation possess, ex hypothesi, feelings of group loyalty. This being the case, we can expect greater support for redistributive welfare programs among members of a common nation than between members of different nations. In short, nationality solves the motivational problem that social democratic societies face.

Miller's argument is, unfortunately rather vague as to how nationality (as he defines it) produces what he considers to be the necessary form of horizontal solidarity. What matters, so it would seem, is a common public culture. Thus he writes:

> The potency of nationality as a source of personal identity means that its obligations are strongly felt and may extend very far—people are

willing to sacrifice themselves for their country in a way that they are not for other groups and associations. But at the same time, these obligations are somewhat indeterminate and likely to be the subject of political debate; in the best case, they will flow from a shared public culture which results from rational deliberation over time about what it means to belong to the nation in question.[26]

Even if we allow that Miller has identified one possible mechanism that leads individuals to support redistributive policies, it is not difficult to think of alternative mechanisms. For many people, support for social democratic policies has less to do with horizontal solidarity and their sense of common nationality than with their own self-interest. Anyone who fears that he will not fare well in a capitalist economy—perhaps because he has no marketable skills—or worries that he will need expensive medical care will have a self-interested reason for favoring social democratic policies. Solidarity grounded in a common national identity may provide one route to the *Sozialstaat*, but self-interest provides another. Abstract principles of fairness provide still another. For some people, social democratic policies follow from some underlying conception of fairness, such as, for instance, a Rawlsian commitment to "the least well-off." For these people, support for social democratic policies has nothing to do with any sense of solidarity with a bounded, national community. They are likely to favor social democratic policies universally in all states.

A further problem with social democratic nationalism is the lack of any compelling empirical evidence to suggest that the *Sozialstaat* presupposes a strong sense of national identity or distinctiveness. Some states with a robust sense of their own national distinctiveness have weak welfare regimes (Japan, for instance), and some states with a weak sense of their own national distinctiveness (the Netherlands, for instance) have strong welfare regimes. For most scholars of comparative politics, the nature and strength of a welfare regime is a function of such factors as the strength of unions, the nature of the party system, the skill profile of workers, and the openness of the economy to international trade. "Nationality," however it is defined, does not seem to have the significance that social democratic nationalists suggest.

Given the account offered in the previous chapter of the requirement of sufficiency, it has to be concluded that social democratic nationalists fail to satisfy this requirement. At most, the social democratic nationalist argument can show that a solidaristic national community is compatible with a *Sozialstaat*. But this is to provide only a weak justification for the eurosceptic project of independent nation-states. A sufficient justification needs something stronger than mere compatibility. Ideally, social democratic eurosceptics need to be able to show that a *Sozialstaat requires* an independent nation-state. Perhaps there is a sophisticated political-economic argument that can fit this bill, but the social democratic nationalist argument—which emphasizes the importance of horizontal solidarity and national identity—simply does not work. The social democratic nationalist case for a Europe of independent nation-states is no more compelling than that of the conservative nationalists.

Welfare

KARL POLANYI's seminal 1944 text, *The Great Transformation*, sought to show how modern efforts to create "a self-regulating market" invariably led to countervailing efforts to ensure that the market served socially desirable ends.[1] While the two poles of Polanyi's dialectical argument—a wholly self-regulating market at one pole, a wholly socialized market at the other—remain, as ever, utterly impractical, political battles continue to be fought over the space between these two poles. Some (market liberals) believe that individuals are best served by a *Rechtstaat*, a polity that does little more than establish the rule of law and enforce contracts; others (social democrats) believe that individuals can flourish only in a *Sozialstaat*, a polity that seeks to ensure both a social minimum and an equitable distribution of wealth.[2]

Not surprisingly, market liberals and social democrats tend to hold sharply opposing views of European integration. They disagree, first and foremost, over the current impact of EU policies. For the market liberal, these policies are market-constraining when they ought to be market-conforming.[3] For the social democrat, in contrast, the EU not only enacts policies that are insufficiently market constraining; it also makes it more difficult for national governments themselves to enact market-constraining policies.[4] In addition to this disagreement over current EU policies, market liberals and social democrats disagree about the policies that a more integrated Europe ideally ought to pursue. While the term "superstate" has come now to signify a centralized Brussels-based polity that enacts market-constraining policies,[5] there is no obvious reason why a unitary European state (a superstate, in other words) must be either social democratic or market liberal in its economic orientation. Its economic orientation, ideally, ought to be a matter for Europe's would-be citizens to decide.[6] Doubtless, some European citizens will favor a social democratic ("market-constraining") Europe, while others will favor a market liberal ("market-conforming") Europe.

The fact that Europeans tend to disagree among themselves about the relative merits of social democracy and market liberalism has not deterred attempts to justify European political integration on the basis of one or another of these economic philosophies. Before examining some of these attempts in more detail, it would be helpful to say something first about the link between these philosophies and the idea of "welfare." Many commentators, whether eurosceptics or europhiles, believe that a commitment to a redistributive welfare state (a *Sozialstaat*, in other words) is a defining feature of something they call the European way of life. Thus, for Tony Judt, "Welfare, in its multiple forms, is the great Western European achievement of recent years. It is what distinguishes the region . . . from the United States, where there is almost no formal community provision for the health and protection of all of its members. . . ."[7] Judt himself remains a eurosceptic, because he thinks—much like the social democratic nationalists encountered in the previous chapter—that the nation-state is a precondition for "welfare, in all its multiple forms." Some proponents of European political integration, however, think the opposite. They believe that globalization has rendered the nation-state obsolete and that Europeans must now look to an integrated European polity to secure a minimally adequate form of welfare.

Notwithstanding the disagreements between social democrats about the relative merits of an integrated Europe or the nation-state, social democrats tend to assume that some form of *Sozialstaat* is essential if we are to achieve a minimally adequate form of human welfare. This assumption is not shared by market liberals. Furthermore, this social democratic argument tends to assume that the welfare provided by the state (and its institutions) is more valuable than the wealth provided by the market. But this distinction between welfare and wealth tends to beg the question in favor of the state and against the market.

Contemporary political philosophers tend to avoid these problems by recognizing that there is as much disagreement about appropriate measures of human well-being as there is disagreement about the political and economic institutions necessary to secure human well-being. To this end, they distinguish (1) the "goods" that define human well-being, whether described as wealth, welfare, "primary goods," "the necessaries of life," or whatever; (2) a principle of distribution; and then (3) the institutions necessary to secure a fair or desirable distribution of these goods. In contrast to this approach, the tendency of proponents and critics of European political integration is to conduct the debate solely in terms of (3). Very little is said about how we should think of (1) the goods that define human well-being or (2) how these goods ought to be distributed. Thus, for Tony Judt—who, in this respect, is quite typical—Europe's achievement is its "welfare state." This claim elides the fact that different European states resort to different institutional mechanisms to provide and distribute a different range of goods.[8] Judt's claim also blithely assumes that Europeans all agree that the bureaucratization of certain aspects of human well-being is an unambiguous "achievement."

Given these difficulties with the standard approach to the "welfare state," it would be better, I think, to conceptualize human well-being in terms of what classical economists used to refer to as "the necessaries and conveniences of life."[9] In the modern world, "the necessaries and conveniences of life" are acquired in three primary ways: (1) through the private provision of friends and family members; (2) through the sale of one's services in the market economy; and (3) through transfer payments by the state. In its classic "Beveridgean" form, the welfare state was designed to employ (3) as a temporary remedy for dislocations or disruptions to (2). On the face of it, there seems no obvious reason why the state provision of "the necessaries and conveniences of life" ought to be viewed as any greater "achievement" than the market provision of these goods. Indeed, if (hypothetically) everyone could secure "the necessaries and conveniences of life" through the sale of services in the market economy, there would be no need for a welfare state, and—more to the point—there would be no grounds for celebrating the welfare state as Europe's defining achievement. As we all know (not least from reading Polanyi), the idea of a wholly self-regulating market is a fantasy. A market economy always produces short-term socially undesirable dislocations: firms can go bankrupt or relocate; unemployment in certain sectors and regions can rise rapidly. If more Europeans could, however, derive more of "the necessaries and conveniences of life" from the market rather than the state, nothing important (caeteris paribus) would be lost. The institutional mechanisms that define a "welfare state" are, in short, remedial. They have no intrinsic value.

In light of these remarks, it should now be clear that a "welfare"-based argument for European political integration must draw a clear distinction between "the necessaries and conveniences of life" and the institutional mechanisms that these aspects of life (or aspects of human well-being) actually require. Furthermore, any valid "welfare"-based argument for European political integration must meet the requirements of a democratic standard of justification. The argument must, in short, satisfy requirements of publicity, accessibility, and sufficiency. The remainder of this chapter examines two different—indeed two diametrically opposed—welfare-based arguments for European political integration: Friedrich Hayek's classically liberal argument and Jürgen

Habermas's social democratic argument. Neither argument succeeds. But they are both instructive in their failures.

Friedrich Hayek, Market Liberalism, and European Political Integration

Hayek took up the question of European integration in his 1939 essay "The Economic Conditions of Interstate Federalism."[10] Although this essay predates the current process of European integration, a process initiated by the Schumann plan in 1950, the argument of the essay is nonetheless germane to the case of "welfare"-based arguments for European political and economic integration. Hayek's 1939 essay addresses the economic implications of interstate federation. In a manner that has now become commonplace, he identifies the gains to prosperity that will result from a common economic regime. A common economic regime, he points out, will realize tremendous economies of scale. The greater prosperity that will result from these economies of scale will, in turn, make Europe more powerful and less vulnerable to external attack.

Hayek also offers a more controversial, classically liberal rationale for an economically unified Europe. Since this rationale foreshadows some of the debates taking place in Europe today, it will be useful to consider this argument in more detail. Hayek's aim in this part of his argument is to show that the multinational character of an interstate federation will prove conducive to the liberal project. His point of departure here is that an economically unified interstate federation will permit "the free movements of men and capital between the states of the federation."[11] In such a federation, there will be a single market, and the prices of goods will vary only by the costs of transport. Labor and capital mobility will furthermore prevent the states in the federation from imposing costs on business or industry that exceed the costs imposed by other states. It will thus be necessary "to avoid all sorts of taxation which would drive capital and labor elsewhere."[12] Federation, in short, will impose severe constraints on the states' capacity to enact interventionist and protectionist policies.

One obvious way for states to overcome these constraints would be for them to transfer regulatory authority from the state (or national) level to the federal (or supranational) level. A transfer of this sort, however, is unlikely to succeed, so Hayek argues, because supranational regulation is much more difficult than national regulation. His argument here is important. For Hayek, the form of solidarity built into the idea of a shared nationality exercises a baleful influence on economic policy. As he puts this point:

> In the national state, current ideologies make it comparatively easy to persuade the rest of the community that it is in their interest to protect "their" industry or "their" wheat production. . . . The decisive consideration is that their sacrifice benefits compatriots whose position is familiar to them.[13]

In an interstate federation, in contrast, this form of national solidarity will be absent. "Is it likely," Hayek asks, "that the French peasant will be more willing to pay more for his fertilizer to help the British chemical industry?"[14] A supranational federation will not be able to pursue either protectionist or redistributive policies, because the members of that federation will lack the solidarity necessary to sustain such policies.

Hayek's argument in support of an interstate federation can be seen as a mirror image of his argument against the nation-state. Hostility to the nation-state—and to nationalism a fortiori—is a recurrent theme in Hayek's work. In the present context, nationalism and the nation-state are damned for their tendency to sustain state planning, protectionism, and redistributive welfare policies. These harmful policies are easier to enact in a nation-state, because of the "comparative homogeneity, the common convictions and ideals, and the whole common tradition of the people."[15] Conversely, Hayek expects an interstate federation in Europe to be ordered on classically liberal principles. Hayek's conclusion is that "there would have to be less government all round if federation is to be practicable."[16]

Notwithstanding the fact that Hayek wrote his defense of an interstate federation in a very different intellectual and political context from that prevailing today, his arguments remain germane to the present debate on European integration. Paradoxically, these arguments are more likely to be heard today from social democratic opponents of European integration than libertarian proponents of it. A number of social democratic theorists, as we have seen in the previous chapter, have noted the dependence of the modern welfare state on a shared sense of solidarity anchored in the idea of a nation. These social democrats fear that European political and economic integration will yield a market cut loose from the political policies that have tempered what they perceive as the market's destructive tendencies. European integration, in short, will triumph at the expense of social justice.[17]

Leaving aside, for the moment, the merits of the very different normative perspectives adopted by Hayek and the social democrats, I want to consider a puzzle that arises if we accept the conclusion that European integration is good for free-market capitalism. The puzzle is this: Why do many promarket parties and politicians oppose European integration? Margaret Thatcher can serve as an example here. She was a fervent admirer of Hayek's economic writings yet a vehement critic of European integration. On one level, the puzzle can be answered easily. The postwar process of European integration created a very different type of interstate federation than that which Hayek had in mind in his prewar essay. Thatcher feared that her own efforts to destroy social democracy in Britain would be jeopardized by a European project to reconstitute social democracy at the supranational level.[18] But to acknowledge this point is to suggest that Hayek's 1939 essay puts too much weight on the role of national solidarity in sustaining protectionist and interventionist state policies.

Hayek's 1939 essay specifies just one mechanism that might conceivably yield protectionist policies: nationalism. From this perspective, the solidarity felt by members of a common nation encourages them to tolerate a lower level of overall prosperity so that some of their number can escape the costs of disadvantageous change. But this is clearly not the only mechanism through which protectionist policies emerge. Consider here, by way of an example, the situation of farmers in both Europe and the United States. On both sides of the Atlantic, farmers are protected against foreign competition and are provided with various governmental subsidies. National solidarity can hardly explain this state of affairs. While Americans might possess a robust sense of national solidarity, Europeans—at least qua Europeans—do not. A more probable explanation is that farmers constitute a well-organized and thus important segment of the vote. Governments appease farmers, because they fear the electoral consequences of subjecting them to market competition.

The organization of producer groups in support of self-serving market-constraining policies provides an alternative mechanism through which protectionist policies might emerge. Adam Smith warned his readers of precisely this mechanism in his *Wealth of Nations*.[19] For Smith, the merchants presented a particular threat in this respect, both because their sectional interest did not coincide with the general interest and because they were the best equipped to ensure that their sectional interests won out.[20] If this line of argument is correct, then the critical question for classical liberals to ask when confronted with the prospect of interstate federation is this: Are interest groups more likely to succeed in their advocacy of protectionist policies in an interstate federation or in a national state? Thatcher and other classically liberal critics of European integration maintain that such policies are more likely in an interstate federation. Hayek, so it would seem, thinks that they are more likely to succeed in a nation-state.

In addition to Hayek's mechanism of national solidarity and Smith's mechanism of sectional interests, a third mechanism that might conceivably yield protectionist policies is the idea of social justice. For better or worse—Hayek clearly thinks for worse—politically significant actors will often favor policies that constrain the market in the interests of what they perceive as social justice.[21] For many European social democrats, the postwar success of Europe resides in its ability to force the market to abide by basic social values. The citizens of Europe's postwar democratic nation-states now expect their governments, as Fritz Scharpf puts it, "to prevent mass unemployment . . . ; to prevent extreme poverty that would force persons to live below socially acceptable levels of income and life chances; and to assure a fair sharing of burdens and tax benefits."[22]

The very attempt to force the market to conform to the dictates of social justice has been sharply criticized by classical liberals. Hayek has argued that the desire for social justice represents a misguided attempt to apply the distributive principles that make sense in small face-to-face communities to the impersonal context of a great modern society.[23] This is to suggest that "social justice" is simply another name for national solidarity. But this suggestion is, I think, mistaken. The members of a great modern society might seek the policies described by Scharpf simply because they wish to insure themselves against the costs of failure in the market order. From this perspective, protectionist policies arise because politically significant actors—whether citizens, political leaders, or administrative officials—believe that they will fare better in a polity that protects against economic distress. As Scharpf puts it:

> The democratic state . . . derives its claim to legitimacy from a commitment to the public interest and to distributive justice, and governments are constrained, through the mechanisms of electoral accountability, to

orient their policies toward the interests of the broad majority of its voters. They are therefore under political pressure to protect groups in the
electorate against the losses caused by structural change, to prevent
mass unemployment, to regulate labor markets and production processes in the interests of the workers affected, and to achieve a normatively defensible distribution of incomes.[24]

Leaving aside for the moment the question of whether governments are
justified in their pursuit of social justice, the point to grasp here is that
this pursuit need not owe anything to the mechanism of national solidarity. The pursuit of social justice provides, in short, a distinctive mechanism through which protectionist policies might emerge. This being
the case, an argument that seeks to defend interstate federation on the
basis that it will thwart national solidarity is unpersuasive insofar as it
fails to consider the alternative mechanisms through which protectionist policies can succeed. Even if we were to share the classical liberals'
animus toward protectionist policies, we thus have no basis for thinking that such policies are any less likely to succeed in an interstate federation than in a nation-state.

This problem with Hayek's argument can be restated in terms of a failure to satisfy what I have earlier called the requirement of sufficiency.
In order to satisfy this requirement, the purported link between European political integration and its justifying values must not rest on weak
or false claims. Yet in the case of Hayek's argument for an interstate federation, his rationale that it would thwart protectionism is the very par-
adigm of a weak claim. His liberal capitalist order—the premise or justifying value of that argument—simply does not require the rejection of
a Europe of nation-states. There are, as I have tried to show, mechanisms
other than nationalism that sustain an interventionist *Sozialstaat*.
Granted the existence of these additional mechanisms, there is no reason to think that a more politically integrated European polity will yield
a *Rechtstaat*. Indeed, if the lessons of the current *process* of European integration are any guide, then each step along the road to political integration will require side payments in the form of subsidies to sectoral
groups. Partly for this reason, some proponents of a liberal capitalist
order—such as the Thatcherite wing of the British eurosceptics—believe that the *Rechtstaat* is better housed within the nation-state than in
any form of European polity. Hayek's argument has little to say to this
sort of eurosceptic. He has no argument, in short, to sustain the claim
that European political integration is a necessary condition for—rather

than being merely consistent with—a liberal capitalist order. In this case Hayek's justification for European political integration thus fails to satisfy the requirement of sufficiency.

HABERMAS'S DEFENSE OF THE EUROPEAN PROJECT

In contrast to Hayek, most proponents today of European political integration tend to be social democrats. They favor European integration on the grounds that it provides greater support than the nation-state for a *Sozialstaat*. This justification for European integration proceeds, in other words, from normative premises diametrically opposed to those shared by classical liberals. Perhaps the best example of such a justification is to be found in Jürgen Habermas's recent writings.[25] These works provide an illuminating point of contrast to those of Hayek. More generally, they highlight the pitfalls of pinning the case for European integration on any substantive conception of justice, whether classically liberal or social democratic.

Habermas's recent writings on European integration begin with an acknowledgement that the European project is desperately in need of a compelling justification, if it is to "mobilize political support around . . . political union."[26] Habermas rightly points out that justifications that worked when the project was in its formative stage no longer suffice. "Neither of the two original motives for integration"—ending interstate war and controlling German power—now provide "a sufficient justification for pushing the European project any further."[27]

Notwithstanding Habermas's recognition of the enormous transformation entailed by the project of constructing a unitary European polity—a federal Europe, as he terms it—he also emphasizes the conservative dimensions of this project. Quite in contrast to Hayek, a federal Europe is necessary, Habermas argues, in order to conserve the achievements already made at the level of Europe's individual nation-states.

To understand Habermas's account of these achievements, it is important to note the sociological and normative standpoints from which his theory proceeds. From a sociological point of view, Habermas assumes that religion and tradition are spent forces that are no longer viable as bases of social integration. And normatively, Habermas is committed to a form of what he terms "Kantian republicanism," according to which the subjects of any legitimate polity must be able to recognize themselves as the authors of the laws of that polity.[28] The great achievement of the European nation-state, Habermas maintains, is that it has secured a form of integration anchored in the laws and practices of constitutional democracy. The European nation-state has been aided here by two further factors, one of which Habermas considers positive, the other negative. The welfare state is the positive factor; it provides the ordinary citizen with a set of social rights and, more generally, ensures that the capitalist economy operates in accordance with the public interest. Exclusionary nationalism, in contrast, is the negative factor. While a feeling of national solidarity has helped in securing identification with the democratic constitutional state, this feeling of national solidarity has often been bolstered by invidious conceptions of ethnic and cultural superiority. The negative consequences of nationality are apparent, so Habermas believes, both in the wars of the twentieth century and in the present difficulties Europe's nation-states confront in integrating cultural minorities.[29]

Habermas wants to conserve the beneficial features of the nation-state (democratic norms and the welfare state) while rejecting the harmful features (invidious conceptions of nationality). He believes that this aim is possible for a federated Europe, because he thinks that integration around democratic norms needs only a thin form of constitutional patriotism rather than a thick national identity grounded in a shared history, culture, or ethnicity.[30] More important, he believes that this aim is necessary, because globalization has rendered the nation-state obsolete.[31]

By globalization—a concept that plays a central role in his argument for European integration—Habermas has in mind a cluster of processes that presents problems and risks that the nation-state, acting either singly or collaboratively, can no longer solve. As he puts it,

> the globalization of commerce and communication, of economic production and finance, of the spread of technology and weapons, and above all of ecological and military risks, poses problems that can no longer be solved within the framework of nation-states or by the traditional methods of agreement between sovereign states.[32]

The constraints imposed by globalization, Habermas contends, have produced negative consequences for the social democratic welfare state. The increase in international competition has led to higher unemployment; the increase in capital mobility has diminished the tax base that states use to finance their social policies; and, more generally, globalization has encouraged a shift toward a neoliberal social model. The upshot is that the nation-state is no longer able to sustain the social democratic rights that are necessary if citizens are to recognize themselves as the authors of their laws. If citizens are to gain political control over global economic forces, they can now do so, Habermas contends, only at the European or transnational level.

In Habermas's earlier writings on Europe during the 1990s, the claim that globalization has rendered the nation-state obsolete served as his principal justification for the European project. More recently, Habermas has offered an additional—perhaps even an alternative—justification. Rather than invoking economic arguments for Europe, Habermas now thinks that Europe must appeal to shared values and an "affective attachment to a particular ethos . . . a specific way of life."[33] Fortunately, Europe already possesses, he argues, a specific way of life, which is located in its commitment to social, political, and cultural inclusion. Europe, in other words, has a distinct identity grounded in its commitment to social justice. This identity sets Europe apart from the United States.[34]

Habermas is not alone in thinking that Europe defines a unique and morally attractive form of life.[35] This is a common refrain of many European critiques of American-led globalization.[36] In Habermas's altogether more sophisticated version of this argument, a federal Europe is necessary to protect Europe's uniquely solidaristic way of life from the ravages of a neoliberal global economy. No single nation-state can, he contends, achieve this goal.

Critics of Habermas's defense of the European project typically focus on what has come to be known as the "no demos thesis."[37] Simply stated, the critics contend that European political integration is impossible, because Europe lacks a "demos"—a politically self-conscious and bounded citizenry. In the absence of this "demos," Europe cannot secure the precondition of a Kantian republic: citizens who think of themselves as both the authors and the addressees of the law. Habermas has responded to this criticism—effectively, I think—taking note of the growth of a Europewide public sphere. But even granting that Habermas is right on this point, there remains a more fundamental challenge to his argument. This challenge, which centers on the idea of social justice, brings Habermas's argument into confrontation with Hayek.

Habermas v. Hayek on Social Justice

Habermas's claim that European integration can be justified in terms of its contribution to social justice invites at least three different criticisms. The first criticism concerns the very idea of social justice, which, according to Hayek, is both philosophically incoherent and unattainable in a modern society.[38] The second criticism concerns the adequacy of Habermas's argument about the impact of globalization on the *Sozialstaat*. And the third criticism concerns the propriety of appealing to a conception of social justice, however sound in principle, to justify the particular project of European integration. Let me consider each criticism in turn.

For classical liberals such as Hayek, "social" justice is a perversion of the concept of justice, which can apply only to individual conduct.[39] If this argument is correct, then Habermas's view is fatally flawed. For this reason, it is worth considering the grounds of Hayek's objection to social justice in more detail.

At its most general level, Hayek's argument rests on the claim that a just distribution of benefits and burdens requires a state capable of effecting that distribution. As a classical liberal who believes in a limited government capable of enforcing the rule of law—a *Rechtstaat*, in other words—Hayek, unlike the anarchist, has no objection to the state as such. It is the state that takes on responsibility for a redistributive social welfare system—a *Sozialstaat*—that poses a problem.

Hayek relies on two different arguments to condemn the *Sozialstaat*. First, he contends that any state that seeks to redistribute benefits and burdens must, ipso facto, diminish individual liberty. Hayek does not possess a natural-rights theory of liberty. Thus he cannot, like some other classical liberals, claim that a social democratic welfare system violates individual rights. Instead, Hayek simply maintains that individuals will have less liberty in a *Sozialstaat* than they would have in a *Rechtstaat*, and that this is undesirable, albeit not a violation of rights.

The second argument Hayek employs against the *Sozialstaat* concerns its effects on the free market. Hayek won a Nobel prize for noticing that the market is "the only procedure yet discovered in which information widely dispersed among millions of men can be effectively utilized for the benefit of all."[40] The *Sozialstaat* does not allow this information-providing function of the market to operate unchecked. A free market informs people through the mechanism of prices. A *Sozialstaat*, in contrast, commands people through the mechanism of coercion. A market order, so Hayek maintains, cannot be preserved while imposing on it a pattern of remuneration defined by social justice. Hayek fears that government intervention in the market to achieve the goals favored by social democrats can only lead to a directed or command economy.[41]

Hayek's arguments against social justice would, if true, be highly damaging, not only to Habermas's case for European political integration, but also to the many European intellectuals who claim that Europe embodies a more humane model of society than such countries as the United States. Yet neither of Hayek's arguments against the *Sozialstaat* is altogether convincing. The claim that the *Rechtstaat* is more conducive to liberty than the *Sozialstaat* is, at best, a provocative suggestion. Judgments about the relative scope of liberty in different social systems are notoriously difficult to substantiate. They always seem to founder on the problem noticed by Isaiah Berlin: "there are many incommensurable kinds and degrees of freedom, and . . . they cannot be drawn up on any single scale of magnitude."[42] Hayek's work lacks any convincing solution to this problem.[43]

Hayek's contention that the pursuit of social justice undermines the market order is similarly problematic. Hayek first advanced this line of argument in *The Road to Serfdom*, which was written during the Second World War.[44] In a sense, Hayek has been refuted by the macroeconomic performance of postwar European economies. During this period, European nation-states have managed to combine a high level of economic growth with a high level of social expenditure. Furthermore, the economies of those advanced industrial states with high levels of social expenditure (for instance Sweden) have not, contrary to Hayek's expectations, performed substantially worse than those with low levels of social expenditure (for instance Britain). Finally, there is little truth to Hayek's suggestion that social democracy leads ineluctably to a command or planned economy. Indeed, European countries have, in recent years, managed to sustain their commitment to social welfare expenditure while concurrently privatizing many of their state-owned industries.[45] These considerations suggest that Hayek's arguments against the *Sozialstaat* are largely incorrect.

The fact that Hayek's case against social justice is unconvincing does not mean, however, that Habermas is right to base his justification of European political integration on this concept. For Habermas's argument to succeed, there must be some good reason to believe that the social democratic welfare state is sustainable only at the European supranational level. But Habermas's arguments in support of this claim are themselves weak and ineffective. Indeed, he relies here on a number of causal claims concerning the impact of globalization on the welfare state that are hard to square with either the facts or any plausible account of social mechanisms. In this respect, Habermas's argument, much like Hayek's, also fails the requirement of sufficiency.

Two of Habermas's claims are, in this context, particularly problematic. First, he argues that "national governments today are increasingly compelled to accept permanently high unemployment . . . for the sake of international competitiveness."[46] And second, he asserts that "economic globalization obviously has an impact on the shrinking tax base the state uses to finance its social policies."[47]

The first claim suggests that European countries face progressively higher rates of unemployment because of international competition. This claim is hard to swallow for a variety of reasons. First, it fails to register the divergence in unemployment rates within Europe: relatively low (less than 5 percent) in Britain and Austria; higher (8–10 percent) in France and Germany; and higher still in Belgium and Spain (more than 10 percent).[48] International competition alone cannot explain this divergence, because international competition, if it is a cause of unemployment at all, is obviously not the sole cause. A more plausible candidate for a monocausal theory of European unemployment—which is essentially what Habermas's argument here relies on—is inflexible labor markets.[49] Even many German social democrats have come to the conclusion that Germany's highly regulated labor markets are a principal cause of Germany's relatively high unemployment.

A second problem with Habermas's argument concerning unemployment is that even if it were correct, it is difficult to understand how European political integration can provide any solution. Eastern European countries, many of which (Poland, Hungary, and Slovakia, for instance) are now full members of the EU, are a principal source of low-wage competition for western European industry.[50] Further European political integration will not protect, say, German workers from seeing German manufacturers flee to Poland. Even in the case of competition from outside Europe—the third-world agricultural sector, for instance—it is not obvious that a "United States of Europe" can or ought to protect its domestic producers. Social democrats like Habermas are committed to improving the material conditions of the least well-off whatever country they inhabit. It is difficult to see how a policy that protects the welfare of European producers at the expense of third-world producers, which is essentially what the Commons Agricultural Policy manages to do, can be justified on social democratic grounds. Insofar as international competition works to the advantage of the global least well-off, it is difficult to understand how a social democrat could object to international competition no matter what its impact on the wages and employment figures of the relatively affluent western European countries.

Habermas's claim concerning the impact of globalization on the tax base of Europe's nation-states is also more complicated than he suggests. How much money is available to a state to fund its welfare system is a function of the overall gross national product (GNP) and the percentage of GNP the state can extract in taxes. A variety of factors affect a state's capacity to tax, one of which is the threat of flight by the individual, group, or company that is to be taxed. On the face of it, globalization does constrain the state's capacity to tax, if only because it increases the possibilities for flight. It is important to recognize here, however, that the state can tax payrolls, consumption, property, and estates, not just individuals or corporations. All taxes are not equally vulnerable to flight. Globalization may mean only that the state has to shift its revenue-raising activities to the less mobile taxable entities. The state's ability to employ these options is likely to depend as much on the willingness of electorates to impose and to bear the cost of taxation as on threats of flight. For some reason, voters appear to be much less willing to approve of high taxation today than in the earlier postwar period, hence the recurrent popularity of populist antitaxation political parties and candidates.[51]

Viewed in this light, Habermas's welfare-based argument suffers from the same failing as Hayek's. Both arguments fail to satisfy the requirement of sufficiency. The creation of a European polity, whether in its sovereignist or postsovereignist forms, is a momentous step. It demands a justification that satisfies certain minimum requirements. The requirement of sufficiency is designed to weed out arguments that are "weak" and "ineffective." Neither Habermas nor Hayek can show that a politically integrated Europe is necessary to achieve their preferred economic regimes. Moreover, even if their arguments could be bolstered to meet this problem, there remains a further problem with the attempt to justify European political integration on the basis of a welfare state. Any such argument, unless very carefully formulated, seems to fall foul of the requirement of publicity.

ECONOMIC PHILOSOPHIES AND EUROPEAN
POLITICAL INTEGRATION

In his dissent to the so-called Lochner case, the US Supreme Court justice Oliver Wendell Holmes put forward the following famous statement of judicial restraint:

> I strongly believe that my agreement or disagreement has nothing to do with the right of a majority to embody their opinions in law. It is settled by various decisions of this court that state constitutions and state laws may regulate life in many ways which we as legislators might think of as injudicious, or if you like as tyrannical . . . A Constitution is not intended to embody a particular economic theory, whether of paternalism and the organic relation of the citizen to the state or of *laissez faire*. It is made for people of fundamentally differing views.[52]

Holmes's judicial philosophy is worth remarking in the present European context, because it stands in marked contrast to the positions defended above by Habermas and Hayek. Whereas Holmes does not think it appropriate for a constitution to reinforce any particular economic philosophy, both Habermas and Hayek seek constitutional protection for their own preferred philosophies. Whatever one might think of the relative merits of the *Sozialstaat* and the *Rechtstaat*, Holmes is surely right when he says that constitutions are "made for people of fundamentally differing views." For better or worse, the people of Europe today hold differing views on the balance between state and market provision of what I called earlier "the necessaries and conveniences of life." Given this undeniable statement of fact, the attempt to entrench in a European Constitution any particular economic philosophy seems misplaced.

Yet once we allow, as I think we must, that Europeans today hold fundamentally different views, not merely on economic philosophy, but also on a wide range of topics—including the role of religion in public life—it becomes difficult to see how any justificatory argument for European political integration could ever gain any political traction. The *requirement of publicity*, which I defended at length in chapter 1, is designed, at least in part, to solve this problem. This requirement is not meant to filter out *all* values over which there is any societal disagreement. Here it is important to register the distinction between, what I called a *general* argument for European political integration and a *public* argument for European integration. Whereas a general argument seeks to appeal to all Europeans rather than a segment of them, a public argument seeks to appeal to all Europeans through publicly acceptable arguments. Publicly acceptable means, in this context, acceptable to a *bare citizen*, which is to say a citizen who accepts as values equality, liberty, security, and prosperity. In contrast to a general argument, which proceeds from a sociological rather than a normative standpoint, a public argument purports to identify a standpoint for identifying the political institutions that *ought* to exist. If we can show that a *bare citizen* has a good reason to accept European political integration—perhaps because it is essential to protect liberty or security—then we have gone some way toward the justification of European political integration. This is not to say, however, that all Europeans will in fact accept such a public justification. People have differing views about the political institutions necessary to protect liberty or security, no less than they have differing views about the political institutions necessary to protect welfare (or what I called "the necessaries and conveniences of life").

These distinctions can help us to clarify where the welfare-based justification for European political integration goes wrong. Rather than work up a justification for an integrated Europe on the basis of some fairly abstract value that all Europeans have good reason to accept, such as securing "the necessaries and conveniences of life," most welfare-based arguments, (including that of Habermas) focus on protecting some more specific institutionalized embodiment of welfare, such as the German-style "Conservative Welfare Regime."[53] Here the problem is not simply that (from an empirical point of view) Europeans have differing views about the merits of this type of welfare state but that (from a normative point of view) there is no obvious reason why Europeans *ought* to support this type of welfare state. The bare citizen, who accepts (ex hypothesi) the need for institutional mechanisms capable of securing "the necessaries and conveniences of life," is under no obligation to accept the "Conservative Welfare Regime." To suggest otherwise is simply to pass off one's own personal prejudices as a public argument that warrants constitutional recognition.

Habermas's more recent efforts to identify a distinctively European way of life that a European polity might protect simply compound these problems.[54] Thus, in a letter cosigned with Jacques Derrida, Habermas offers a highly tendentious view of European identity. "Are there," he asks, "historical experiences, traditions and achievements, which provide us with the awareness of a shared political destiny which can be arranged together for European citizens?"[55] Habermas's answer to this question is worth quoting in full, because it includes a variety of references that are neither generally nor publically shared by all Europeans.

> In European societies secularization has progressed relatively far. Here citizens regard trespasses beyond the border between politics and religion rather suspiciously. Europeans have a relatively great confidence in the organizational abilities and directive capabilities of the State, while they are sceptical with regard to the efficiency of the market. They . . . hold no unbroken optimistic expectations with regard to technical progress. They have a preference for the security guarantees of the welfare state and for solidaristic regulations.[56]

To the extent that European political integration is designed (à la Habermas) to secure an identity-defining consensus on secularization, the welfare state, and collective regulations, then it is hard not to sympathize with some of the fears of eurosceptics. A common suspicion of eurosceptics is that the European project is all a plot by left-leaning secularists to push through policies for which they cannot gain democratic support at the national level. This suspicion is, I think, misplaced. Nonetheless, it is important that proponents of the European project recognize that a Europe that sees its "achievement" in terms of a "welfare state" and "solidaristic regulations" runs the risk of alienating many otherwise committed Europeans. More troubling still, this vision of Europe seems to hobble Europeans with an outmoded set of socioeconomic institutions and policies. Indeed, if Europe is to become an effective global counterweight to the United States, as Habermas and others hope, then Europe needs an economy at least as vibrant and productive as that of the United States. The Anglo-Saxon model of capitalism—which is less regulated, more innovative, and (somewhat paradoxically) more congenial to women and immigrants—provides far better guidance here than the ossified, dirigiste models of Continental Europe.[57]

This chapter has been highly critical of some influential attempts to justify European political integration on the basis of the welfare state. It does not follow, however, that all welfare-based justifications for European political integration must necessarily fail. My only claim is that any convincing justification needs to be able to satisfy a democratic standard of justification. A welfare-based argument must, in short, rest on values that a *bare citizen* could endorse. This requirement would force proponents of the welfare-based justification to shift their attention away from very narrow specifications of a particular type of welfare state. Instead, they would be required to base their arguments on something akin to "the necessaries and conveniences of life," leaving it an open question whether these "necessaries and conveniences" are better secured by the market or by the state.

Whereas the requirement of publicity forces proponents of welfare-based justifications to express their argument in terms of a public value that all can share, the requirement of sufficiency demands an argument showing that the European level of government actually is necessary. It will hardly suffice to demonstrate that a European level of government is merely *consistent* with, say, securing "the necessaries and conveniences of life." The creation of a unified European polity—the goal of proponents of the European project—entails far-reaching changes that require a more demanding justification. It will not do to argue, as do some advocates of a Europeanwide welfare state, that globalization is a problem that only a European polity can solve. Globalization, in the form of boundary-crossing flows of capital and trade, would pose just as many problems for a Europeanwide welfare state as it poses now for national welfare states. Proponents of a welfarebased justification for the European project need to be able to show—in ways that they have not yet been able to—that Europe offers an effective and efficient solution to these problems of globalization. Perhaps there is a convincing welfare-based justification for European political integration. But no one has yet produced one.

Security

Proponents of European integration often claim that European integration has ensured—and continues to ensure—that Europe remains peaceful. From this perspective, the European project finds its justification in Europe's own lamentable history of war and interstate conflict. If European integration can bring this history to an end, then the European project has all the justification it needs. Viewed more closely, however, this security-based argument for European integration (as it might be termed) tends to fall apart. Indeed, there are at least three problems with this line of argument.

The first problem with the security-based justification is that Europe is already stable and peaceful. Simply put, if Europe has been peaceful for the last fifty years or so, why is it now necessary for Europe to take the further step toward full political integration? Indeed, it might be argued—as some eurosceptics have done—that further political integration would only jeopardize important elements of the postwar international order, including NATO and the bipolar balance.[1] There is a certain paradox here. The success of western Europe in avoiding war since 1945 makes it more, rather than less, difficult to invoke a security-based argument for European political integration. Perhaps the security-based justification would be more plausible if Russia were to develop imperial aspirations with respect to other European states. But this does not seem likely. Nor does this prospect seem to call for European political integration. Indeed, NATO probably remains the best means of dealing with Russia. There is no obvious reason why European political integration would provide the answer to a resurgent Russia.

A second problem with any security-based argument for European integration is that it begs the question of why the value of security should weigh so heavily in the scales. A eurosceptic might allow that the project of European integration makes violent conflict within Europe somewhat less likely, but nonetheless contend that the preservation of national sovereignty outweighs whatever gains to security that political integration might yield. In order to meet this objection, the proponent of European integration needs to explain why security—and what form of security—matters.

A third problem with a security-based justification for European political integration is that it can succeed only at the expense of some very well-entrenched perspectives on current international relations. For both "realists" and "liberals"—the two dominant schools of international relations—the idea of European political integration is neither feasible nor desirable. For "realists," states seek relative power with respect to each other under conditions of international anarchy. Most realist scholars view the EU as an artifice of the Cold War, which will either continue in its present form or dissolve into a competitive multipolar state system. For "liberals," dominant societal groups force states to maximize the interests of these groups by constructing mutually beneficial international institutions. From this perspective, the EU represents a successful example of such an international institution. It is supported by dominant societal groups who lack any interest in the creation of a more politically integrated Europe.

These three problems with a security-based justification for the project of European political integration provide the agenda for this chapter, which identifies a conception of security suitable for arguments that seek to justify—or criticize, for that matter—European political integration. I consider these three objections in the following three sections of this chapter, reverse order. First I consider the challenge posed by realist and liberal theories of international relations. Next I offer an account of what security is and why it matters. And finally I propose an international relations framework suitable for considering the implications of a more politically integrated Europe on individual security.

EUROPEAN INTEGRATION AND INTERNATIONAL RELATIONS THEORY

The point of departure for all realist theorists of international relations is the fact of anarchy—the fact, in other words, that the interactions between states take place in the absence of a binding form of political authority. Under these conditions of anarchy, states must pursue relative power. The behavior of states can be explained—and perhaps even ex ante predicted—on the basis of this view of state motivation.

The first generation of realists—so-called classical realists—sought to provide statesmen with a view of interstate conflict that emphasized the role of power politics and to warn them against the temptation of utopian, world-transforming projects.[2] Thus Hans Morgenthau, probably the most influential of these classical realists, encouraged statesmen to pursue the national interest defined in terms of power.[3] Morgenthau was deeply skeptical of the capacity of international law and transnational institutions to temper the self-interested behavior of states.

The best illustration of the classical realist approach to European integration can be seen in the statecraft of politicians such as Charles de Gaulle and Margaret Thatcher. While these politicians were willing to support the process of European integration at certain of its formative stages, they always made it clear that European institutions were valuable only insofar as these institutions served their own state's national interests. Thus Margaret Thatcher was an early advocate of the Single European Act, because she believed that its economic provisions were in the interests of British industry. Both de Gaulle and Thatcher were quite candid in their instrumentalist conception of European integration. They never ceased to remind their followers that their own states' national interests remained the sole touchstone of their policies toward Europe. At the point when European laws and institutions threatened national interests, they became very hostile to European integration.

For present purposes, the classical realism of Morgenthau, de Gaulle, and Thatcher is less germane than the so-called structural realism of Kenneth Waltz and his followers.[4] It is this version of realism that remains influential in academic circles.[5] For all its differences with classical realism, structural realism retains, as we shall see, a profound skepticism of European political integration.

Waltz's reworking of the realist approach to international relations draws on the idea that states form part of an international system. He holds that the aim of any theory of international relations is to understand how the *structure* of the international system produces patterns of state behavior. Waltz, in short, maintains that the structure of the international system exercises a greater impact on state behavior than the domestic characteristics of states themselves. This structure, as he conceptualizes it, possesses two salient features: (1) anarchy, which is to say, absence of an effective overarching political authority; and (2) unequal distribution of power. Waltz seeks to derive valid generalizations concerning the behavior of states primarily on the basis of the distribution of power in the international system. The most reliable generalization, he argues, is that states will seek to maintain their independence by balancing against dominant states. As Waltz puts this point:

Balance of power theory leads one to expect that states, if they are free to do so, will flock to the weaker side. The stronger, not the weaker side, threatens them, if only by pressing its preferred policies on other states.[6]

In an extension of these views concerning the propensity of states to balance against each other, Waltz formulates a number of generalizations concerning the link between the distribution of power in the international system and its stability. Bipolarity (a system with two dominant powers) is, he argues, more stable than multipolarity, which itself is more stable than unipolarity. For Waltz, the present international system is unipolar, which he considers "the least durable of international configurations."[7]

Waltz's views concerning European integration reflect his theoretical assumptions concerning the international system. These assumptions suggest that states, the principal actors in the international system, will strive to maintain their relative positions in the system. They pursue this goal as a condition of achieving security and maintaining an autonomous way of life.[8] Given this view of states, Waltz generally dismisses international institutions such as NATO and the EU as little more than epiphenomena of underlying national power. Thus, for most realists like Waltz, the EU owes its present institutional configuration to the effort of weaker European states to curtail the potential power of Germany.[9] Realists like to highlight the extent to which states pursue their national interests through these new international institutions.

More recently, Waltz and other structural realists have speculated on the likely response of states to the new era of US unipolarity.[10] Waltz's structural theory predicts that other leading powers in the international system will eventually, acting either singly or collectively, balance against the United States. "Unbalanced power, whoever wields it," so Waltz argues, "is a potential danger to others. . . . In international politics, overwhelming power repels and leads others to balance against it."[11] This would mean that China, Japan, and the European powers can be expected to balance against the United States. Interestingly, when Waltz considers the case of Europe as a challenger to the United States, he expects Germany—the dominant power in Europe—to take the lead. As he puts this point: "In the absence of radical change, Europe will count for little in international politics for as far ahead as the eye can see, unless Germany, becoming impatient, decides to lead a coalition."[12] Waltz also seems to suggest that if Europe is successfully to check American dominance, it would have to become a unified state, but he thinks that this is unlikely. Indeed, given the emphasis he places on states and their pursuit of autonomy, it is difficult to see how his theory could even allow for the possibility that states would sacrifice their sovereignty in a wider politicallyintegrated Europe. Waltz's structural realism, in short, represents a formidable obstacle to those who believe that there is a security-based justification for European political integration.

Realism, whether in its classical or structural forms, represents only one, albeit influential, approach to international relations. In its emphasis on conflict and the pursuit of power, it stands in sharp contrast to those so-called liberal approaches that emphasize the possibility for cooperation in international politics. At first glance, these liberal approaches would seem to lend more support to the idea of European political integration. The European Union represents one of the most successful examples of an international institution facilitating cooperation between sovereign states. The EU—the current product of European integration—is not, however, the aspiration of proponents of the European project of integration. The European project seeks, as its terminus, either a unitary sovereign European superstate or a postsovereign European polity. Liberal approaches to international relations are less obviously supportive of this project. Moravcsik's recent formulation of a liberal theory can serve here as an illustration of this point.[13]

Like Waltz's structural realism, Moravcsik's liberal theory seeks to formulate valid generalizations about the pattern of state behavior. Unlike Waltz, Moravcsik seeks to explain state behavior as a function of domestic or societal interests. The fundamental actors in international relations are thus not states, as they are for realists, but the individuals and social groups that lobby their states to advance their preferences or interests. States themselves "do not automatically maximize fixed, homogeneous conceptions of security, sovereignty, or wealth per se (as realists assume . . .) . . . Instead . . . they pursue particular interpretations and combinations of security, welfare and sovereignty preferred by powerful groups."[14] Of course, this is not to say that powerful groups, even in the most powerful states, always get their way. While Moravcsik does not subscribe to the idea that an international system determines state behavior, he does allow that the configuration of interdependent state preferences constrains state behavior. In other words, states seek to get their way in a world where other states are seeking to get their way. Moravcsik wants to conceptualize the resulting clash of interests in terms of the concept of "policy interdependence." What he means is that states will have different stakes in different policies. Outcomes in international relations will depend less on the power of states than on the strength of underlying state preferences and the extent to which these preferences are shared by, or in conflict with, the preferences of other states. In contrast to realists, Moravcsik and other liberal international relations theorists allow that, in many policy arenas, state preferences will be harmonious, and, when they are not, intensity of preference matters more than state power.

Although Moravcsik's liberal theory of international relations is not as state centric as Waltzian realism, his theory also does not lend any direct support to the project of European political integration. Indeed, liberal theory explains the current arrangement of the EU in terms of the interests of societal actors. Thus Moravcsik's own account of European integration emphasizes the role played by domestic business interests in all of the formative treaties creating the EU.[15] Neither federalist ideas nor security considerations played, he argues, much of a role. The implication of this view is that any change in the direction of greater political integration must await a shift in preferences of business groups in Europe's leading states. Absent this shift in preference, the EU will remain in its present "intergovernmental" form.[16]

The project of European integration is, at base, a normative project. It postulates a terminus, whether a sovereign state or a postsovereign polity, that *ought* to be attained. From this perspective, it might initially seem that these realist and liberal theories of international relations are beside the point. Yet if arguments in support of the European project are to be anything other than hortatory, they must engage with social scientific theories that purport to describe and explain how international relations actually work. To ignore these theories is to run the danger that the project of European integration will be dismissed as a utopian goal—a goal that is not attainable either in principle or in practice. No less importantly, arguments in support of the project of European political integration must make certain inferences concerning the impact of a European sovereign or postsovereign polity on the resulting pattern of international relations. These inferences must rest on plausible assumptions concerning the behavior of individuals, groups, and states in the international system.

Since the view of international relations that informs the argument of this chapter departs from both Waltz's structural realism and Moravcsik's liberalism, it would be useful to register the areas of divergence. The first point to note is the standing of normative inquiry in their respective theories. For all their differences, Waltz and Moravcsik seek a theory of international relations that is capable of valid, lawlike generalizations concerning the behavior of states. Indeed, they reject each other's approaches on the basis of alleged failures to yield sufficiently robust, nontrivial generalizations. It is not my aim here to assess the empirical adequacy of the generalizations that these theories yield. It suffices to say only that a theory of international relations can seek other aims than lawlike generalizations concerning the behavior of states. Normative theories of international relations seek to identify the international arrangements most likely to protect or advance some normatively desirable state of affairs. A normatively desirable state of affairs might include such values as "world peace," "global democracy," "sustainable development," or even, say, the "American national interest." A principal task of any normative theory of international relations is to justify the chosen normative standpoint. In this chapter, I take as my normative standpoint "individual security." I wish to consider the question of whether the project of European political integration contributes to individual security.

In focusing on the individual, the approach adopted here might seem to share more in common with Moravcsik's liberal theory of international relations than with Waltz's structural realism, which focuses primarily on states and *their* security. This is not to say, however, that a normative commitment to individual security entails a liberal theory of international relations. Indeed, it is wholly consistent to combine a normative commitment to individual security with a sociological perspective that recognizes that configurations of power remain the principal determinant of international politics. In illustration of this point, I want to consider the problems that arise when this "realist" dimension of international relations is, as in Moravcsik's work, neglected.

For Moravcsik, as we have seen, state behavior is primarily a function of the preferences of dominant societal groups and not, as realists believe, a function of the distribution of power in the international system. Yet for this "liberal" approach to be fruitful, the preferences of dominant societal groups must be exogenous to the relative power of the state to which these groups belong. If the preferences of these groups are, in any important sense, a function of the relative power of their state, then it would make little sense to accord explanatory primacy to these preferences.

A more plausible interpretation of the relationship between preferences and power would recognize that individuals and groups belonging to powerful states have a wider range of options available to them. These options are themselves a function of the distribution of power within the international system. The international political options available to the wealthiest company in a weak state are certainly more limited than the international political options available to the wealthiest company in a powerful state. The preferences of the business interests in these two countries will be selected from the menu of options made available to them by the relative power of their respective states in the international system. Power, in short, determines the options that preferences select. Consider here, by way of example, the options made available to US banks and automobile companies by US power in East Asia. On a whole range of issue, US political leaders pressured—sometimes successfully, sometimes not—the Japanese government to enact policies favorable to US financial and manufacturing interests.[17] US power, in other words, can and does create options for dominant societal groups. The preferences of these societal groups thus cannot provide the point of departure for a theory that seeks to explain how the current international political and economic systems operate.

The current power imbalance between the United States and European countries provides a further illustration of the extent to which the preferences of states and dominant societal groups are shaped by the configuration of capabilities. Whereas political elites in the United States are actively engaged in debates about when and how "regime change" ought to occur, European political elites are, for the most part, advocates of nonintervention. Although a liberal theory of international relations might account for this disagreement in terms of underlying differences in ideas, interests, and culture, the more plausible explanation—controversially espoused by Robert Kagan—is that Europeans' preferences are a function of Europe's relative weakness. As Kagan puts this point:

> When the United States was weak, it practiced the strategies of indirection, the strategies of weakness; now that the US is powerful, it behaves as powerful nations do. When the European great powers were strong, they believed in strength and martial glory. Now, they see the world through the eyes of weaker powers.[18]

From Kagan's realist perspective, Europeans' hostility to unilateralism in international relations is a function of their own state's weakness. The preferences of dominant societal groups are, in short, curtailed by the options that the power of their states makes available.

Yet if preferences do not provide the point of departure for a social scientific theory of international relations, can it not be said that they provide the point of departure for a normative theory of international relations? Certainly, any normative theory sympathetic to liberalism must take preferences seriously. "The only freedom which deserves the name," as John Stuart Mill famously put it, "is that of pursuing our own good in our own way."[19] From this perspective, it might be argued that preferences ought to be the ultimate arbiter of normatively desirable outcomes in international politics. This position would, however, be rather embarrassing for a proponent of European political integration, because prevailing preferences in Europe today do not support European political integration. But only a very crude normative theory would take prevailing preferences as the last word on the desirability of an outcome. A normative theory, in short, seeks to persuade people to modify their preferences in accordance with a justified criterion of value. A liberal normative theory thus seeks to persuade people to adopt preferences compatible with liberal ends. These ends can be detailed in a more or less comprehensive way. For the reasons identified in the previous chapter, normative theories of international relations would do well to avoid any appeal to thick or comprehensive conceptions of the good. In keeping with this ambition, the normative theory of international relations pursued here privileges individual security. The task remains to provide a fuller account of this normative standpoint.

What Is Security? And Why Does It Matter?

International relations theorists have, at least until recently, taken a very narrow view of security.[20] Typically, they assume that security is a predicate of states, and that states achieve security through maximizing their relative military and economic power. More recently, various scholars have suggested that we think of security more broadly.[21] In the wake of these suggestions, many international relations scholars have come to acknowledge that security can be predicated of individuals and groups rather than, or in addition to, states. They also acknowledge that "security" can be extended beyond military security to take in such concerns as economic security, food security, environmental security, and even cultural security.

There is a lot to be said for expanding the focus of the concept, but there is also a danger that "security" might become a term that names just any value deemed worthy of priority attention. The state of the nation's schools or the erosion of the nation's religion could then, for instance, become a security issue. Although any account of security used in a moral or political theory must be tailored to the purposes of that theory, my account here cannot depart too far from customary usage. To this end, it is worth identifying the various ways that the term "security" has been employed in our moral and political language. Viewed from the perspective of the history of Western political thought, it would seem that the concept "security" has functioned in three somewhat different ways: (1) as a presupposition of individual well-being; (2) as itself an element of individual well-being; and (3) as a state of a collectivity.[22]

The idea that security constitutes a precondition for individual well-being finds its canonical expression in the political writings of Thomas Hobbes. For Hobbes, our duties to each other are exhausted by our obligation to keep the covenants that create the state. Ultimately, it is the state that guarantees the social conditions of mutual security. So long as we do nothing to jeopardize the Sovereign, our duties to each other are complete. It is important to recognize here, however, that the Hobbesian Sovereign matters only insofar as it provides its individual members with the conditions of security. From an ontological point of view, Hobbes is a thoroughgoing individualist. The state matters only because of what it provides the individual. Hobbes assumes that in an absolutist state, individuals would be free to pursue what he terms a "commodious life." In other words, security is not the ultimate aim of human existence. Consider, for instance, Hobbes's account of the obligations of the Sovereign:

> The office of the sovereign, be it a monarch or an assembly, consisteth in the end for which he was trusted with the sovereign power, namely the procuration of the safety of the people, to which he is obliged by the law of nature, and to render an account thereof to God, the Author of that law, and to none but Him. But by safety here is not meant a bare preservation, but also all other contentments of life, which every man by lawful industry, without danger or hurt to the Commonwealth, shall acquire to himself.[23]

While Thomas Hobbes's political theory suggests that sovereignty is both a necessary and a sufficient condition for the security of the individual, Adam Smith's writings suggest a somewhat different view. For

Smith, security is not indivisible; it is for Hobbes, who believes that no one is so wealthy or so powerful that he could be secure in the absence of a Sovereign. In his account of the progress of commerce in Book III of the *Wealth of Nations*, Smith shows how some segments of society can be more or less secure than others.[24] Thus those living in the towns of medieval Europe were more secure than those in the country, and those who were wealthy were more secure than the poor. These differences were significant, because they affected the relative productivity of the cities and the country, the rich and the poor. In the absence of security, the progress of commerce was stymied. And in the absence of a flourishing commercial society, individuals could not acquire what Smith terms "the conveniences of life." From Smith's perspective, the political authorities in medieval Europe were, moreover, as much a threat to, as a source of, security.

John Stuart Mill's *Principles of Political Economy* follows Smith in viewing security as a presupposition of the progress of commerce. Like Smith, Mill also describes how the security of individuals and communities was often jeopardized by rapacious individuals, arbitrary governments, and belligerent foreign powers. But Mill makes the further point that as societies become more progressive, security—in the sense of freedom from sudden attack—becomes a condition that all individuals can enjoy. As he puts these points:

> Another change, which has always hitherto characterized, and will assuredly continue to characterize, the progress of civilized society, is a continual increase of the security of person and property. . . . Even in semi-barbarous Russia, acts of spoliation directed against individuals, who have not made themselves politically obnoxious, are not supposed to be now so frequent as much to affect any person's feelings of security. . . . Of this increased security, one of the most unfailing effects is a great increase both of production and of accumulation. Industry and frugality cannot exist where there is not *a preponderant probability* that those who labour and spare will be permitted to enjoy.[25]

An interesting feature of this argument is that it introduces the psychological observation that arbitrary attacks against some individuals bear upon the feelings of security of others.

Mill also introduces the idea of security into his moral and political thought. Thus notwithstanding the very specific account of individuality, which Mill relies on to identify a liberal conception of the good, Mill assigns security a more foundational role in his theory of justice. In his "Utilitarianism," Mill describes security as "the most vital of all interests." He then goes on to explain why:

All other earthly benefits are needed by one person, not needed by another; and many of them can, if necessary, be cheerfully foregone, or replaced by something else; but security no human being can possibly do without on it we depend for all our immunity from evil, and for the whole value of all and every good, beyond the passing moment; since nothing but the gratification of the instant could be of any worth to us, if we could be deprived of anything the next instant by whoever was momentarily stronger than ourselves.[26]

The idea found in Hobbes, Smith, and Mill that security is a precondition for the good or commodious life must be distinguished from the very different idea that security is itself a component, perhaps the highest component, of the good life. This usage of the term "security" derives, as Emma Rothschild has pointed out, from the Latin *securitas*, which means, among other things, "tranquility."[27] Thus for Cicero and Seneca, *securitas* described a state that the fortunate few could attain. "It denoted composure, tranquility of spirit, freedom from care, the condition that Cicero called the 'object of supreme desire,' or the absence of anxiety upon which the happy life depends."[28] Mill too (as in the quote above) uses security to refer to a condition of individuals, but there is nothing terribly elevated about his "feelings of security"—they appear simply when individuals are free from threats of attack or arbitrary appropriation.

Rothschild also notes a third sense of "security": a condition of a collectivity. This usage, she argues, first became prominent at the time of the French Revolution and the Napoleonic Wars. Thus it became common to speak—as international relations scholars now do—of the security of the state. One obvious drawback of restricting the usage of the term solely to states or collectivities is that it can lead to the mistaken view that state or collective security is a sufficient condition of individual security. But this is clearly not the case. Rousseau recognizes the possible disjuncture between individual and state security when he notes,

It will be said that the despot assures his subjects civil tranquillity. Granted; but what do they gain, if the wars his ambition brings down upon them, his insatiable avidity, and the vexatious conduct of his ministers press harder on them than their own dissensions would have done?[29]

While the danger of considering "security" as exclusively a predicate of the state is now well known, it is important to note that there are comparable dangers in thinking of security as a precondition of individual well-being (the usage suggested, for instance, by Mill in his "Utilitarianism"). The danger here is that if security is, as Mill suggests, the most important of our interests—something on which we depend "for all our immunity from evil, and for the whole value of all and every good"—then there would seem to be no limit to what political authorities might do in its name.[30] Thus, in the name of security, political authorities might be persuaded to discount other values such as liberty, privacy, and democracy.

The fact that "security" is a value that can be used and has been used to justify limitations on other values underscores the importance of specifying the nature of security and its relationship to the other values we have reason to care about. To understand security, it is useful to begin with its close relative: a threat. A threat (T) can, in this context, be understood as a function of the magnitude of the potential harms (H) that an individual faces in any given period of time multiplied by the probability (p) of those harms actually happening. In other words,

Threat (T) = potential harms (H) $\times$ probability of occurrence (p).

At first glance, it might seem that we could represent security as nothing more than the absence of—or, at least, a very low level of—threats. But this brief account of threats neglects the role of various safeguards that might be in place at any given time to protect us against potential harms and their likelihood of happening. Clearly we are more secure the greater our confidence in the safeguards we possess relative to probable harms (Hp). In other words, threats, as measured above, might increase—potential harms may be more catastrophic; their likelihood of occurring greater—but our overall security could nonetheless increase so long as we had greater confidence in our safeguards against such threats. The adequacy of safeguards (G) might itself be conceptualized as a function of two further factors: one, *belief in the efficacy of the measures (E)* that have been taken in protection against Hp; and two, the *compatibility of these measures with basic societal values (V)*. In other words,

adequacy of safeguards (G) = efficacy (E) $\times$ value consistency (V).

No one can know, in advance of any actual attack, just how effective (E) the existing protective measures are. E is thus a measure of subjective belief: how confident, in other words, we are that current measures

101

will prove effective. Yet while E includes an irreducible subjective component, E remains a matter that is susceptible to modification in light of new evidence and rational argument. It is possible to consider rationally how well various measures have fared in the past against particular threats. It is also possible to consider a range of counterfactual threats and gauge how well existing plans and institutions will respond. It will sometimes be possible to protect against threats by adopting policies that are at odds with basic societal values.[31] The incidence of terrorism, for instance, could probably be cut by allowing the state to open all mail, tap all phones, detain and torture "profiled" suspects. Likewise, street crime could probably be cut by imposing a nighttime curfew on all males between the ages of fourteen and thirty. We do not adopt these protective measures, because they conflict with basic societal values such as privacy and liberty. Given these possibilities, it is important to include in the concept of adequate safeguards some measure of their compatibility with basic values.

In order to conceptualize security, it is necessary to combine the equations for threats (T) and adequacy of safeguards (G). The greater the level of the threats we face relative to the adequacy of our safeguards, the less secure we are. In short,

$$\text{security } (S) = \frac{\text{adequacy of safeguards } (G)}{\text{threats } (T)} = \frac{(E)(V)}{(H)(p)}.$$

If the concept of security is to do any real work, something further needs to be said about the substantive content of the terms V and H. Insofar as we are interested here in a conception of security sufficient to justify European political integration, we need a conception of V and H suitable for a modern liberal European society. There is, in short, a difference between *security as a concept* and a *liberal conception of security*, which will allow only a certain range of V and H. For a liberal, the harms that matter most are those that affect the physical safety of the individual, the individual's enjoyment of basic liberties, and life's "necessaries and conveniences." By the same token, a liberal conception of security must construe basic societal values (V) in a broadly liberal way. Modern European societies all remain committed to a liberal conception of political legitimacy. They will thus seek safeguards that do not sacrifice their commitment to, say, due process and limited government. This point is nicely captured in John Locke's response to proponents of the absolute state such as Robert Filmer and Thomas Hobbes:

For if it be asked what security, what fence is there in such a[n absolute] state against the violence and oppression of this absolute ruler, the very question can scarce be born. They are ready to tell you that it deserves death only to ask after safety. Betwixt subject and subject, they will grant, there must be measures, laws, and judges for their mutual peace and security. But as for the ruler, he ought to be absolute, and is above all such circumstances; because he has a power to do more hurt and wrong, it is right when he does it. . . . This is to think that men are so foolish that they take care to avoid what mischiefs may be done them by polecats or foxes, but are content, nay, think it safety, to be devoured by lions.[32]

There is one further important dimension of basic liberal values that must be taken into consideration in any liberal conception of security: democratic self-government. The members of a modern liberal society will measure the adequacy of safeguards against potential threats, at least in part, in terms of their ability to democratically control those safeguards. They will be no more willing to purchase security at the price of democratic self-government than at the price of their liberty. The idea that members of a modern liberal society—"bare citizens," as I described them earlier—can control their political institutions involves a certain amount of fiction. Democracy in a modern society is not what it was in the Athenian polis. Active citizenship, which is to say genuine participation in political decision making, is not an option in a complex modern society. Yet even if the idea of democratic self-government has grown more attenuated and the idea of democratic control has become largely fictive, these ideas are nonetheless important. They help sustain what might be termed a liberal conception of self-worth.

I say a lot more about democratic self-government and how it bears on the justification of the European project in chapter 7. It suffices here to note that that the idea of democratic self-government enters a liberal conception of security at two points. It enters into the measure of potential harms (H), and it enters into the conception of basic values (V). As a component of (V), democratic self-government limits the adequacy of safeguards that rely on the power of persons or entities that cannot be—either in actual practice or even in a fictive sense—democratically controlled. I will pursue this line of argument below to expose the difficulties that arise in all proposals that suggest that Europeans can rely for their security on the United States or some other foreign power. To conclude this present section on the nature and value of security, I merely want to relate the conception of security outlined here to the earlier discussion of different possible understandings of the concept of security.

For some theorists—Hobbes and Mill, for instance—security is not only a necessary good but the presupposition of all other goods that we might value. One difficulty with conceptualizing security in this way is that it suggests that there can be no limits to the measures that might be taken to safeguard security. (Hobbes and Mill draw on additional aspects of their moral and political theories to mitigate this problem.) Rather than conceptualizing security as a presupposition of other goods, it is possible, as some theorists have done, to think of security as one good among others. Security, whether conceived as a state of tranquillity or as relative freedom from insecurity, must be balanced against other goods like privacy and liberty. Henry Kissinger had this sense of the term in mind when he reported,

> The important thing in foreign policy is this: There are a lot of important objectives: democracy is one of these; security is another; prosperity is another. So you have to see how you give emphasis to these objectives at any moment of time.[33]

There are difficulties, however, with the idea that security can be conceptualized in isolation from other goods, against which it must be balanced.[34] Such a view suggests that that there is a state of security that can be described independently of the other values we care about. In contrast to that view, the approach adopted here conceptualizes security as a relational concept, which balances potential threats and adequate safeguards. Viewed as a relational concept, security still possesses the status of a necessary good that a person with the commitments of a "bare citizen" could not do without. In the remaining sections of this chapter, I want to consider how European political integration might bear on this conception of security.

Security, European Integration, and International Order

Now that we possess a clearer conception of individual security, I want to return to the task of considering security-based arguments for European political integration. The assumption behind security-based arguments, as I understand them, is that European political integration (whether it takes a sovereignist or postsovereignist form) can be justified in terms of contributions to European peace, stability, or (the term I prefer) security. Typically, this argument focuses solely on the prospects for an enduring peace among Europe's separate peoples and states. Since 1945, western Europe has managed to avoid the problem of interstate violence that plagued the continent over the preceding centuries. Europe now possesses, what Karl Deutsch has termed a "pluralistic security community": a cooperative arrangement among states that makes defense against each other unnecessary.[35] It is difficult to know how much credit the process of European integration can claim in the achievement of this "pluralistic security community." But whether the credit is great or small, the fact that Europe already possesses a "pluralistic security community" diminishes the plausibility of any argument that seeks to invoke security as a justification for the further political integration.

Yet while crude versions of the security-based justification for European political integration—versions that habitually crop up in the speeches of Europe's political leaders—lack credibility, this does not necessarily mean that more sophisticated versions of this justification also lack credibility. Intuitively, the creation of a sovereign or postsovereign European polity is likely to have major ramifications not just for politics within Europe but also—and more importantly—for politics between Europe and the rest of the world. It thus seems incredible to believe that Europeans would enjoy the same level of security in a Europe of nation-states, in a unitary federal Europe, and in a postsovereign Europe. This would be to suggest—to introduce some terms that I will explain further below—that a "world order" could remain constant notwithstanding fundamental changes in the "international state system" and "international society." Such a suggestion is, for the reasons I now wish to explain, implausible.

Let us begin with the idea of security developed in the previous section. International relations scholars typically work with a very crude conception of security. Simply put, security is a predicate of states, and security is present when war is absent.[36] A more plausible account of security would recognize that security is a predicate of individuals, who achieve security when they have adequate safeguards against potential threats. While this more plausible account of security focuses on individuals rather than states, the state nonetheless enters into considerations of security in at least three different and important ways. To grasp the impact of the state on individual security, it will be helpful to keep in mind the following:

$$\text{security } (S) = \frac{\text{adequacy of safeguards } (G)}{\text{threats } (T)} = \frac{(E)(V)}{(H)(p)}.$$

At one level, the state enters into considerations of security in its capacity as a protector or safeguard. Any well-ordered state will effectively protect (E) the individual against potential harms (H) without jeopardizing core values (V). Yet at another level, the state itself can pose a threat to individual security. In thinking of the state as a threat, it is important to distinguish between the domestic and international activities of the state. Domestically, the state threatens only its own members. Internationally, the state threatens other states, their members, and indirectly—if other states respond militarily—the state's own members themselves. A liberal theory of security will focus on harms—whether originating domestically or internationally—to personhood, basic liberties, and material prosperity; it will also ensure that political measures taken to safeguard against these threats do not themselves jeopardize these basic liberal values.

This is not to say, however, that the state poses the sole threat to individual security today. Some political sociologists have argued that a striking feature of late modern societies is the extent to which states have lost power to nonstate actors (whether powerful individuals, multinational corporations, transnational social movements, or loosely organized networks of terrorists).[37] Nonstate actors can certainly pose a threat to individual security. Violent criminals and loosely organized networks of terrorists are perhaps not, in most cases, as capable of harming individuals as is the state itself, but they can, nonetheless, pose a potential harm to the security of the individual. This potential harm becomes a more likely occurrence (p) when the state is weak or ineffective. In other words, individuals have reason to fear living in both strong arbitrary states and weak ineffective states.

The principal threats to individual security can now be summarized in the following way: (1) *private violence,* which is to say violence by individuals or groups in one society against other individuals or groups in that society; (2) *state-controlled violence,* which is to say violence directed by the state against its own subjects and citizens; (3) *interstate violence,* which is to say the organized violence of one state directed against another; and (4) *terrorism,* which is to say violence organized by nonstate actors, whether domestic or foreign, for political purposes.

Although this list of threats is not meant to be exhaustive, it serves to remind us that threats to individual security come from a variety of different sources (other individuals and groups, one's own state, other states). For this reason, the framework necessary to conceptualize all these potential threats to security needs to relate both the domestic and the international aspects of political order to each other. In this respect, the general approach of Hedley Bull and the so-called English school of international relations theory is more useful than the dominant "liberal" and "realist" paradigms favored by many American international relations theorists.[38] Bull's approach is useful because it draws a clear set of distinctions between "world order"—conceived as a normatively desirable state of affairs—the "international state system," and "international society." A modified version of Bull's approach to "world order" provides, as I now wish to show, the best perspective from which to consider security-based justifications for European political integration.[39]

"World order," as understood here, is a normative concept that refers to an arrangement of the international state system and international society that protects a normatively desirable state of affairs. Different theorists will embrace difference conceptions of the normatively desirable. Bull himself interprets order as "a pattern of human activity that sustains elementary, primary, or universal goals of social life."[40] Following the argument provided in the previous section, world order, as I understand it, is an arrangement of the international state system and international society that sustains individual security. Policies are thus "order enhancing" when they increase individual security. Policies are "order diminishing" when they decrease individual security. I am interested in the question whether, and under what circumstances, European political integration can be construed as an order-enhancing project. Notice that this focuses on something other than "peace" narrowly conceived. By tying "world order" to individual security—itself conceived as adequate safeguards against potential threats—the focus shifts to a broader set of concerns than the absence of war. From the perspective of "world order," moreover, the only ontological significant entity is the individual and his or her security. States matter only insofar as they are "order enhancing," which is to say conducive to individual security.

Although states have no privileged ontological status in the conception of world order, this is not to say that it is possible to ignore the presence of the "international state system." This analytical term refers to precisely those features that Waltz emphasized in his theory of international relations: international anarchy, states, and the unequal distribution of capabilities among states. Waltz disavowed any interest in normative questions. He was concerned primarily with the question of system stability. But one can draw on his account of the propensity of states to balance against each other to consider what arrangements of the international state system are more or less conducive to world order. It thus becomes possible to ask whether a unipolar state system is more or less "order enhancing" than a bipolar or multipolar international state system.

The least plausible aspect of Waltz's international relations theory lies in his view that international anarchy imposes on states a remorseless logic of self-help through the pursuit of power. Clearly, there is more to the interaction of states than this. Hence the need for a third concept: "international society." "International society" refers to those norms, rules, and institutions that moderate the interaction of states in the international system. These norms, rules, and institutions make it possible for states to pursue goals other than relative power over their neighbors. International norms, laws, and institutions have, in certain periods of history and in certain geographical regions, sometimes exercised a profound influence over state behavior. Perhaps the most important international norm in operation today is the norm that recognizes certain self-governing, territorially limited polities as "sovereign states." Conceived as such a norm, sovereignty provides states with an internationally recognized status and a set of rights, powers, and privileges that attach to that status. It is impossible to understand international and domestic politics today without understanding the role that this norm plays. From the perspective of "world order," it is possible to consider whether this norm is more or less "order enhancing" than other possible norms. Would it, for example, be "order enhancing" to abolish sovereignty in its present form for a set of international norms that provided international recognition and support only for those self-governing, territorially limited polities that provided their members with a certain threshold level of security? Would it—to cite an example closer to home—be "order enhancing" to replace the norm of sovereignty with a norm that encouraged states to delegate authority to transnational institutions?

This tripartite distinction between a normatively defined "world order" and an analytically distinguished "international state system" and "international society" enables us to adopt a more comprehensive assessment of the link between individual security and European political integration. Conceptualized as peace, security provides little purchase in arguments—whether pro or con—about European political integration. Conceptualized as adequate safeguards against potential harms, security can do more work. It now remains to be seen how this more complex account of security fits into the attempt to justify European political integration.

CONCLUSION

Most arguments in support of European political integration rely on some conception of peace or prosperity. This book has conceptualized these arguments in terms of "welfare" and "security." These are abstract concepts, which, if they are to do any justificatory work, must be given greater specificity. Furthermore, these concepts must be put to work in such a way that they do not fall foul of the democratic standard of justification (defended in detail in chapter 1). As we saw in the previous chapter, many of the leading welfare-based arguments for European political integration came a cropper here. Not only did these welfare-based arguments employ conceptions of welfare that were inconsistent with the requirement of publicity. They also drew connections between welfare and the overall political configuration of Europe that failed to satisfy the requirement of sufficiency.

This chapter has done little more than pave the way for consideration of a security-based argument for European political integration. Given the importance of security, any proponent of any eventual European political configuration—whether a European superstate, a postsovereign Europe, or a Europe of nation-states—must believe that his or her own preferred option will yield the requisite form and amount of security. To a certain extent, disagreements on this point flow from different assessments of the threats and of the adequacy of the various safeguards that might be taken against these threats. When it comes to threats, people will disagree not only on their probability but also on their understanding of the cost of various "harms." Likewise, when it comes to "safeguards," people will disagree not simply on the technical question of "efficacy" but also—and more importantly—on the suitability of these safeguards with respect to basic societal values.

Given the fact that any concept of security can operate with different accounts of "harms" and "basic societal values," it is possible to distinguish different conceptions of security. Insofar as "harms" and "basic societal values" are understood in terms of the "bare citizen," it is then possible to identify what might be termed a "liberal conception of security." This conception of security is readily compatible with the requirement of publicity. It remains to be seen, however, whether any particular type of European polity can be justified on the basis of this conception of security. The remaining chapters of this book explore the implications of this conception of security for a postsovereign Europe, a European superstate, and a Europe of nation-states.

✳ CHAPTER 6 ✳

A Postsovereign Europe

THE project of European political integration has two very different possible ends: one, a European superstate; and two, a postsovereign European polity. The European superstate—also sometimes described as a "federal Europe"—remains the eurosceptics' worst nightmare. Before this European superstate can become a reality, it will require the dissolution of all of Europe's current sovereign nation-states. So controversial is the idea of a European superstate that most proponents of the European project prefer to rally behind the idea of a postsovereign European polity—also sometimes described as "a confederal Europe."

Whether a postsovereign polity represents a more modest, less transformative aspiration than the superstate remains, however, a matter of dispute. Some proponents of the postsovereign polity claim that the European Union (EU) is now already a postsovereign polity. For these people, "the promised land," as it were, has already arrived.[1] What tasks remain are those of fine-tuning the institutions and spreading the good news. Thus, for Neil MacCormick, neither Europe's member states nor the EU are sovereign.[2] Postsovereignty describes the situation prevailing in Europe today.

In contrast to those who believe that Europe is already postsovereign, other europhiles believe that the promised land still lies ahead and will not be reached until Europe has removed more (if not all) of the vestiges of national government. These people entertain a variety of different conceptions of the form of a postsovereign Europe. This more radical vision of a postsovereign Europe draws inspiration from the writings of a number of contemporary political philosophers who believe that the sovereign state has profound, disabling weaknesses.[3] From this postsovereign perspective, the sovereign state is necessarily hostile to the "deep diversity" present in modern societies; it is indifferent to the welfare of those outside its borders; it resists the establishment of an overarching conception of cosmopolitan law; and it establishes a fixed and final set of rights rather than an open-ended process of constitutional dialogue. Europhiles inspired by this vision propose a radically decentered polity that is held together by practices of dialogue and contestation.[4]

The assumption of this book is that the project of European integration involves a fundamental transformation in the political architecture of Europe. The European Union in its present form remains predominantly, despite some supranational features, an intergovernmental organization. In other words, there remains a substantial difference between the project of European political integration and the current product of integration. The postsovereign polity—especially that form of it envisaged by proponents of agonistic democracy—would represent a radical step beyond the intergovernmentalism present in the contemporary EU. Such a step requires a strong justification.

This chapter examines the justifications that can and have been put forward in support of a postsovereign polity in Europe. In keeping with the general aim of this book, my focus lies not on the precise institutional configuration of this polity but on the values and justifications that lend support to such a polity. The institutional configurations recommended by advocates of the postsovereign polity interest me only insofar as they embody these values and justifications.

The argument of this chapter proceeds in four sections. The first section describes the postsovereign polity advocated by the legal theorists Neil MacCormick and Joseph Weiler. It then assesses the plausibility of the "nationality-based" justifications that these two theorists offer in support of a postsovereign Europe. The second section discusses the more radical vision of a postsovereign Europe favored by some contemporary "agonistic" democrats. The third section discusses a civic-republican justification for a postsovereign Europe. And the fourth section considers the suggestion that a postsovereign Europe take the form of a civilian power in a cosmopolitan legal order.

Nationality and the Idea of a Postsovereign Polity

Neil MacCormick's writings contain some of the most cogent defenses of a postsovereign European legal order.[5] Like many advocates of a postsovereign Europe, MacCormick—both a Scottish nationalist member of the European parliament and an eminent legal theorist—is dissatisfied with the modern sovereign state. He takes particular issue with those defenders of sovereignty—Hobbes, Austin, Bentham, and Dicey among others—who claim that a sovereign state is a necessary presupposition of a legal order. Against this view, MacCormick argues that a legal order can exist and function effectively even in the absence of that particular type of political system established and sustained by sovereignty. MacCormick further wants to suggest that the "external sovereignty" of a state—the state's independence from outside interference—does not require "internal sovereignty," which is to say a centralized hierarchically organized locus of decision making. Federal states, such as the United States, possess, as he sees it, external but not internal sovereignty.

MacCormick draws these distinctions—between legal and political systems and internal and external sovereignty—because he wants to show that neither the EU nor its member states can be legitimately described as sovereign. Despite the absence of a sovereign European polity, Europe possesses a legal order to which Europe's member states are subordinate. In Europe today, member states have, in short, lost their sovereignty without the EU gaining it. In an arresting metaphor, MacCormick suggests that we think of the loss of sovereignty as more akin to the loss of one's virginity than to the loss of one's property: "something that can be lost by one without another's gaining it—and whose loss in apt circumstances can even be a matter of celebration."[6] To describe Europe's current situation, in which neither the member state nor the EU is sovereign, MacCormick introduces the term "postsovereignty."

MacCormick wants to do more, however, than describe; his principal concern is to defend this postsovereign legal order. He wants to convince us that a postsovereign Europe is preferable to a Europe of nation-states. He also wants to make suggestions for institutional reform, the effect of which would be to diminish the current privileges of nation-states in Europe's political system.[7] The most important—and revealing—of these institutional reforms concerns the representation of minority nations such as the Scots, the Welsh, and the Catalans. MacCormick would like to see these nations given representative weight in Europe's political system equal to that of comparable-size nation-states. Thus, since Scotland and Denmark both have roughly the same population, they should get an equal number of representatives in the European parliament. MacCormick also calls for stricter adherence to the so-called principle of subsidiarity, which requires that decision making proceed at the lowest, most decentralized level possible.[8] The overall consequence of these reforms would be to reproduce a form confederation within Europe's nation-states, while these nation-states themselves would form confederal units of Europe—a genuine postsovereign confederation of federations.[9]

Before inquiring into the justificatory arguments that support MacCormick's defense of postsovereignty, I want to consider the slightly different version of a postsovereign Europe defended in Joseph Weiler's writings. Like MacCormick, Weiler is a legal theorist whose writings on European integration are grounded in a detailed knowledge of Europe's current legal order.[10] More than any other contemporary writer on Europe, Weiler has brought home the distinctive character of the legal relationship between Europe's member states and Europe's supranational legal and political order. Weiler does not use the term "postsovereignty" to describe this arrangement. Instead he prefers to speak of a "Supra-national community ideal," which he contrasts with a "Supra-statal unity ideal."[11] Weiler and MacCormick are thus both in agreement about the undesirability of sovereignty, whether located at the nation-state level or the European level. Where Weiler differs from Mac-Cormick is in his belief that the European Union, as it is now constituted, has already achieved the "supranational community ideal." In other words, the transformation has already taken place.[12] "Europe," as Weiler puts it, "has charted its own brand of constitutional federalism. It works. Why fix it?"[13] The task now, presumably, is to defend it.

At first glance, there is something puzzling in Weiler's attachment to the EU, which most other people, whether europhiles or eurosceptics, tend to criticize. He describes an EU that is much more virtuous, much more worthy of support, than many people have realized. Weiler identifies two particular virtues of the EU: one, it practices "constitutional" tolerance rather than "constitutional" compulsion; and two, it habituates us to rule with and rule by culturally diverse peoples. "Constitutional" tolerance is very important for Weiler; it distinguishes the EU from both a European superstate and a Europe of nation-states. As he describes the way that "constitutional" tolerance works,

> Constitutional actors in the member states accept the European constitutional discipline not because as a matter of legal doctrine, as is the case in the federal state, they are subordinate to a higher sovereignty and authority attaching to norms validated by the federal principle, the constitutional *demos*. They accept it as an autonomous voluntary act; endlessly renewed on each occasion of subordination, in the discrete areas governed by Europe, which is the aggregate expression of other wills, other political identities, other political communities.[14]

Europe, in short, is held together by voluntary compliance to a legal order that lacks the force of a *pouvoir constituant*. Weiler celebrates what proponents of a European superstate bemoan: the absence of a constitutional document expressing the will of "we the people of Europe."[15]

The peoples of Europe are thus *invited* to obey "constitutional" norms, whereas the members of other federal states are told they must obey. "The Quebecois," as Weiler points out, "are told: in the name of the people of Canada, you are obliged to obey. The French or the Italians or the Germans are told: in the name of the peoples of Europe, you are invited to obey."[16]

The second virtue of the EU in its present unconstitutionalized form concerns its impact on intercultural relations in Europe. Weiler makes some bold claims here concerning the influence of EU laws and institutions on Europe's citizens and officials. Conceived as a supranational community that coexists with national governments, the EU encourages citizens to see themselves as both nationals and Europeans. Moreover, each person will be habituated to following norms and laws that have been authored by Europeans, including one's fellow nationals and foreign nationals. The message that Europe drives home to its members is this:

> We are willing to submit aspects of our social ordering to a polity composed of "others" precisely because we are convinced that in some material sense they share our basic values. It is a construct which is designed to encourage certain virtues of tolerance and humanity.[17]

Europeans learn this message not as an abstract ideal but through the daily practice of encountering the laws authored by the cultural other. The overall effect of this message is to improve human decency.

Weiler's characterization of a nonsovereign European "constitutional" order appears, at least on the face of it, highly attractive. Who but a xenophobic brute could not be seduced by a "constitutional" order that instills affection for diversity? Who would not prefer to live in a polity that invites rather than compels its members' obedience? Weiler's characterization of the EU as a "constitutional" order is not, however, the full story. Indeed, it is not obvious whether he means this characterization as a description of what the EU does or as a normative model of how it ought to operate. For the most part, Weiler's defense of European integration takes place against those who would like to provide Europe with a *written* Constitution, which would turn Europe into a statelike entity. Weiler describes the EU as it exists in the absence of a conventional Constitution because he wants to draw out the EU's hidden values. His description has a normative dimension. Thus, for Weiler, Europe's "unique brand of constitutional federalism—the status quo—represents not only its most original political asset but also its deepest set of values."[18]

It would be a mistake to let Weiler's description of Europe's deepest values pass as an accurate account of the EU (the current *product* of European integration, as I prefer). It would also be a mistake to simply assume that these "deepest values" are values that can belong in a democratic justification of the European project. As a description of what the EU does, Weiler's focus on its "unique brand of constitutional federalism" is, at best, somewhat one-sided. Weiler himself recognizes this. In a description of Europe's capacities, Weiler points out that Europe has the ability

1. to enact norms which create rights and obligations both for its Member States and their nationals, norms which are often directly effective and which are constitutionally supreme;

2. to take decisions with major impact on the social and economic orientation of public life within the Member States and within Europe as a whole;

3. to engage the Community and, consequently, the Member States by international agreements with third countries and international organization; and

4. to spend significant amounts of public funds.[19]

From this description, it is clear that the EU is much more than a "constitutional" order. Its decisions structure the social and political lives of all Europeans. While it is not my intention here to assess the EU's social and economic accomplishments, it must be noted, however, that they are not all unambiguous achievements. Even the most ardent europhile would be hard pressed to justify the Commons Agricultural Policy (CAP) as a net contributor to human decency. Not only is the CAP—which consumes nearly half the EU budget—riddled with fraud; it is regressive (because poorer households spend a larger proportion of their income on food); and it is harmful to the agricultural sector of developing countries. An overall assessment of the EU would also have to come to terms with criticisms of the EU's impact on national welfare systems, the position of labor with respect to management, and the general quality of democracy in Europe.[20]

Even if we focus solely on Europe's unique form of constitutional federalism, Weiler's description is a bit hard to swallow. There are two particularly indigestible portions of this description. First, it is misleading to describe Europe's "unique brand of constitutional federalism" as an invitation to belong. There is nothing invitational about EU directives. They are transposed into national law, which can be disobeyed by citizens—Mr. Stephen Thoburn, "the Metric Martyr," for instance—only at the price of a criminal record. The notion of voluntary subordination is also hard to square with the policy the EU follows in regulating the budget deficits of member states. Those states that exceed the stipulated 3 percent limit are not *invited* to tighten their belts. They are told that they *must* comply; if they do not, they face stringent financial penalties.[21]

The second problem with Weiler's description of the EU concerns his emphasis on the role of the EU as a facilitator of ethnocultural sensitivity. At one level, Weiler's account of why ethnocultural membership (or nationality) matters follows the standard Herderian view of such cultures as central components of human well-being.[22] Thus, for Weiler (as for Herder), nationality provides people with "belonging" and "originality."[23] Weiler's twist on the standard Herderian argument is, however, to concede an important element of the antinationalists' objections to nationality. The erotic appeal of nationality is, so Weiler allows, dangerous; it tends to produce a nasty form of "we" against "they" politics. Nationality, as Weiler puts it, tends to be abusive of boundaries; it creates and injures outsiders. Europe's nation-states have historically been among the very worst abusers of boundaries. Fortunately, the EU provides a solution to this problem. As long as the EU resists the temptation to become a superstate, it provides a cold legalistic check on the excesses of nationality. As Weiler sees it, "supranationalism expressed in the community project of European integration . . . is not meant to eliminate the national state but to create a regime which seeks to tame the national interest with a new discipline."[24] By depriving nationality of a codified expression in statal and legal form, the EU tames nationality while protecting it as an "authentic, internalized, [and] a true part of identity."[25]

Weiler is not alone in advancing a nationality-based argument for a postsovereign Europe. Neil MacCormick makes the same move. The premise of MacCormick's argument is that individuals are dependent on a cultural context. Among the most important of these cultural contexts is a national community, from which individuals derive a sense of identity, individuality, and belonging. MacCormick couples this sociological observation with a Kantian principle of respect for persons. In MacCormick's rendering of this principle, respect for persons involves respect for "whatever goes into their individuality."[26] The last stage of his argument draws a political conclusion:

> If many individuals . . . include in their subjective sense of individuality and identity the idea of belonging to a certain nation or national cul-

ture, then respect for persons as contextual individuals must include respect for that aspect of their individuality. Moreover, it is likely that individual self-fulfillment will require a political context involving some opportunity for collective self-government.[27]

Conceived as a justificatory argument for postsovereignty, this argument is open to the obvious objection that respect for persons does not involve respect for whatever goes into their individuality. It would be more plausible to think that respect for persons entails only respect for their *capacity* to develop a sense of identity and individuality.[28] Indeed, sometimes respect for persons requires the expression of disdain for their actual self-identity, which might take a range of individious forms. But even if we allow that MacCormick's argument has the resources to distinguish noninvidious and invidious conceptions of self-identity, this still leaves the larger question of whether this type of argument can justify a European postsovereign polity.

I have dwelled on Weiler's and MacCormick's nationality-based argument for postsovereignty because their work contains the strongest, most persuasive and influential versions of a popular position. For better or worse, many people in Europe today believe that a politically integrated Europe will prove more supportive of the variety of minority nations and ethnocultural groups present in Europe today. In assessing this argument, it is important to distinguish at the outset (1) the role of nationality (broadly conceived to include minority nations and ethnocultural groups) in the justification of a postsovereign Europe, and (2) the role of nationality in the policies and institutions of a well-ordered polity. This distinction is important, because it is quite possible to think that any well-ordered polity ought to recognize minority rights—including the right of national minorities to practice self-government and even perhaps, in extreme circumstances, to secede—and yet to deny that nationality can justify European political integration. There is no obvious reason, in short, why the debate over the rights of national minorities in Europe must necessarily bear on the justification of a postsovereign European polity. Thus, while Neil MacCormick seeks Scottish national independence in an overarching European postsovereign polity, other Scottish nationalists seek independence in a Europe of sovereign nation-states.[29]

Insofar as the nationality argument is understood as a justification for a European postsovereign polity, then this argument must meet certain democratic requirements, including those of publicity, accessibility, and sufficiency. The principal difficulty here comes from the requirement of publicity, which serves to ensure that any arguments put forward in support of European political integration rest on "public values." There is, as was argued in chapter 1, an important difference between a general argument for European political integration and a public one. The former rests on values that all people do in fact embrace, the latter on values that all people ought to embrace. Clearly, the nationality-based argument is not, in this sense of the term, *general*. Nor, more importantly, is it *public*.

Certainly, all people in Europe today grow up in a specific culture. Furthermore, all people in Europe today are citizens, in the sense of enjoying a set of legal, political, and social rights. Throughout much of Europe's recent history, Europe's principal unit of political membership—the nation-state—presupposed and reproduced a fusion of culture and citizenship, nation and state. More often than not, this fusion was purchased at the price of local minority cultures (Welsh, Catalan, Basque, and Breton, for instance), which faced powerful assimilative pressures. In a very general sense, it might be argued that all Europeans today need full membership in a polity that has successfully fused together culture and citizenship. Ernest Gellner (as we saw in chapter 3) contends that this type of fusion is an essential feature of the modern world. Yet even if he were right about the importance of this fusion, this claim would do little to enhance the argument for a postsovereign Europe. Indeed, insofar as nationality is interpreted (à la Gellner) as the fusion of nation and state—the fusion, in other words, of a school-transmitted high (national) culture with a set of civic and political rights—then the nationality-based argument would seem to support either the maintenance of a Europe of nation-states or the creation of a European superstate.

Neither MacCormick nor Weiler, however, understand nationality in this Gellnerian sense. They view nationality in terms of a set of historical memories, distinctive customs, conventions, and practices. For Weiler (especially), a national culture matters because it is a repository of meaning and originality. This is to view national culture in precisely the same way as do most minority nationalists and multiculturalists. The question arises whether nationality understood in this Herderian sense can justify a postsovereign Europe. The difficulty here is that there is no general agreement on the value of nationality understood in this way. While there are people who warm to the call of their ancestral customs, there are also many of us who remain tone-deaf to this call. To claim that all people have a national identity, understood in this sense,

119

is simply false. For better or worse, some people prefer to think of themselves as rootless cosmopolitans rather than romantic nationalists. Indeed, some people view romantic nationalism as dangerous nonsense. These people will, at the very least, have little reason to support the creation of a postsovereign Europe that will give greater scope to this type of nationalism.

Proponents of the nationality-based argument for a postsovereign Europe might allow that their preferred form of nationality is not a general value but is itself linked to one or another of the public values that inform what I have called the *democratic standard of justification*. These public values were listed, in chapter 1 above, as the moral equality of all individuals; personal security; personal and political liberty; and material prosperity (or "the necessaries and conveniences of life"). These values express a provisional conception of a modern European way of life. They remain few in number and abstract in nature because they register the extent to which people in a modern society pursue different projects, embrace different lifestyles, and value different ends. Some people structure their lives in accordance with one or another of the Abrahamic religions. Others, to use Max Weber's evocative phrase, are religiously tone-deaf. Nationality (understood in the Herderian sense) is much like religion. It does not matter to many people, nor do these people have any good reason why it ought to matter to them. Nationality is simply not a public value. The attempt to construct a justification for a postsovereign Europe on the shoulders of nationality violates the requirement of publicity. It attempts to justify a transformative project on the basis of sectarian values that not all Europeans either do or can share. Neither MacCormick nor Weiler, in short, possess a satisfactory justification for a postsovereign Europe. From this conclusion, it does not, however, follow that there is no better justification available for a postsovereign Europe. Before considering what I think is a stronger justification, it would be useful to say something further about the nature of a postsovereign polity.

More Radical Forms of Postsovereignty

The form of postsovereignty defended by Weiler and MacCormick does not require the withering away of Europe's national governments. These governments—and the nations that they represent—would merely coexist with subnational and supranational political entities in such a way that no level of the overall polity would be sovereign. Indeed, the mutual checking of levels is for both of these theorists an important point in favor of a postsovereign Europe. Some political theorists, in contrast, envisage a more radical form of postsovereignty in which the nation-state has disappeared in toto. Philippe Schmitter has imagined one such destination for the European project, a destination he terms a *condominio*.[30]

Conceived as a *condominio,* the European polity would contain multiple and various territorial and functional constituencies. Schmitter describes the result in the following way:

> Instead of a single Europe with recognized and contiguous boundaries, there would be many Europes: a trading Europe, an energy Europe, an environmental Europe, a social welfare Europe, even a defense Europe, and so forth. Instead of one "Eurocracy" that coordinated all the distinct tasks involved in the integration process, there would be multiple regional institutions acting autonomously to solve common problems and produce different public goods.[31]

In this type of polity, the state, as we know it, would no longer exist. Indeed, instead of a recognizable central government, the *condominio* would be regulated by a variety of mechanisms of governance. The concept of *governance,* which means different things to different people, is especially popular among advocates of postsovereign and postmodern forms of polity. For Schmitter, governance signifies "A method/mechanism for dealing with a broad range of problems/conflicts in which actors regularly arrive at mutually satisfactory and binding decisions by negotiating and deliberating with each other and cooperating in the implementation of these decisions."[32]

Schmitter himself is not an advocate of Europe becoming a *condominio.* Indeed, he thinks that the problems of coordination in such a polity would be so great that no proponent of the European project would seek this as a goal. If a *condominio* were to emerge, it would be as a consequence, so Schmitter thinks, of a series of successive compromises. The idea that no one would advocate a *condominio* as an ideal is not, however, wholly accurate. This type of polity possesses precisely those qualities of flexibility and flux that a number of postmodernist legal and political theorists celebrate. Typically, these theorists base their normative prescriptions on what they term an agonistic or contestatory

121

form of democracy. From this perspective, the enemy of democracy is a fixed and final constitutional settlement that takes the rights and duties of political membership off the day-to-day political agenda.

James Tully's writings provide perhaps the clearest articulation of the values that might support a radically decentered *condominio*.[33] Writing primarily with the Canadian constitutional experience in mind, Tully has argued that the constant renegotiation of constitutional settlements is not necessarily a negative. Thus, for Tully, citizens ought to be able to define and redefine their basic political architecture. What matters is that they negotiate with each other in accordance with the conventions of what he terms "mutual recognition, consent, and cultural continuity."[34] In his more recent writings, he has extended these ideas to the European context. For Tully, the fact that the EU currently lacks a settled constitution is a positive accomplishment. "What makes a constitutional arrangement legitimate," he argues, "is . . . its openness to democratic contestation."[35] In an ideal polity, citizens will develop multiple and different sites of democratic contestation, where they will negotiate and renegotiate the terms of political association. The European *condominio* with its multiple forms of governance is precisely the type of polity called into existence by this contestatory or agonistic form of democracy.

Building on the ideas of James Tully and others, a number of political and legal theorists have described (prescribed would be the better term) a future European polity—postsovereign in nature—that combines three distinctive features: (1) asymmetrical incorporation, (2) an open method of coordination, and (3) a dialogic order rather than constitutional fixity. These three elements are already present, at least to some extent, in the EU, but advocates of a postsovereign Europe would like to elevate them into the basis of a new type of polity.

Simply stated, asymmetrical incorporation describes a situation whereby some jurisdictional units are incorporated into Europe on a different basis than others. The model here is something like the Canadian polity, in which Quebec has different rights and responsibilities—different "competences," to use the European terminology—than other provinces. The EU in its current form already allows for asymmetrical incorporation. Thus some European states (including Britain, Denmark, and Sweden) are not part of the "euro" common currency. Proponents of asymmetrical incorporation believe that the future of Europe lies in such a modular design. Jurisdictional units that wanted to form closer ties of integration could do so. Schmitter's *condominio* represents the extreme version of this type of asymmetrical incorporation.

The open method of coordination (OMC) is a form of governance that is already, at least in certain limited areas, current practice in the EU. The OMC, which was initiated at the Lisbon European Council of March 2000, is designed to coordinate policies throughout Europe on the basis of something other than a centralized law or directive. The aim is to improve mutual learning among decentralized national and subnational jurisdictional units. More specifically, the OMC coordinates certain policy issues—including pensions, employment policy, and immigration—through the establishment of benchmarks, peer review, and the identification of "best practices." This approach builds on the notion that "governance" provides a less coercive, less uniform, and less hierarchical basis of rule than "government." Some observers of OMC have seen it as a way of extending a form of deliberative democracy throughout the EU's numerous committees and administrative bodies.

Finally, the idea of a dialogic order rather than constitutional fixity seeks to preserve openness and flexibility in the very basis of membership in Europe. Joseph Weiler, as we have seen, has celebrated this aspect of the EU. He thinks that the EU is distinctive in offering its members an invitation to belong, an invitation that they can, if they wish, refuse. Proponents of a dialogic order simply extend this observation a step further. They welcome a European polity, the basis and nature of membership in which would be constantly up for negotiation and renegotiation. From this perspective, the idea of a Constitution as a settled, once-and-for-all statement of the rights and responsibilities of membership is anathema.

The proponents of these more radical versions of a postsovereign Europe offer a variety of justifications in their support. Many of these justifications focus on the improvements in governance and the quality of democracy that such a polity would make possible. A major problem with these arguments is that they frequently appeal to values—such as radical conceptions of participatory democracy—that are not generally or publicly shared by modern European citizens. The type of "agonistic democracy" celebrated by Hannah Arendt—the inspiration of many who favor a postsovereign Europe—rests on a conception of human flourishing that is no more suitable for a Europe of diverse citizens than a conception of human flourishing grounded in one or another of the Abrahamic religions. If a postsovereign Europe is to be justified at all, it must be justified on the basis of values that all Europeans can at least share. Perhaps the most promising candidate here is to base the justification of a postsovereign Europe on a republican conception of security.

A Civic Republican Conception of Security

One way of justifying the various forms—some more radical than others—of postsovereignty is to appeal to a republican conception of politics. A number of proponents of a postsovereign Europe have adopted this approach. Republicanism, as they understand it, requires an active form of citizenship as a means of limiting the individual's dependence on the arbitrary will of others. For advocates of this form of republicanism, freedom as nondependence is best achieved through something akin to the postsovereign polity described in the preceding section. Republican theorists differ among themselves on the precise form that a postsovereign polity would ideally assume. But they share a common opposition to the form of state sovereignty defended by Thomas Hobbes.

Viewed as an account of human flourishing—a description of the good life—the republican celebration of active citizenship will not take us very far in the effort to justify a postsovereign Europe. The problem is obvious. Insofar as arguments in support of a transformative project like a postsovereign Europe must meet the requirements of a democratic standard of justification, they must, as an element of that justification, satisfy a requirement of publicity. Active citizenship, in the form of direct democratic participation in deliberative forums, is simply not an activity that all people do, or even ought to, embrace. It may well be, however, that the republican approach to politics can be interpreted in a way that is more consistent with a publicity requirement. The republican emphasis on nondependence can, as now I want to show, be reformulated as a component of our concern for personal security.

The concept of security can itself be understood—following the account in the previous chapter—in terms of the threats that an individual or a society faces. These threats can in turn be conceptualized as a function of the magnitude of the potential harms (H) faced in any given period of time multiplied by the probability (p) of those harms actually happening. Threats must be set against the adequacy of safeguards (G) that are available. These safeguards might further be conceptualized as a function of two more specific factors: *belief in the efficacy of the measures*

(E) that have been taken in protection against *Hp*; and the *compatibility of these measures with basic societal values* (*V*).

This concept of security will give rise to a variety of more specific conceptions of security, depending on how the terms *V* (basic societal values) and *H* (harms) are conceptualized. The defining claim of republicanism is that "harms" must include not just the standard forms of coercion and injuries to bodily integrity but also forms of "dependence." We are, from this republican perspective, made insecure when we have to depend for our security on capricious or arbitrary organizations. This problem crops up at the level of either the threats that we face or the safeguards that we might take against those threats.

To lend more precision to this line of argument, it would be helpful to bear in mind the powerful articulations of the republican position found in the writings of Philip Pettit and Richard Bellamy.[36] Although Pettit himself has little to say about security per se, his arguments concerning "freedom as nondependence" (or "nondomination") clearly have an important bearing on this concept. Thus Pettit notes that it is possible to escape many of the harms of ill-treatment by putting oneself "under the grace or favor of the powerful."[37] Yet, as he adds, "the price of liberty in such a world is not eternal vigilance but eternal discretion. The person lives in the power or under the mastery of others; they occupy the position of a *dominus* in his or her life."[38] For Pettit, the answer to the problem of *dominus* is through *imperium*: the establishment of political authorities that act in a nonarbitrary way. He defines "nonarbitrary," quite plausibly, as action that tracks people's "commonly avowable interests," which is simply another way of saying that political authorities must pursue what I have described as "public values." Unfortunately, Pettit does not pursue very far the further task of identifying the political institutions that are necessary to protect against *dominium* in the modern world. He is crucially silent on the question—the central question for any applied political theory—of how we are to rank and order the different forms or sources of *dominium* in the modern world. The answer to this question will determine, at least in part, any decisions we might take about the creation of an *imperium* (whether located at the national or the European level).

Pettit's republican theory has relatively little to say about the organizational or institutional dimensions of a republicanism suitable for contemporary Europe; this gap has been filled by Richard Bellamy.[39] For Bellamy, a republicanism designed to avoid domination by arbitrary powers will seek a form of "mixed government," which disperses and balances power. Bellamy draws his inspiration here from republican theorists, such as James Harrington, who wrote in opposition to the form of sovereignty defended by Thomas Hobbes. Bellamy thinks that a mixed government (or "mixed constitution") will lack any centralized unitary locus of command. The guiding principle of such a polity is *audi alteram partem* ("listen to the other side"); its dominant political practice is one of mutual agreement and consultation. Under a mixed government, as Bellamy puts it,

> No agent or agency holds the power of supreme authority. Unity here depends not on authoritative command but on norm agreement between the various parties. Indeed, it is the inability of any agent or agency to force a decision that partly motivates the search for such an agreement.[40]

Bellamy believes that the EU in its present form is evolving into a mixed governmental system that is capable of realizing the virtues of a republican system. Whereas sovereignists complain about the incoherence of the EU's current political arrangements, republican proponents of a mixed governmental system—which is essentially a "postsovereign Europe" under another name—welcome its "healthy balance between transnational, national, and supranational interests."[41] Once we view this model of Europe as a way of enhancing security—understood as a form of nondependence on arbitrary forms of power—there is no reason to believe that the requirement of publicity poses any problem for a postsovereign Europe.

While a republican defense of a postsovereign Europe can be grounded in a conception of security—thereby satisfying the requirement of publicity—this approach still faces certain profound (and ultimately, I think, disabling) difficulties. There are three principal difficulties: (1) *dominium* (dependence on the arbitrary power of others) is only one of a number of different threats to our security; (2) there are worse forms of *dominium* than that posed by Europe's national sovereign states; and (3) a postsovereign Europe does not seem to be well equipped to handle the full range of threats that Europeans currently confront. Let me say something more about each of these difficulties.

Dependence on the arbitrary power of others (whether individuals, groups, or organized political authorities) is clearly a threat to our security. To be fully secure is to be free of this form of dependence on others. Republicans are quite correct to emphasize this point. But *dominium* is not the only—or even the most important—threat to our security.

More fundamentally, security is a matter of physical safety. We cannot be secure if we live in an environment where we are exposed to violent attack by private individuals, domestic terrorists, foreign terrorists, or foreign states. Sometimes we may have to put up with an arbitrary sovereign state as a condition of achieving basic physical safety.

Even if we were to confine our attention to the threat to our security posed by dependence (or *dominium*), we could hardly limit our concerns to the threats posed solely by our own state. True, Europeans today must worry about the arbitrary power exercised by political authorities organized at the national and European levels. But they must also worry about the arbitrary power exercised by political authorities located outside Europe. While a postsovereign Europe may dutifully track the "commonly avowable interests" of all Europeans, this will hardly matter if Europeans are dominated by a global hegemonic power.

In recognizing the problems posed to Europeans by more powerful foreign states, it is difficult not to recall why the republican form of mixed government ultimately disappeared. The modern world has been dominated by sovereign states because this type of polity proved to be far more successful as a war-fighting entity. A system of government that had multiple centers of power, balanced carefully against each other, simply could not respond militarily to the concentrated power of a national sovereign state. Here it is instructive to bear in mind Tocqueville's comment on the mixed form of republican government that he found in the United States in 1835.

> I cannot believe that any confederate people could maintain a long or an equal contest with a nation of similar strength in which the government is centralized. A people which, in the presence of the great military monarchies of Europe, should divide its sovereignty into fractional parts would, in my opinion, by that very act abdicate its power, and perhaps its existence and its name.[42]

Ultimately, the United States came to abandon its "confederal system"—a "mixed government" in other words—in favor of a more centralized federal system. Indeed, while the United States lacked "internal sovereignty" (understood in MacCormick's sense), the United States found it very difficult to resist British and French intrusions into its territories.[43]

If the republican conception of a postsovereign Europe fails, as I think it does, to provide Europeans with a full measure of security, then some other grounds for must be found for justifying a postsovereign Europe.

It is far from clear that any such grounds are available. The nationality-based argument for a postsovereign Europe fails, for the reasons specified earlier. The republican defense of postsovereign Europe, if understood as involving an appeal to a comprehensive conception of human flourishing, also fails the publicity requirement. Interpreted as a claim about security, however, the republican conception avoids this problem but then runs into difficulties from the requirement of sufficiency. A politically integrated Europe, whether it takes a sovereignist or a postsovereignist form, must be able to protect the values that purport to justify it. Although I have not yet fully established this point, a postsovereignist Europe cannot provide for the security of Europeans. Either it will be vulnerable to the power of more centralized sovereign states (such as the United States, Russia, or China), or it must depend on one or another of those states for its security. Insofar as security requires some form of nondependence, then a postsovereign Europe will always be insecure. The following chapter substantiates these claims. But before concluding the present chapter, something further needs to be said about the approach of postsovereignists to Europe's international security and defense needs.

CIVILIAN POWER IN A COSMOPOLITAN LEGAL ORDER

Proponents of a postsovereign Europe often like to suggest that the only alternative to this form of political integration is violent conflict. Thus Neil MacCormick states that postsovereignty diminishes "the probability of recurrence to the barbarisms of time recently past."[44] Likewise, Philippe Schmitter fears that were Europe to revert to what he terms "its *status quo ante integratio*," it would mean "constant threats of violence, [and] unstable balances of power punctuated by international war."[45] The notion that European political integration, whether in its sovereignist or postsovereignist forms, offers an antidote to war is a frequently reiterated claim, too, of many of Europe's prointegrationist political leaders.

Even if postsovereignists are correct in thinking that a postsovereign Europe diminishes the likelihood of violent conflict within Europe, this would be to adopt an unduly narrow perspective on the security threats facing Europe today. These threats include terrorism and conflict with foreign states. The postsovereignist solution to these more pressing problems is to look to the following three developments: (1) Europe as a "civilian power"; (2) Europe's membership in the United Nations and NATO; and (3) the emergence of a cosmopolitan legal order.

The idea that Europe would form a so-called civilian power was popularized in the 1970s by Francois Duchene.[46] To a certain extent, this strategy represented at that time the only feasibile option for Europe's nascent economic community. But Duchene thought that there were virtues in not being a strong military power. Europe could focus instead on being a responsible leader, a "civilian power" that would spread around the world democratic and egalitarian values. Similar ideas have been recommended by a number of other observers. Many europhiles think that Europe should model itself on the postwar experience of Scandinavia.[47] Much like Sweden, Europe could then represent to the world a set of normative ideals; this would be its contribution to world security. In perhaps the most well-developed recent version of this argument, Jan Zielonka has argued that Europe should make clear to itself and to the world that it has no desire to become a global power.[48] "[A]spiring to military power status would be an expensive, divisive, and basically futile exercise for the Union," so Zielonka argues, whereas " . . . [o]pting for a civilian power Europe would represent one of the basic choices that could help the Union acquire a distinct profile."[49]

There is an obvious difficulty with the idea that Europe should become a civilian power. The difficulty is this: a civilian power is, as Hedley Bull pointed out in a response to Duchene, a contradiction in terms.[50] It is one thing to hope that the promotion of democratic and egalitarian values will make the world a better place. But it is difficult to see how this strategy contributes to the security of one's own citizens. For Bull, the idea that Europe ought to become a "civilian power" simply means that Europe would be condemned to superpower domination. In response to this line of criticism, contemporary advocates of a "civilian power Europe" point out that the era of superpower rivalry is over. "The world has become more civilized in recent years," points out Zielonka, ". . . the politics of violence and brutal force have been largely confined to areas outside the Western world and do not threaten the wealth and integrity of the Union as such."[51]

A civilian-power strategy for Europe might seem to be implausible, if it were pursued wholly in isolation from a more general foreign and strategic policy. Europe could not successfully become isolationist and demilitarized in the way that postwar Scandinavia has done. The idea of a Europe as a normative ideal is, however, consistent with the pursuit of a foreign and strategic policy through international alliances and organizations such as NATO and the United Nations. In other words, a postsovereign Europe could take its place as a "civilian power" within a NATO and United Nations that continued to rely heavily on US military power. The model here would build on the *relative* successes of Kosovo—*relative* in comparison with Europe's failures in Bosnia—where decisive American political action, backed up by US air strikes, drove the Serbian armies out of Kosovo.[52] Although the Europeans were initially reluctant to use force, they eventually contributed a sizable number of troops to Kosovo to act as peacekeeping and police forces. There is, on the face of it, no reason why the Kosovo experience could not be repeated in other areas around the world. Sometimes interventions would take place under NATO auspices and sometimes under UN auspices.

For Europe to remain primarily a civilian power, however, Europe would have to rely on the United States to supply the military teeth of NATO and the United Nations. Postsovereignists generally believe that any problems that might arise in the dependence of Europe on US military force could be minimized by bolstering international norms, laws, and institutions. To this end, a postsovereign Europe would bolster institutions like the International Criminal Court and the World Trade Organization. Furthermore, Europe would encourage—by force of its own successful example—other parts of the world to follow its own postsovereign path and to achieve security through the encouragement of mutual trust and transparency. Europe's experiences with the treaty on conventional forces could serve as an example to the world here. Under the terms of this treaty, weapons were destroyed and mechanisms were set in place that allowed states to inspect each other's territories. In a world of postsovereign polities, this type of mutual transparency should be easier to implement.

It might be argued that a postsovereign Europe would not need to rely for its security solely on international institutions. A postsovereign Europe could develop its own military force, which would be able to act independently of NATO and the United Nations if necessary. This militarized postsovereign Europe could still claim to be a "civilian power." Its independent military force would merely mean that it could employ modest military means toward limited ends, to promote and project democratic values outside its borders.[53] Supporters of this perspective might point here to the example set by the EU's announced intention of developing a sixty-thousand-strong rapid deployment force.

The description presented here of a postsovereign Europe as a civilian power in a cosmopolitan legal order faces a number of difficulties. First, Hedley Bull's critique of Duchene's notion of a civilian power as a contradiction in terms still remains apt. Bull wrote this critique at a time in the early 1980s when the relations between the superpowers had soured. He feared that a Europe without its own military forces would be vulnerable to superpower domination. In the current era of unipolarity, Europe does not need to fear invasion. But it does need to worry about abdicating the capacity for autonomous military action solely to the United States. More often than not, the United States and Europe will have congruent interests. But there is no guarantee that this will always remain the case.

The second problem with Europe as a postsovereign civilian power concerns the durability and effectiveness of multilateralism in an age of unipolarity. Realist international relations scholars such as Kenneth Waltz and John Mearsheimer have predicted that multilateralism will not survive the age of unipolarity.[54] The dominant power in the international system will act unilaterally. Multilateralists such as Joseph Nye hope that the dominant power will recognize that its long-term interests lie in maintaining and acting within the constraints of multilateral institutions. Given the trajectory of President George W. Bush's foreign policy, it would be difficult not to conclude that the realists' predictions have won out over multilateralists' hopes. There is no necessary reason why a dominant power must act unilaterally; it is possible that George W. Bush will be succeeded by a president with a scrupulously multilateralist agenda. But prudence—always the first rule in the formulation of a foreign policy—dictates that Europe must assume a worst-case scenario. It is reckless in the extreme to construct a foreign and military policy on the *hope* that the dominant power will respect multilateral norms and institutions.

The third problem with a postsovereign European civilian power concerns the suggestion that it develop its own military force capable of autonomous action. Granting the need for such a force, especially in light of the problems with a unilateralist United States, the question becomes one of feasibility. We know already, from the experiences with the Common Foreign and Security Policy, that the EU in its present form has faced enormous difficulties in developing a centralized foreign policy decision-making apparatus. These difficulties have been compounded by the absence of a common defense procurement policy and ever diminishing defense budgets. If this is the current situation—the situation of an intergovernmentalist EU—then what is likely to happen when Europe becomes progressively more postsovereign? How likely is it that a European *condominio* will be able to make rapid foreign policy decisions and project military force outside its own borders? It hardly seems likely at all. Indeed, the very features that advocates of a European "mixed government" celebrate—dispersal and decentralization of power, multiple points of contestation, dialogue, and so forth—are precisely the features that would render any such polity ineffective as a war-fighting unit. This would not matter in a world where all other polities were equally ineffective and where war was wholly obsolete. But as we are reminded by the Yugoslavian wars of the 1990s and by the events of September 11 in New York and March 11 in Madrid, this is not, sadly, the world we now inhabit. As the world grows more dangerous, as security becomes a more salient issue, Europe needs to evolve accordingly. The next chapter examines the case for a sovereign European superstate.

A Sovereign Europe

Political theorists have often remarked on the ambiguity of the term "sovereignty." Indeed, one theorist concluded his discussion of the concept with the suggestion that we give up "so Protean a word."[1] Such difficulties have not, however, deterred many eurosceptics from making sovereignty their rallying cry. The loss of sovereignty, as they see it, provides a specific justification for rejecting the project—and perhaps also the current "intergovernmental" product—of European integration. This chapter seeks to understand why sovereignty matters, and whether there is any compelling justification for locating sovereignty at either the national or the European level. Clearly, the value of sovereignty cannot be taken for granted. If we are to take the eurosceptics' arguments seriously, we need to gain a clearer view of what they think sovereignty is—which is not obviously the same as what those critical of sovereignty think it is—and what human purposes or values it serves. To this end, I begin with Noel Malcolm's brief but lucid statement of the eurosceptics' case against European political integration, a case that rests solely on the claim that *national* sovereignty is both necessary and desirable.[2]

Following a discussion of Malcolm's eurosceptic account of sovereignty, the second section of this chapter discusses "sovereignty" as it functions in international society. It is crucial, I argue, to understand this international dimension, because the organization of sovereignty has important international ramifications. The third section draws on this international relations perspective on sovereignty to consider a security-based justification for a European superstate. The fourth section addresses some of the problems with a European superstate. And the fifth section argues that whatever problems the European superstate faces, these problems cannot, contrary to the claims of many Eurosceptics, be remedied by a Europe of nation-states.

A Eurosceptic's Account of Sovereignty

Noel Malcolm's euroscepticism proceeds by way of a careful analysis of the nature and importance of sovereignty. In some respects, Malcolm's argument retraces the steps taken by Enoch Powell (whose accounts of sovereignty and euroscepticism we discussed in chapter 3 above). But since Malcolm directs his argument at the post-Maastricht EU, his account focuses on aspects of European political and economic integration that Powell (writing in the early 1970s) neglected. Unlike the many publicists and politicians who confuse, so he believes, sovereignty with power or the capacity for independent action, Malcolm ties the concept of sovereignty to the idea of authority. A state is sovereign, so he argues, "when it possesses plenary and exclusive competence, a matter of enjoying full authority internally and not being subordinated to the authority of another state."[3] Sovereignty requires, in other words, a legal order, which in turn has to be validated by political authority. A condition of political authority, so he further contends, "is that it is recognized, or granted, or willed, or believed in by the people who are subject to it."[4] Malcolm's emphasis here on the role of will and belief is crucial, as we shall see below, for his argument *against* European political integration.

From Malcolm's perspective, since sovereignty entails a legal order backed up by an ultimate political authority, it is a mistake to think that a political constitution can itself limit sovereignty. Rather, a constitution simply states the rules for the ways in which political authority can be exercised. Thus the United Kingdom Constitution "enables sovereign authority to be exercised in a peculiarly direct and simple way through legislation; other states have more complicated rules, but the sovereignty is the same in every case."[5] It is also a mistake, so Malcolm contends, to think that sovereign authority cannot be delegated. "The difference between delegating the exercise of sovereign authority to another state and becoming constitutionally dependent on that state is usually quite clear." Thus Britain delegates, as Malcolm points out, "a very important part of the exercise of its sovereign authority by becoming a part of NATO." But this form of delegation does not jeopardize Britain's sovereignty, because NATO lacks "the competence to determine its own competence."[6]

With these distinctions in play, Malcolm turns to Europe. In principle, he has no objection to the delegation of some areas of authority to European political bodies. He does, however, draw the line at delegation to a law-making body that makes decisions on the basis of majority vote. Here his argument is worth quoting in full:

> The Council of Ministers is a law-making body, and its laws have "direct effect" in Britain, overruling British laws. So long as the Council of

Ministers reached its decision unanimously, *we could pretend* that the whole procedure was still contained within the rules for our own exercise of our own authority. . . . With majority voting, however, it is difficult to keep up this *pretense*: whenever we are in the minority, it becomes obvious that we have delegated the exercise of legislative authority to a body which we do not control [emphasis added].[7]

Malcolm concludes that even if delegation is not itself a threat to sovereignty, when delegation extends to issues of greater importance and becomes increasingly hard to reverse, the member state becomes more readily suited to form "a subordinate part of a federal constitution."[8]

Malcolm's account of sovereignty incorporates the idea that a sovereign state is both a legal person (equipped with a cluster of rights, powers, and privileges) and a moral person, whose authority depends on belief, imagination, and "pretense." This conceptual argument does not itself, however, provide us with a justification for supporting the nation-state and rejecting a putative European state. A proponent of European political integration could, in other words, argue that given the current stage of the process of European integration, neither Europe's nation-states nor Europe's political bodies retain sovereignty.[9] The pretense necessary to sustain a belief in national sovereignty now strains, so it might be argued, credulity. On this view, it would be less pretentious—not to mention economically and militarily more advantageous—to reinvent sovereignty at the European level.

Malcolm resists this application of his argument by insisting that a sovereign legal authority requires a validating political authority, which itself requires, so he contends, "the same customs, political traditions, and, above all, the same language."[10] What his argument amounts to here, in effect, is a nationalist argument that makes an antecedent set of customs and traditions the condition of legitimate political authority. A European state would lack, so Malcolm believes, a genuine political community: "it will have a kind of political authority derived not from any sense of real participation in real political life, but only from a hazy mixture of wishful thinking and benign indifference."[11] Malcolm allows that a European state could in time generate a genuine Europeanwide political community. In this respect, his euroscepticism is contingent rather than principled. He is not, to use the terms of chapter 2 above, a conservative nationalist eurosceptic who fears that European political integration will destroy so many hundreds or thousands (pick your number) of years of distinctive history. Malcolm's argument turns instead on the belief that Europe's current nation-states retain viable political traditions currently absent at the European level.

Before reaching any final conclusions concerning the merit of this argument for national sovereignty, it is worth adding a few more conceptual distinctions. First, it is important to bear in mind the distinction between the *nature of sovereignty* and the *value of sovereignty*. And second, it is worth distinguishing between the *source of an authoritative command* and the *content of that command*.

Malcolm's account of the *nature of sovereignty* is, on its face, uncontroversial. It corresponds to what is commonly thought of as *external (or Westphalian) sovereignty*—freedom from subordination to an external political authority.[12] Malcolm does not have much to say about *internal (or Hobbesian) sovereignty*—a unitary centralized locus of political decision making. Thus the argument he presents here in support of external sovereignty is, in theory, consistent with a considerable degree of internal separation of powers and federal decentralization. Malcolm need not apologize for focusing on external sovereignty, because this is precisely the issue that upsets most eurosceptics. Stephen Thoburn—the "Metric Martyr" whom we encountered in the opening chapter—was worried about precisely this issue. He objected to the outside interference from Brussels into affairs (weights and measures) that he believed rightly belonged to the Westminster parliament.

To define sovereignty as freedom from subordination to an external political authority is to say something about the *nature of sovereignty*. It does not tell us anything about the *value of sovereignty*. What, in other words, is wrong with subordination? To answer this question, the distinction between the *source of an authoritative command* and the *content of the authoritative command* becomes useful. One reason for worrying about the source of authoritative commands is that the content of these commands is likely to prove to be disadvantageous to the commanded. This was a principal reason why, for example, the American colonists sought independence from Britain. By the same token, some eurosceptics—social democratic nationalists, for instance—oppose European political integration because they fear that the content of the legislation that is likely to emanate from a European polity will jeopardize values they hold dear. But this is not the line of argument pursued by all eurosceptics. The "Metric Martyr," for instance, seems to oppose European political integration not because of the content of the legislation likely to be produced but because of the source.

This points to another reason for worrying about the source of authoritative commands. Sometimes the source is, for one reason or another, held to be an insult to the dignity or sense of worth of the commanded. A grievance of this sort informed many of the anticolonial movements of the nineteenth and twentieth centuries. The Irish independence movement of the early twentieth century, for instance, was less exercised by the content of authoritative commands than by their source. Even when Irish adult males had the same voting rights as those in Great Britain, this did not remedy the problem. These authoritative commands, regardless of their content, were perceived as alien. Some eurosceptics likewise object to EU laws and directives because of their source, which they consider to be less legitimate than the laws that emanate from their national governments. But this is not Malcolm's argument. His argument, interpreted in its strongest form, suggests that in order for the source of an authoritative command to be effective, the source must be able to call on an underlying sense of popular legitimacy, which in turn requires (or grows out of) common customs, traditions, and language. Malcolm develops his argument in such a way that it leaves open the possibility that any source of authority would be acceptable if it could call on an underlying sense of popular legitimacy. Europe's nation-states already possess this sense of popular legitimacy; European political institutions do not. There is, therefore, no good reason *as yet* to support the project of European political integration.

One of the principal tasks of this chapter is to weigh Malcolm's ostensibly quite compelling defense of national sovereignty against arguments that might be put forward in support of a European superstate. Proponents of a European superstate—a unitary European polity, in other words—remain committed to the idea of sovereignty; they disagree, however, on the appropriate locus of sovereignty.

THE FOUR DIMENSIONS OF SOVEREIGNTY

To define sovereignty as freedom from subordination to an external political authority (as Malcolm and many other eurosceptics do) is not the best place to start with a concept as tricky and multifaceted as sovereignty. The place to begin is with the recognition that sovereignty functions on more than one level. Sovereignty serves (first level) as an ordering principle of international affairs. It does so by according a privileged status (second level) to certain territorially limited, self-governing polities. This status qualifies these polities (third level) to claim a set of rights, powers, and privileges, including, most importantly, the Westphalian right to be free of unwanted external interference into their own domestic authority structures. Sovereignty, in short, is at once an *ordering principle* of international affairs, a *status* that attaches to some territorially limited, self-governing polities, and a *set of rights, powers, and privileges*. (There is, as we shall see, a fourth dimension to sovereignty—internal sovereignty—which is not obviously entailed by these three other forms of sovereignty. For the moment, I will set this fourth dimension of sovereignty aside.)

Viewed from this perspective, sovereignty (at least the first three dimensions) might be conceived as a convention, a socially constructed norm, that makes territorially limited self-governing polities (states, in other words) the fundamental units of international affairs.[13] A state has the status of sovereignty bestowed on it by the international community of sovereign states. It is they that decide which territorially limited self-governing polities constitute sovereign states and which do not. Thus the international community has decided that Colombia is a sovereign state—even if its government does not control anywhere near the full territory of Colombia—but the Palestinian Authority is not. This feature of sovereignty can easily be missed if we focus on sovereignty as de facto control. Weber's famous definition of the state as involving "a successful claim to the monopoly of legitimate physical force in a determinate territory" is, in this respect, somewhat misleading.[14] No matter how successful the Palestinian Authority is in monopolizing physical force in, say, the Gaza Strip, the Palestinian Authority will not constitute a sovereign state unless it receives external recognition as such. Only then will it be invited to join the United Nations, to receive diplomatic immunity for its foreign officers, to send a team to the World Cup, and to apply for IMF loans. By the same token, the inability of many sovereign states to monopolize physical force in their territory—the situation in Colombia, Afghanistan, and many of the states of equatorial Africa—does not detract from their status as sovereign states. No matter how limited their internal control, these states—"quasi-states," as Robert Jackson calls them[15]—retain the status of sovereignty and are accorded the rights, powers, privileges, and immunities that go along with this status, including the most important right, the Westphalian right to be free of unwanted external interference in domestic political authority structures.

This account of sovereignty as an interrelated three-level concept (*organizing principle*, *status*, and *set of privileges*) helps clear up a common misconception concerning the delegation of so-called sovereign powers.[16] A sovereign state does not cease to become a sovereign state merely because it has delegated certain of its rights, powers, and privileges to a transnational institution. Britain will remain a sovereign state whether its monetary policy is set by the Bank of London or the European Central Bank. A state can also retain its status as sovereign even when it has delegated powers and privileges to transnational institutions whose decisions it cannot veto. States can, however, reach a point—when they have delegated so many of their most important rights, powers, and privileges to transnational institutions—that other states cease to recognize them as sovereign states. Europe's member states could, for instance, delegate so many of their powers and privileges to European-level political institutions that other world leaders would rather meet with the president of the European Commission than with any leader of a member (national) state. More generally, one can imagine a situation where all states have delegated their most important powers and privileges to transnational institutions, at which point it becomes possible to question whether sovereignty still remains an ordering principle of international affairs.

Neorealist international relations theorists tend to ignore sovereignty as an ordering principle of international affairs. They focus instead on "anarchy."[17] The term "anarchy" serves to register the fact that the international system consists of independent states that coexist under conditions where they lack any higher effective political authority and, as a consequence, must rely on their own power to survive as independent entities. The term "sovereignty" conveys, in one of its usages, something of this information. But the term also adds the further information that independent states owe their independence, at least in part, to the convention of according each other a common status that brings with it certain rights, powers, and privileges.

Power is not, however, altogether absent in the operation of sovereignty as a norm or convention. There remains, as Stephen Krasner has pointed out, a considerable amount of "hypocrisy" in the application of the convention of sovereignty.[18] While sovereignty bestows a common and equal status on all states, some states are more equal than others. Not all states, for instance, are equally capable of making effective their claim to the rights, powers, and privileges bestowed by sovereignty. Even the right to be free of unwanted external interference in domestic authority structures is sometimes violated by the most powerful states when it is in their interest to do so. (Consider, for instance, the history of the United States in its dealings with Central American and Caribbean states.) Powerful states, in other words, have the capacity to flout conventions. Powerful states also have another capacity: they get to decide, usually in conjunction with other powerful states, what cluster of rights, powers, and privileges generally attach to sovereignty as a status. Consider here, for example, the introduction by the United States of the idea of "regime change," which denies Westphalian rights to those "rogue" states that support global terrorism. It remains an open question whether the United States will succeed in legitimating, either to its own citizens or to other powerful states, "regime change" as a new international norm. But the larger fact remains that only a powerful state such as the United States is capable of modifying the relationship between sovereignty as status and sovereignty as a cluster of rights, powers, and privileges. Thus, if the United States gets its way, only "non-rogue" sovereign states—those that refrain from supporting global terrorism—will be able to claim the full complement of rights, powers, and privileges that sovereignty as a status typically bestows.

In mentioning the role of power in enabling some (more powerful) states to ensure that the norm of sovereignty works in their favor, the fourth dimension of sovereignty—internal sovereignty—becomes germane. In this sense of the term, sovereignty describes a particular type of domestic authority structure: one that is centralized, undivided, and absolute. Although there is no necessary analytical link between internal sovereignty (sometimes also called *"Hobbesian" sovereignty*) and the earlier three usages, many social and political theorists—including Hobbes himself—have argued that internal sovereignty is a precondition for the enjoyment of effective external sovereignty. In other words, if a state is to ensure that other states respect its external sovereignty, that state must possess a centralized, undivided, and absolute domestic authority structure. It cannot rely on a mere convention. The claim that internal sovereignty is a presupposition for external sovereignty is best interpreted as a sociological claim. From this perspective, a centralized domestic authority structure is necessary if states are to pursue a coherent foreign policy, make decisions rapidly, and raise the revenue to fund military operations. States that lack internal sovereignty can sometimes survive—the norm of sovereignty will prop them up—but their external sovereignty is always vulnerable.

To draw together these remarks concerning the various dimensions of sovereignty, it would be useful to relate the present discussion to the discussion in chapter 5 of the framework that incorporated a normatively defined "world order," "the international state system," and "international society." "World order," as understood here, is an arrangement of domestic and international affairs that sustains, as its primary goal, individual security. Whether sovereignty—in any of its four dimensions (organizing principle, status, set of rights, domestic authority structure)—contributes to world order is an open question. The idea of world order does not itself entail any particular organizing principle of international and domestic affairs.

The idea of "world order" introduces a normative dimension into the study of international affairs, but it is pointless to ignore the fact that the present arrangement of international affairs lacks any effective institutionalized legal and political authority. No entity in the world today can claim a legitimate global monopoly of violence; there is no global Leviathan. In the absence of any such entity, the present state of international affairs is dominated by self-governing territorially limited polities (or states), some of which are very much more powerful than others. It is with this point in mind that we can speak of "sovereignty" as an organizing principle of international affairs.

The interaction between these "sovereign states" can be conceptualized from two different analytical perspectives. One analytical perspective focuses on the distribution of power between the various states in the so-called international state system. Those who focus exclusively on this analytic perspective—Waltzian neorealists, for instance—believe that the distribution of power in the international state system determines state behavior. To the most single-minded advocates of this approach, it is enough that we know whether the international state system is "unipolar," bipolar," or "multipolar." States, if they value their own security—and if they do not, they will not exist very long—will, so neorealists contend, have to balance against dominant powers. From another analytical perspective, the idea that the interactions between states can be understood solely with reference to the distribution of power between states is untenable. Hence the need for an analytical perspective that focuses on "international society," a perspective that recognizes the role of norms, customs, and cooperative practices in international affairs. The idea of sovereignty as a convention fits into this latter analytical perspective more readily than it fits into the former analytical perspective. Indeed, it might be argued that neorealists—who emphasize the notion of the international state system as "a self-help system" that requires states to maximize their power as a condition of their own security—will find it difficult to account for the norm of sovereignty. They have no basis to explain why the more powerful states in the international system would recognize as equals those states that are clearly inferior to them in power.

Any adequate theory of international relations will need to draw on all three levels of analysis—world order, international state system, and international society. An international relations theory that lost interest in the larger normative questions of world order would be uninteresting. Yet a purely normative international relations theory that neglected the play of power in the international state system would be irrelevant. The analytical task is to find some way of reconciling the fact that power matters in the international state system with the no less important fact that the international state system is always embedded, to a greater or lesser extent, in an international society. The normative task is to identify the distributions of power and the levels of embeddedness that are most conducive to world order.

It is important to situate discussions of European sovereignty into a broader framework of international relations, because the arguments between eurosceptics, federalists, and postsovereignists clearly have important international ramifications. It is one of the many perverse features of the debate over European political integration that these international ramifications are rarely discussed. They certainly do not figure very prominently in the writings of the many legal and political theorists who advocate some form of European political integration. Thus, while the topics of European citizenship and Europe's democratic deficit have been extensively covered, legal and political theorists have rarely noticed that the choice between a Europe of nation-states, a federal Europe, and a postsovereign Europe is, at the same time, a choice that will bear on world order.

A Case for European Sovereignty

Viewed as a sovereignist project, European political integration involves the transfer of the status of sovereignty from Europe's member states to a unitary federal Europe.[19] A change of this magnitude requires a robust justification. Some proponents of European integration have focused on the *content* of the authoritative commands that would be possible in a federal Europe. Habermas's arguments in support of a federal Europe can be read in this way. Europe's member states, so he contends, are no longer able to provide their members with the goods and benefits they have come to expect. The globalization of the world economy has rendered the territorially limited self-governing nation-state obsolete. A federal Europe could provide Europeans with the goods and benefits that the nation-state can no longer secure. A federal Europe, in other words, is not supposed to generate a qualitatively different set of authoritative commands from those generated by Europe's nation-states. The difference lies solely in the ability of a federal Europe to translate these authoritative commands into genuine benefits for their members. As I concluded in chapter 3, this argument, despite its initial plausibility, falls short of providing the robust justification necessary to support the project of European integration. Globalization does not pose as great a problem for the nation-state as the Habermasian argument requires; and even if it did, the project of European integration would fail to supply the answer.

A more promising basis on which to justify the sovereignist project of European integration is premised on the contribution a federal Europe would make to individual security. Earlier chapters have defended a concept of security according to which individuals achieve security when they have adequate safeguards against probable threats. On the face of it, European political integration might seem to have no great bearing on the security of individuals in Europe. Whether Europe remains a Europe of nation-states or becomes a unitary federal state, it is likely, so it might be argued, that Europe will remain an ally of the United States and will depend on the NATO alliance for its military security.

There are, however, certain problems with this *plus ça change* perspective. It assumes, for one thing, that the present relationship between the United States and Europe is both desirable (in the sense of optimal for "world order") and sustainable. To understand some of the problems with this perspective, it is necessary to notice only two features of the current international state system: one, it is unipolar; and two, it is likely to remain so unless Europe decides to pursue an independent foreign and security policy outside NATO.

Neorealists have long argued that a unipolar system is unstable, because the dominant power in the international state system will abuse its power and will provoke a balancing coalition on the part of other states in the international state system. Thus, for Waltz, "unbalanced power, whoever wields it, is a potential danger to others."[20] From this perspective, European states, acting singly or together, must—and eventually will—balance against the United States as a condition of remaining secure and autonomous. At first glance, the suggestion that the United States might constitute a "potential danger" to Europeans seems absurd. This view seems to ignore a number of important factors that together minimize any potential danger that the United States might pose to Europe. First, the United States is generally committed to maintaining a stable international order defined by laws, institutions, and multilateral cooperative arrangements. Second, Europe and the United States share an overlapping set of values including democracy, the rule of law, and a commitment to some form of market capitalism. Third, the United States and Europe possess highly interdependent economies. And fourth, the United States remains an "offshore power"; it lacks, in other words, a contiguous border and as such poses less of a threat to Europe than either European states pose to each other or Russia poses to Europe.

Notwithstanding these mitigating factors, Waltz's contention that unipolarity poses a "potential danger" deserves further consideration. Up to a point, this danger can be conceptualized in abstraction from the many policy disagreements that have recently arisen between the United States and Europe. Indeed, it is possible to present an idealized account of a range of hypothetical scenarios for a conflict involving (1) a dominant (or unipolar) power; (2) leading powers; and (3) weak (or subordinate) powers.

In *scenario one*, the dominant power uses its relative military superiority to coerce leading and weak powers. In the present international order, this scenario is extremely improbable. Although the dominant power does sometimes militarily coerce weak powers (Iraq, Panama, Haiti), this typically happens only when a weak power has fallen outside the boundaries of acceptable behavior as defined by international society. The dominant power lacks either the desire or the capability to coerce leading powers such as Russia, China, Japan, or any of the European states.

In *scenario two*, the dominant power uses its military and economic power to structure international society in ways that are conducive to its own interests and values. Realists, who tend to minimize the role of international society in constraining the self-interested behavior of powerful states, believe that a dominant power will always act in this way. Multilateralism is, from the realist perspective, a myth. Whatever one thinks of the realist view of international order, this scenario is certainly a more likely prospect than scenario one. It is worth noting here, however, that the dominant power's actions will prove more costly to leading and weak powers the greater the variance between its interests and values and their interests and values.[21]

In *scenario three*, the dominant power might provoke, intentionally or unintentionally, a third party—whether a leading power, a subordinate power, or a terrorist organization—to attack all allies of the dominant power. Thus, in a world structured in accordance with the values and interests of the dominant power, there will always be some disgruntled states and groups, which might strike against dominant and leading powers without discrimination. In this way, a dominant power poses a mediated threat to leading powers. In thinking about this mediated threat, it would be helpful to further distinguish between mediated threats that arise from the "underreaction" of the dominant power and those that arise from the "overreaction" of the dominant power. An underreaction takes places when the dominant power either refuses to respond—or blocks all responses—to a threat to the international order that is disproportionately costly to leading and weak powers. An overreaction takes place when the dominant power responds to a threat to the international order that is disproportionately costly to itself.

The scenarios described here are logical possibilities, which do not depend on any thick descriptions of the characteristics or particular circumstances of the dominant power, the leading powers, or the subordinate powers. To describe these scenarios as *only* logical possibilities is to depart from the structural determinism of Waltz's neorealism. There is no necessary reason, nothing inevitable, in a conflict between a dominant power and other powers. Nonetheless, once it is conceded that the distribution of power in the international state system has a bearing on world order—that some distributions of power are more "order enhancing" than others—there exists a rational basis, as I now wish to show, for a security-based justification for European sovereignty. This case can be constructed in two steps.

Step One: The Costs of Unipolarity

Some of the disadvantages to leading and subordinate powers of an international state system that contains a dominant power can be captured with reference to some of the points made earlier concerning the role of sovereignty as a convention. While sovereignty bestows a common and equal status on the constituent members of the international state system, the *effective* rather than the *nominal* rights, powers, and privileges of sovereignty remain vulnerable to the play of power politics. A single, overwhelmingly dominant power in the international state system has the capability to determine how sovereignty as a convention will operate in international affairs. We can see this happening, at least to a certain extent, in the statements of the Bush administration, which has declared both its own immunity from international norms that constrain sovereignty and its own right to abrogate the "external sovereignty" of those countries that it deems threatening. The Bush administration's recently announced policy of "unilaterally determined preemptive self-defense" is a policy that reflects this worldview.[22] More to the point, it is a policy option that is available only to a polity like the United States, which enjoys an overwhelming preponderance of power in the international state system.

In many cases, the actions taken by the United States in its capacity as the international state system's dominant power will be "order enhancing" and thus conducive to individual security. Actions undertaken to stop erratic groups of terrorists getting hold of weapons of mass destruction are clearly in the interests of all Europeans who care about security. But there will be circumstances—as the logically possible scenarios described above make clear—when the efforts of the dominant power to increase its own military security threaten the security of individuals outside its borders. Insofar as this situation applies today for Europeans, they have a security-based interest in modifying US behavior. This point is relatively uncontroversial. The more controversial point concerns the role of power in determining and modifying US behavior. If either US international behavior is a function of its own power or the European capacity to modify that behavior requires a comparable amount of power, then Europeans have a prima facie reason to balance against the United States.

There is another security-based strand to arguments that seek to show that the present form of American unipolarity is less than optimal for the security of individual Europeans. Insofar as security requires, as I have argued, both basic physical safety and nondependence on the arbitrary will of others (whether individuals or organizations), then the dependence of Europe on the United States for its military protection is a form of insecurity. Insofar as the security of individual Europeans is, in short, in the hands of a foreign power over which they have no control, they are less secure than they need be. Whether this cost to security is outweighed by the efficacy of the safeguards afforded by the dominant power is an open question. But it is crucial to acknowledge the cost involved here. In the past, to the extent that Europe belonged to a military alliance of equals (the official description of NATO), the security costs of this alliance could be ignored. But in an age of unipolarity—an age when the United States not only *is* the world's sole superpower but *acts* as such—the myth of NATO as an alliance of equals is no longer credible. While eurosceptics are sensitive to the deficits to democratic self-government involved in membership in the EU, these deficits are no less pronounced in the case of membership in NATO.

Step Two: From European Superpower to European Superstate

The idea that Europe ought to become a superpower has long been a dream of many proponents of European integration. Romano Prodi, for instance, stated that one of the aims of European integration is to "create a superpower on the European continent that stands equal to the United States."[23] Even Tony Blair, considerably more eurosceptic than Prodi, has said that he would like to see Europe become a superpower without becoming a superstate. If the arguments of step one are valid, then there is a good security-based justification for Europe to develop foreign and military capabilities that would make it less dependent on the United States. It is far from clear, however, that Europe could become a superpower without also becoming a superstate. A denial of Blair's wish for "a superpower but not a superstate"[24] forms the second step in the case for European sovereignty.

This step in the case for European sovereignty draws on the fourth dimension of sovereignty, *internal sovereignty*—which refers to a domestic authority structure that is centralized, undivided, and absolute. There is, as noted above, no necessary link between internal and external sovereignty. But there is a range of historical and sociological evidence to suggest that states that lack internal sovereignty have a difficult time, despite the assistance provided by the status of sovereignty, maintaining their freedom from external subordination. There is also plenty of evidence to suggest that states that lack internal sovereignty are at a relative disadvantage when they find themselves in conflict with states that possess more centralized, undivided, and absolute domestic authority structures. To provide just two illustrations of this point: Consider, first, the early difficulties that confronted the Confederate States of America when the Confederacy sought to protect its external sovereignty from attacks by the British, the French, and Indian tribes. It was not just that the American Confederacy found it difficult to raise the necessary funds to support an army and a navy. Lacking a centralized locus of decision making, the member states found it difficult to prevent foreign powers from playing one state off against another.[25] Decades earlier, James Madison had recognized this problem. His pamphlet *Vices of the Political System of the United States* relies very heavily on the foreign policy implications of the United States' domestic authority structure to make his case against the Articles of Confederation and in favor of a new Constitution.[26]

The difficulties that confronted the early American republic can be generalized into a second, larger illustration of the value of internal sovereignty. The rise of the sovereign state with a centralized, undivided, and absolute domestic authority structure was, in large measure, a function of the relative success of this type of polity over polities with more loosely organized authority structures.[27] Internal sovereignty, as Hendryk Spruyt has argued, was a consequence of something akin to a Darwinian process of selection.[28] Those polities that lacked the capacity to raise the necessary funds to equip armies and to make decisions quickly simply disappeared. In early modern Europe, a superstate was thus an essential precondition for becoming a superpower.

At first glance, it might seem that the domestic authority structure of the United States, in its present form, contradicts the claim that internal sovereignty is necessary to project power abroad. The Founding Fathers of the American Constitution chose a system of government that dispersed decision-making authority. They selected a federal form of government that left the states in control of most policy issues, and they divided government between three different branches. In contrast to the British, the Americans lacked any notion of sovereignty residing in a single person or office (whether Parliament or the King-in-parliament). Yet despite these institutional designs, the American system of government has evolved in such a way as to make internal sovereignty the de facto if not the de jure authority structure. Particularly in the formulation of foreign and military policy, the American system of government centralizes decision-making authority in the president (the commander in chief) and his closest advisers. The United States thus confirms, rather than offers a counterexample to, the claim that a superpower requires a superstate, which is to say a state with a centralized, undivided decision-making structure.

These examples provide some initial plausibility to the claim that if Europe is to become a superpower—a polity with the power to balance, if necessary, against the United States—then it will have to reorganize its domestic political institutions in such a way that they are capable of making decisions quickly and mobilizing support for policies that project power abroad. Europe, in short, will have to become much more like the United States in its domestic authority structure. This does not mean that Europe need become as centralized as France. Nor does it mean that it will have to abolish all traces of Europe's separate peoples. But it is difficult to understand how Europe could even begin to match the power of the United States without becoming a unitary federal polity.

These two steps in the argument for European sovereignty are, in the present climate, deeply controversial. Certainly, there is very little support in Europe today for a unitary federal Europe. My presentation of these two steps in an argument for European sovereignty is meant to be illustrative rather than decisive.[29] In its present form, the argument is merely meant to show that, working with a relatively uncontroversial conception of security and a set of plausible assumptions concerning the behavior of states in the international state system, it is not difficult to make an argument that Europe ought to become a superpower (step one). Many proponents of European political integration claim to support this goal. Most still believe, however, that even if it is desirable for Europe to become a superpower, it is unnecessary for Europe to acquire internal sovereignty (step two). Step two is certainly more controversial than step one. But even step one will be resisted, both by eurosceptics (who want to return to a Europe of relatively independent nation-states) and by defenders of the EU in its present form (who see no need for Europe to develop more robust and independent defense capabilities). Satisfaction with the current status quo forms, as we shall see, the basis for a strong case against European sovereignty

A Case against European Sovereignty

An obvious objection to the security-based justification for European political integration developed in the previous section is that it seems to require the unraveling of the military alliances that have kept the peace in Europe for more than half a century. If individual security is of paramount importance, then it seems, on the face of it, not only unnecessary for Europe to develop a more robust and independent defense policy but positively dangerous even to contemplate such a course of action. For some observers, the EU in its present form represents the optimal arrangement for Europeans. Despite the fact that the EU in its present form is militarily weak—and likely to remain so in the future—Europeans have no grounds for worrying about their security. There are a number of different versions of this argument. This section considers some of the most cogent statements of this position.

One source of confidence in the status quo is NATO. This military alliance, which was originally designed as a response to the threat posed by the Soviet Union, has defied expectations that it would disappear and has added new members and new responsibilities. True, NATO is something of a lopsided alliance in that the United States contributes the vast bulk of the weapons, the leadership, and the personnel. But NATO nevertheless provides the basis, so its supporters claim, for continuing multilateral cooperation between European countries and the United States. Moreover, European countries have announced that they will in future acquire more capabilities, so that they can do more of the "heavy lifting" in NATO operations. In recognition of the fact that Europe might need military options outside the NATO framework, Britain and France have taken the lead in planning for a European Rapid Reaction Force.[30] Although this new force has not progressed as far as some have hoped, it shows that European countries working within (and occasionally outside) NATO can meet all the legitimate security needs of Europeans.

A further source of confidence in the prevailing status quo is provided by Europe's unique so-called civilian power, which enables it to exert a powerful influence in international affairs. While this concept, which we introduced in the previous chapter, means a number of different things to different people, it generally refers to the idea that Europe can dispense with a preponderance of military power and rely instead on a combination of the following: one, its economic power; two, its diplomatic skills; three, its promise to neighboring countries of future membership; and four, its willingness to pool its sovereignty in transnational institutions. Although the idea of "civilian power Europe" was subjected to a withering criticism by Hedley Bull in the early 1980s, the idea has recently caught on with a number of advocates of the current EU status quo. In one of the most vigorous statements of this position, Moravcsik has argued that "Europeans already wield effective power over peace and war as great as that of the United States, but they do so quietly through 'civilian power.'"[31] Moravcsik thinks that the Europeans can and do match American military power with their own "uniquely European instruments," which include trade, foreign aid, and peacekeeping forces.[32]

The message of Moravcsik's argument is that the Europeans can play an indispensable role even when they cannot match American military power. Europeans and Americans, in other words, enjoy a common set of goals; they merely divide responsibilities for the attainment of these goals. The premise of this argument is that European and American interests can be enhanced by a broader multilateral agenda. Joseph Nye shares a similar view. He worries, however, that the current Bush administration no longer realizes that multilateralism remains in its own self-interest. Nye seeks to warn American policy makers against the temptation of unilateralism. For Nye, unilateralism will not work. The United States must cultivate the goodwill of its European allies, even if this means embracing some of their own fondness for transnational laws and institutions.[33]

Robert Keohane has advanced a slightly more nervous version of this multilateralist argument. Like Moravcsik and Nye, Keohane believes that it is crucial for Europe and the United States to remain close allies and to support, when necessary, transnational laws and institutions. Yet Keohane recognizes the difficulty of future cooperation between a United States that jealously guards its sovereignty and a Europe that has "adopted a pooled conception of sovereignty." For Keohane, the United States and Europe thus constitute fundamentally different types of polity. As he describes the status quo in Europe today,

> States that are members of the EU have broken sharply with the classical tradition of state sovereignty. Sovereignty is pooled, in the sense that, in many areas, states' legal authority over internal and external affairs is transferred to the Community as a whole, authorizing action through procedures not involving state vetoes.[34]

Keohane further maintains that Europe's success in pooling its sovereignty is potentially very significant, for it shows to other "troubled regimes" that internal and external sovereignty are not necessary to be a successful polity. Keohane acknowledges, however, that the United States has not followed Europe down the road toward a postsovereign polity. The United States remains very much a classic sovereign state. He further recognizes the problems that this divergence might cause. The United States' domestic authority structure enables it to act decisively, and it often does; Europe's domestic authority structure prevents it from acting decisively, and therefore it favors diplomatic compromise.

Americans then become irritated with "Euroweenies," while Europeans condemn Americans as "reckless cowboys."[35] Or as Keohane puts it,

> Different conceptions of sovereignty could make it even more difficult for Europeans and Americans to understand one another. Differences in geopolitical roles and interests, societal values, and the role of state security institutions, all pull the United States and Europe apart. The language of sovereignty has long been the language of diplomacy; but in this sense, the United States and Europe now speak different languages.[36]

Despite these differences, Keohane nonetheless thinks that Europe and the United States share a sufficient amount in common that they can cooperate in the establishment of a mutually beneficial global order.

Like all positions in the debate on European integration, the case for preserving the status quo—and thus dispensing with any steps toward European sovereignty—has certain weaknesses. Many of the arguments concerning the benefits of the present military alliance between the United States and Europe assume that these two regions share common values and interests. Yet in a whole range of different areas, the United States and Europe seem to have quite divergent—and even conflicting—values and interests.[37] Some observers believe that the United States and Europe will proceed along different paths in the future, each representing a different variety of modernity. Certainly, there is some evidence to suggest that Europeans and Americans share different understandings of the relationship between state and market, public and private, sacred and profane.[38] Americans are, for instance, much more religious that Europeans. This piety leads the current US government to limit stem cell research and to favor abstinence programs as a means of combating global overpopulation. Americans, to cite another example, are much more hostile to the state than are Europeans; they have lower personal taxation but much higher incarceration rates; they execute criminals; and they appear to be willing to condone torture as a means of combating terrorists. No less important, the United States and Europe—especially continental Europe—have very different norms of corporate governance. Finally, Americans possess a very different strategic culture than Europeans; the military is less prestigious in Europe and military action more controversial. Although the idea of a distinctively European form of solidarity cannot provide the basis for a justification of European political integration—for the reasons identified in chapter 4 above—the differences between Europe and the United States are now sufficiently pronounced that they generate a range of conflicts concerning the laws and norms governing international society. In such circumstances, the notion that the Europeans can afford to let the United States take the lead in international affairs becomes increasingly less plausible.

A second problem with these defenses of the status quo is that they tend to assume that the United States is interested in acting multilaterally and for the good of all, rather than in acting unilaterally and for the good of itself. Thus, to Nye, the Bush administration's willingness to act unilaterally is an aberration, a betrayal of its own best traditions and interests. But there is an alternative explanation of US unilateralism: overwhelming US power. The United States, in other words, acts unilaterally because it can. There is no obvious reason why, in the absence of any European action to punish such behavior, the United States will cease acting unilaterally. Thus, when it is in the interests of the United States to act under the auspices of NATO or the United Nations, it will. But, as Secretary of Defense Rumsfeld put it, "the mission defines the coalition," which is to say that the United States will not feel constrained to act multilaterally when it can achieve its ends unilaterally.[39]

A third—and much the most important—problem with the claim that the present status quo represents an ideal situation for Europeans is that the present situation constitutes a form of asymmetrical dependence. The United States currently possesses a veto on independent European military action. While this situation might contribute to peace narrowly defined, the concept of security entails a more demanding evaluative standard. Insofar as Europeans are committed to a liberal conception of security, they seek adequate safeguards against potential threats. The notion of an adequate safeguard contains two components: one relates to the efficacy of the protective measures undertaken; the other relates to basic societal values. For a liberal, self-government is a basic societal value. Safeguards against potential harm that require any substantial infringement on self-government must be viewed as undesirable. Now a supporter of the status quo might argue here that the gains to European security are such that they outweigh any cost to the value of self-government. A supporter of the status quo might also argue that NATO remains an alliance of equals with a proper level of consultation and participation by all members. The first of these two counterarguments may well be true, especially insofar as Europe has no alternative to relying on the American alliance. But this does not diminish the force of the more general claim that a liberal conception of security calls for "order-enhancing policies" that bolster basic liberal values like self-government. The second of these two counterarguments, however, is certainly false. NATO is obviously an organization that relies so much on American weapons and willpower that Europe's political classes have grown accustomed to playing a subordinate role in foreign affairs. True, they might complain about the United States' actions and inactions. But they do not want, nor are they capable of playing, a more prominent or independent role. The inability of Europeans to act decisively during the destruction of Bosnia is one of many examples that might be cited in support of the observation that without the United States, Europe cannot act decisively in foreign affairs.[40] The fact that Europeans later supplied the peacekeeping forces hardly makes up for their ineffective dithering while thousands were being killed.

Euroscepticism Reconsidered

Many eurosceptics rally behind the idea of sovereignty. Now that we possess a clearer view of the multidimensional nature of sovereignty and the costs and benefits of locating it at the national or European level, it is possible to reach some conclusions concerning the cogency of the eurosceptics' position on sovereignty. The first point to recognize is that sovereignty-based euroscepticism is not necessarily based on a nationalist political ideology. For nationalist eurosceptics, national sovereignty is valuable either because the nation possesses a venerable identity or character that would be lost in a politically integrated Europe, or because the nation defines a solidaristic community. Sovereignty-based euroscepticism, in contrast, focuses on the content and/or source of authoritative commands. Eurosceptics want to preserve national sovereignty because they fear that the authoritative commands that emanate from a European sovereign will be deficient, in one form or another, relative to the authoritative commands that emanate from national capitals.

For those eurosceptics who worry about the content of the authoritative commands that would emerge from a unitary federal Europe, the concern is that the policies that would emerge from European political institutions would be less favorable than those that emerge from national political institutions. In other words, eurosceptics fear that the median voter in Europe lies to the left or to the right of the median voter in their national electoral system. Thus left-wing British eurosceptics in the 1960s and 1970s would argue that the EEC (as it then was) was a "businessman's charter" that would block the regulatory measures favored by British socialists of the day. Similarly, right-wing British eurosceptics in the 1980s and 1990s would argue that the EU would favor regulatory measures to protect workers and the environment.

The content-based critique of European political integration has a certain prima facie plausibility. The critique draws support from the perception that democracy, as a form of government, ought to be responsive to the preferences of the governed. If a local majority finds that their preferences would be nullified in a larger jurisdiction, then it is natural that they would oppose political integration. It must be conceded, however, that this content-based critique of European political integration is not a principled critique. It does not rest on any conception of political value other than partisan preference. The content-based critique of European political integration is, in this respect, no better than a content-based justification for European political integration. In either case, the justification amounts to little more than the claim: "I am for/against European political integration, because it will enhance/diminish the likelihood of my policy preferences being adopted." This type of argument falls foul, so I have argued, of the requirement of publicity, which holds justifying arguments up to a standard of what I have called democratic justification.

The more interesting challenge posed by eurosceptics concerns the source of authoritative commands. We encountered a sophisticated version of this argument earlier in the chapter. Noel Malcolm's defense of national sovereignty derives from a claim concerning the effectiveness of sovereign commands. To be effective, commands must draw on a form of authority that, as Malcolm puts it, "is recognized, or granted, or willed, or believed in by the people who are subject to it."[41] National sovereignty possesses the requisite form of authority; European sovereignty would lack it. Case closed.

Advocates of European sovereignty need not, however, accept the suggestion that there is anything mysterious in the process of granting or recognizing an authoritative source of commands. This process lies at the very basis of the modern state. It is certainly possible to think of this process as the outcome of a rational choice. Hobbes's *Leviathan* conceptualizes political authority in precisely this way. A Sovereign, in Hobbes's account, becomes the representative of the people and exercises authority on their behalf. As Hobbes puts it,

A Multitude of men, are made One Person, when they are by one man, or one Person, Represented; so that it be done with the consent of every one of the Multitude in particular. . . . Every man giving their common Representer, Authority from himselfe in particular; and owning all the actions the Representer doth.[42]

The decision to transfer authority to a Sovereign is, for Hobbes, wholly rational. It is done to for reasons of individual security. A centralized, absolute, and unitary form of sovereignty constitutes, so Hobbes argues, a necessary condition—an effective safeguard, in other words—against potentials harms.

Hobbes's account of sovereignty as an effective safeguard focuses almost exclusively on domestic threats to security. He has very little to say concerning international threats. The thought here, presumably, is either that the domestic threats were more serious or that an effective safeguard against such threats was also an effective safeguard against international threats. Rousseau pointed out the problem with such a position:

as man with man, we live in the civil state and subject to laws; as people with people, each one enjoys natural liberty: and our situation is far worse than if these distinctions were unknown. For living at the same time in the social order and in the state of nature, we are subject to the inconveniences of both, without finding the security of either.[43]

The weakness of the eurosceptics' position on the source (or locus) of sovereignty is roughly comparable to the weakness Rousseau perceived in Hobbes's position. The eurosceptic thinks that the efficacy of the state's political authority can be gauged independently of the place of the state in the international state system. It is sufficient, for the eurosceptic, that the state's political authority is recognized and accepted. But this is to ignore, not just the "inconveniences" that might arise from the international context, but the threats to individual security that might arise from the same context.

The eurosceptic might still insist that these threats do not warrant any departure from a Europe of nation-states, that each nation-state has the wherewithal to protect itself and its members from international threats, and that NATO still provides the best solution to the problem of world order. The strongest case for European sovereignty rests, from the eurosceptics' perspective, on an exaggerated assessment of international threats, unwarranted skepticism of the United States, and an overly expansive conception of individual security. It is not my aim in this book to resolve this disagreement. It suffices to note that an argument cast in terms of security and international relations represents the type of argument that Europeans—whether for or against European political integration—ought to be conducting about their future political arrangements.

Enough has been said, however, to expose some of the deficiencies of those forms of euroscepticism that focus exclusively on the domestic basis of political authority. The fact that the nation-state successfully "represents" the polity's members, who accept its commands as authoritative, cannot be the last word on the question of European political integration. The nation-state exists in a broader international context—a context defined by an international state system and an international society—which is a source of potential harm. If we take seriously a conception of individual security that recognizes the dangers of dependence on arbitrary forms of power, then it simply will not suffice to focus on a narrow conception of security as the mere absence of war. For most eurosceptics, a politically integrated Europe poses much more of a threat to Europe's own security than the NATO military alliance poses. It is nonetheless odd that this sensitivity to national political autonomy tends to disappear when the eurosceptic considers his nation's place in the broader international context. Any single European nation-state—independent of either the EU in its present form or a more politically integrated Europe—will likely face a far more constrained set of options than as a member of the EU.

To pose the question in terms of the options confronting nation-states is, however, to concede too much to the eurosceptic. Ultimately, individuals are the only morally significant entities. Security and self-government must be predicated of individuals rather than nations. The case for European political integration need only claim that individuals would be more secure in a world where Europe was at least as powerful as any other state. Whatever limitations Europeans face in controlling Europe's political institutions, these limitations are negligible when compared with their ability to control powerful foreign allies.

Conclusion

Imagine that, on September 11 next year, terrorists based somewhere in the Maghreb fly hijacked passenger jets into the Westminster parliament, the Reichstag, the Vatican, and the Louvre. These attacks kill thousands. Let it further be imagined that the United States is either preoccupied with China or, in the wake of the recent disasters in Iraq, has lost all appetite for foreign military intervention. After years of complaining about US unilateralism, Europeans now fulminate against US isolationism.

It is worth bearing this scenario in mind, because given existing military capabilities, Europe's nation-states, acting either singly or jointly, would be unable to conduct anything resembling the operation that the United States conducted to destroy Al Qaeda camps in Afghanistan in October and November of 2001. If terrorists based in camps in the Maghreb—perhaps protected by a friendly host government—promised to repeat their attacks, there would be little that European powers could—other than fulminate against US isolationism—do about it.

It is partly in recognition of Europe's current military weakness and its one-sided dependence on the United States that a number of European political leaders have said that Europe needs to become a "superpower." Most of these political leaders want to see Europe become a "superpower" without becoming a "superstate." Some intellectual proponents of a postsovereign Europe believe that Europe could become a "superpower"—albeit a "superpower" of a new and different type—while operating under a radically decentered form of "mixed government."

The arguments of the last few chapters have tried to show that when situated in a context of violence, conflict, and wide disparities of power between states, many of the prevailing assumptions about European political integration look rather naïve. The widespread belief that the sovereign state is now obsolete seems increasingly difficult to accept, not least because the most powerful political units in the world today—the United States, China, and Russia among them—all jealously guard their sovereignty. Indeed, the United States—the world's only genuine global power—is, in many respects, a classic nation-state, which possesses a centralized locus of decision making (at least in the key areas of foreign and military policy) and a national culture constituted by a powerful unifying creed.[1] If the United States were able to take military action abroad only with the approval of all fifty state governors, then it would become a much weaker state more easily dominated by unscrupulous rivals. Yet it is precisely this type of weak postsovereign state that some proponents of European political integration eagerly seek. One of the central aims of this book has been to raise some doubts about this proposed destination for the European project.

These issues of security and sovereignty might seem very distant from the place where this book started: a fruit stall in the north of England. There we encountered Mr. Steven Thoburn, the "Metric Martyr," who wanted to know why he could no longer sell his bananas in imperial measures. Thoburn's skepticism of the European Union is not exceptional. Recent European elections show that apathy and outright hostility are becoming growing problems. Too few people in Europe seem to have a clearly formed view of the point or purpose of European integration. Efforts to make European political institutions more transparent and to establish a European constitutional treaty seem only to have exacerbated these problems.

For many critics and supporters of the EU, Europe's principal problem is its "democratic deficit." The EU's political institutions, so it is argued, are too bureaucratic, too complex, and insufficiently sensitive to the democratic will of a majority. In a slightly more sophisticated version of this argument, Europe's problem is not so much the democratic quality of its institutions—which are hardly any worse than most national democratic institutions—but the fact that Europe lacks a "demos." From this perspective, Europe can never gain legitimacy and popularity without Europeans self-identifying themselves as such. As long as people think of themselves as national first and Europeans second or not at all, the EU will remain illegitimate and unloved.

In contrast to most political philosophers who address European integration, I have had very little to say in this book about this "democratic deficit." My reason for ignoring this topic is that I have been less interested in the institutions and policies of the EU (the current *product* of European integration) than in the *project* of European integration, the telos of the process of European integration. This project preoccupies both eurosceptics and europhiles. It is important to assess the merits of arguments that wholeheartedly endorse and wholeheartedly reject this project. The quality of the EU's current democratic institutions is not, I suspect, the principal basis of most peoples' assessments of this project. Much more important are issues such as nationalism, welfare, and security. The case for or against the European project must be constructed out of such issues.

The effort to think about the arguments that might be advanced in favor or against European political integration immediately raises a more philosophical question concerning the criteria of adequacy for such arguments. European political integration is transformative: it entails a fundamental transformation in Europe's "polity" and "regime." Such a transformation requires, so I have argued, arguments that can satisfy the democratic requirements of publicity, accessibility, and sufficiency. Many of the most widely employed arguments put forward in favor of European integration fail one or more of these requirements. Many of the economic arguments for European political integration— arguments that I have not spent a lot of time on—fail the requirement of accessibility. The average European citizen simply cannot be expected to understand and evaluate, for instance, the optimal conditions for a currency union. It makes little sense to base European integration on matters of such complexity.

More influential than economic arguments are welfare-based arguments for European political integration. For many europhiles, Europe possesses a deep-seated and distinctive commitment to a *Sozialstaat*, which is now no longer viable at the national level. From this perspective, European political integration thus redeems the possibilities of a solidaristic welfare state that are now lost in the nation-state. This book has criticized this argument on a number of grounds. First, this argument rests on a partisan view of the role of the state in the provision of what I have called "the necessaries and conveniences of life." The aim of the publicity requirement is to filter out conceptions of the good that not all Europeans have a good reason to share. The precise role of the state in the provision of life's "necessaries and conveniences" is an issue best left up to democratic majorities. It cannot form the grounds for the very existence of a European polity.

A second reason for questioning this welfare-based argument for European political integration is that it appears to rest on a set of bogus claims about the impact of globalization on national welfare states. There is no reason to believe the arguments of those social democrats who believe that a politically integrated Europe is necessary to protect against the shift of manufacturing industries to lower-cost developing countries. These arguments fail, in other words, the requirement of sufficiency. They rest on empirical claims and causal mechanisms that are wrong and weak.

A more plausible basis for European political integration, so I have argued, is a security-based argument. Security is one of the central tasks that any polity must perform, not least because all citizens have a good reason to place the very greatest importance on their security. This book has conceptualized security in terms of the adequacy of safeguards against likely threats. Individuals in Europe today face a variety of threats. In order to deal with these threats, it is important to recognize their multiple and different sources, including other individuals, private groups, one's own state, and foreign states. To be fully secure, one needs not only an effective state but also an order-enhancing international society. The debate about European political integration must be situated in this broader context. Whether Europe forms a unitary polity or not bears on the capacity of international society to sustain a desirable form of order. An international society with two roughly equal "Western" powers would, so I have argued, be far more secure than the current situation, in which the United States is the sole global power and acts as such.

The security-based argument in support of European political integration does not rely solely on the claim that a Europe acting as a co-equal to the United States enhances the basic physical safety of Europeans—by, for instance making them less likely to be dragged into unnecessary wars, or by enabling them to decide themselves whom to treat as friends and enemies. The security-based argument rests on two additional claims. First, security is, as many civic republicans have pointed out, jeopardized not merely by threats to physical safety but also by dependence on the arbitrary power of other individuals or organizations. A Europe dependent on others for its military protection, unable to take autonomous action, unable to define its own friends and enemies, is, in this broader sense of the term, insecure. Second, a Europe that is capable of assuming the role of a great power and of adopting an autonomous foreign and military policy cannot afford to adopt the radically decentered polity advocated by postsovereignists. It is no accident that the nation-state emerged as the dominant type of political unit in the modern era. It is no accident that the world's sole global power, the United States, is a nation-state. If Europe is to play any comparable role, then it must adopt a comparable type of polity. Europe must, in short, become a "superstate." Those who refuse to accept this conclusion are either deluding themselves or they are prepared to see Europe remain a weak and dependent power.

The suggestion that Europe ought to become a "superstate" will provoke the immediate objection that such an option is nothing but a pipe dream. Hardly anyone—apart from a few federalist dreamers—seeks such a radical telos for the European project. Furthermore, a federalist European superstate is further from being a viable option today than at any time in Europe's postwar history. As the recent wrangles over a European constitution have revealed, neither Europe's political classes nor its voters favor anything resembling a federal Europe. Observers who suggest that Europe's intergovernmentalists have vanquished the federalists are largely right. Even more troubling for the dwindling ranks of federalists, an increasing number of European voters have become eurosceptics. In Britain, the UK Independence Party—a political party that seeks immediate withdrawal from the EU—earned 20 percent of the vote in the 2004 European elections. Parties seeking a similar goal have emerged in a number of other European countries.

These observations about the current unpopularity of the European project—while doubtless of enormous psephological significance—have very little bearing on the argument put forward here. This is not a work of futurology: it does not seek to predict the political arrangements that will eventually emerge in Europe. The book merely seeks to identify the normative arguments that might satisfy a democratic standard of justification. Contrary to what most people believe, a security-based justification for European political integration can satisfy requirements of publicity, accessibility, and—given the prevailing nature of the threats that Europeans must confront—sufficiency. Does this mean that Europeans, fearful for their security, will quickly rally behind the banner of a federal Europe? Clearly not. A lot of people in Europe care more about preserving their national sovereignty than they do about their security. An inward-looking, past-oriented nationalism remains, sadly, the animating ideology of many people in Europe today. Before saying more about such people, it would, however, be useful to review the steps that Europe might conceivably take toward greater European political integration. What process of European political integration would be most likely to bring about a unitary European polity?

For much of Europe's postwar history, the process of European political integration has relied on a neofunctionalist strategy of incremental integration. This so-called Monnet method was designed to avoid any direct democratic involvement. Jean Monnet's Europe was, in short, an elite-led project. It would be wrong, however, to think that the history of European political integration from 1950 to 2004 was solely the work of European bureaucrats exploiting the minutiae of rules, regulations, and court decisions. The key steps toward European integration—formulated in the principal treaties of 1950, 1986, 1993, and 2004—were the work of the political leaders of Europe's member states. Invariably, these political leaders were motivated largely by the economic interests of their own states. It is possible, but highly unlikely, that Europe will, through this method, take one further decisive step toward political integration. The difficulty for proponents of this method is that Europe is no longer viable as an elite-led project. Following the Maastricht Treaty, Europe's citizens have demanded, quite rightly, to be consulted and to have the final say in any further steps that Europe might take toward political integration. While the European Union (or European Economic Community, as it was then called) focused primarily on economic matters, citizens believed that they could safely ignore much of what went on in Brussels. But now that European political laws and institutions bear on employment policy, welfare policy, and—given the scope of the European Charter of Fundamental Rights—almost every other aspect of human existence, it is reckless to ignore what goes on in Brussels. European political integration can not go anywhere now without the support of its citizens.

The European Convention of 2002–3 and the subsequent Constitutional Treaty of 2004 represent an attempt to bring European citizens, through their national elected representatives, more directly into the process of European political integration. While it remains too early to say how this Constitutional Treaty will ultimately fare, the events of 2002 through 2004 can hardly be described as a ringing success. The attempt to make the EU more transparent and to bring it closer to its citizens has done little more than open up deep divisions within Europe—divisions between large and small states, pro-US and anti-US states, and states more and less enamored of market-restricting regulations. The Constitutional Treaty itself, which must be ratified by all twenty-five member states in order to take effect, merely papered over these divisions by including at least some constitutional provisions for everyone. Unfortunately, this approach is likely to make the ratification process more difficult—especially in those countries where a referendum is planned—because each side (whether pro– or anti–European integration) can point to constitutional language that it finds unacceptable. Given the problems with the convention and the Constitutional Treaty, it seems unlikely that Europe's next steps toward political integration will proceed in precisely this way.

Perhaps a more probable, if more troubling, possibility for Europe's future political integration is that it will be crisis driven. Thus, rather

than being planned (whether incrementally or through intergovernmental councils), the process of European political integration will involve a challenge-response model. Europe's member states will, in other
words, confront challenges to which they cannot respond effectively unless they adopt a very different type of political structure. This happened in the aftermath of the Second World War, when a number of European states, most notably France and Germany, realized that they
could not function as effective nation-states unless they pooled some of
their governing functions. Given the very grave threats to security that
Europe now faces, it is not too far-fetched to think that the only available response will be to forge a very much closer federal union.

It is in the context of this challenge-response model that it becomes all
the more important for European citizens to think through the fundamental questions of European political integration. Here it is crucial to
focus attention less on the EU in its present form than on the more general question of why (if at all) people in Europe today even need a European level of government. The efforts of some europhiles to close this
question down, to treat European political integration as if it were a
done deal, do not help matters here. There are, as this book has shown,
some compelling arguments in support of a politically integrated Europe. Unfortunately, these arguments will be unlikely to get a fair hear-
ing while so many Europeans remain transfixed on the EU's institutional and policy deficiencies.

In an effort to remedy some of these deficiencies, the EU would benefit by doing more in some policy areas and much less in others. The EU
in its present form does not distribute in a sensible way the appropriate
competences at the appropriate levels. This is an area that clearly needs
greater intellectual investigation. Europe needs a political philosophy
that works out which areas of policy ought to be settled at what level of
government and why. The recourse to the vague term "subsidiarity"
hardly suffices here. This debate needs to be conducted with reference
to specific policy areas, including foreign and defense policy, employment policy, environmental policy, and educational policy. Although
this book has contributed little to this urgent task, it has suggested that
Europe assume responsibility for foreign, military, and defense policy.
This is to ask Europe to take over functions that nation-states guard
most jealously. If this suggestion were adopted, then Europe's nation-
states would, in effect, cease to exist.

An obvious objection to this far-reaching conclusion is that given the
general level of incompetence with which the EU conducts many of its

other responsibilities—the Common Agricultural Policy, for instance—it is madness to suggest that it assume responsibility for something as important as foreign and defense policy. There can, so it might be thought, no better way of endangering the security of Europe's hapless citizens. Compounding this problem, Europeans generally identify more closely with their national institutions than with European institutions, and—more important still—they self-identify as nationals rather than Europeans. Who would die for an abstraction like Europe? For nationalists, this state of affairs is ideal. For some academics, this state of affairs is unavoidable, given the salience of peoples' different traditions and historical memories. In conclusion, I want to respond to each of these objections.

The case against Europe taking on responsibilities for security and defense has been forcefully argued by Mette Eilstrup Sangiovanni. She identifies at least four specific reasons why, as she puts it, "a common security and defence policy is bad for Europe."[2] First, Europe simply cannot afford the costs of becoming a global military power. Second, Europe, even if it were willing to bear the costs of its own independent military forces, would simply be wasting its money given existing political divisions among its members. Third, Europe lacks any will to exert itself outside multilateral organizations like the UN. And fourth, an independent European security and defense capability would undermine the Atlantic Alliance.

Let me consider each of these claims in turn. First, the claim that Europe cannot afford to fund its own military force must be treated with considerable skepticism. People who make this argument typically compare extrapolations of US military spending with extrapolations of European military spending. This argument ignores the fact that, under current circumstances, Europe does not need to spend much on its defense. While the United States is willing to commit money and resources to the defense of Europe, Europeans would be chumps to duplicate these efforts. Why spend good money on something you can get more or less for free? Present European military spending patterns are, in short, no guide to what Europeans could and would spend if they confronted genuine threats to their own security. Second, the claim that Europeans lack sufficient unity of purpose to operate their own military policy needs to distinguish between Europe in its present political form and Europe under a common sovereign state. Mette Eilstrup Sangiovanni is quite right to say that an intergovernmental Europe could not operate its own security and defense policy, but she draws the wrong conclusion from this observation. Europe's current institutional deficiencies do not provide a sufficient reason to abandon the quest for an independent security and defense policy. These institutional deficiencies provide a justification for a unitary European polity.

Sangiovanni's third argument for rejecting an independent European military force turns on an assessment of the advantages to Europeans of acting exclusively through the United Nations and other multilateral institutions. The trouble with this argument is that it exaggerates both the extent to which these institutions adequately protect European interests and the threat posed to these institutions by Europeans acquiring their own independent military force. The principal problem with an exclusive reliance on multilateral institutions is that Europeans—to reiterate a point made many times in this book—inhabit a world that contains powerful states that follow their own national interests. Anyone who doubts this point need only consult the Bush administration's *National Security Strategy of the United States of America* (September 2002).[3] That document makes it quite clear that the United States reserves the right to reject multilateral norms and act outside multilateral institutions when this serves its national interests. This document also makes it quite clear that the United States believes that its own national interest requires it to prevent any other state from acquiring any power comparable to its own. These are statements of a state that believes that it lives in a world of power politics. For Europeans to pretend that this is a world that we have now happily left behind is both naive and a threat to their own security. There is no reason to think that a Europe equipped with its own military force must therefore reject multilateralism. This force merely provides Europeans with an additional option when multilateral institutions fail to serve their interests.

Finally, Sangiovanni's fourth argument against an independent European security and defense policy is that it would endanger the Atlantic Alliance. It is difficult to know ex ante what to make of this claim. But let us assume that it is true. The Atlantic Alliance was a function of the wars against fascism and communism. Now that these wars have ended, it is not surprising that the ties between the Atlantic Allies have become somewhat frayed. A number of realist thinkers predicted that in the aftermath of the Cold War we could expect the United States and Europe to pull apart. There is no necessary reason to regret this occurrence. Over most global issues, the United States and Europe—the two leading Western liberal democracies—are likely to share common cause. The fact that they might sometimes disagree and pursue different paths is not the catastrophe that some devotees of the Atlantic Alliance like to think.

The more troubling challenge to the idea of a common security and defense policy comes from those who worry that the EU lacks the competence to handle such policies. There are two points that can be made in response to this challenge. First, it might plausibly be claimed that many of the EU's weaknesses and deficiencies have everything to do with the fact that it remains an intergovernmental organization designed to reach decisions by consensus. This type of political structure is wholly unsuited to taking quick and effective action. But this fact does not mean that a Europe equipped with a sovereign state could not act quickly and effectively. Second, the present skepticism and suspicion of the EU does, I think, disqualify Europe from taking over anytime soon responsibilities for foreign, military, and defense policy. This point takes us back to the earlier discussion of the process of European integration. Even if one were to think that a sovereignist European project has a lot to recommend it, this does not entail any specific view of the *process* of European integration. Nor, more to the point, does it entail any very positive view of the current *product* of European integration. But this combination of views—enthusiastic toward the project, skeptical of the current product—does require that careful thought be given to the process of European integration.

Europe can, I think, best demonstrate its suitability for assuming greater responsibilities not, as some europhiles like to assume, by making its institutions more democratic or by devoting more of its resources to public relations. Europe has reached a stage in its development where it needs to establish nonduplicative but parallel social and political organizations. In the area of military and defense policy, Europe's member states would be best advised to spend a certain percentage of their defense budgets on a self-standing European military force, which, at least in its formative stages, could operate as something akin to the French foreign legion. Based outside Europe, this small European military force would be employed, first and foremost, to prevent humanitarian catastrophes. Only if and when this independent European foreign legion demonstrated its professional competence would the European Union deserve to be allowed to assume greater responsibilities for Europe's security and defense.

The idea that the process of European political integration ought now to proceed through the development of parallel, nonduplicative social and political organizations has a number of additional applications. It would allow, for instance, for the establishment of a parallel system of higher education designed to train people to operate Europe's administrative agencies. This system of higher education would probably need to be reinforced through a common European secondary education qualification, a European baccalaureate. These proposals—a European foreign legion, a European college of higher education, and a European baccalaureate—are not designed to replace existing national armies, national educational systems, or national secondary examination qualifications. They are designed to introduce nonduplicative organizations and standards that can grow in influence and prestige only if and when they earn it. In this way, the process of European integration would avoid the present suspicion that Europe is a plot designed to replace much-loved national institutions.

Here, finally, at the mention of much-loved national institutions, we return to nationalist-inspired euroscepticism. The greengrocer who wanted to sell his bananas in imperial measures represents for me a noble democratic figure. Refusing to accept without good reason a restriction on his freedom, Mr. Steven Thoburn helped provoke a debate about the justification for a European level of government. This debate forced onto the agenda some basic questions about the European Union that Europe's elites had been happy to ignore. Thoburn and his supporters demanded, in short, a justification for the very existence of a European level of government. Why, in other words, ought people who remain relatively content with their national institutions endorse a project that envisages the ultimate disappearance of these institutions?

Convincing answers to this question are much harder to come by than most europhiles like to acknowledge. A convincing answer does, however, exist. Once we recognize that the preservation of national sovereignty—and, by extension, the preservation of a Europe of nation-states—has important ramifications for the security of Europeans, then the basis exists for a security-based justification for the European project. People like Mr. Thoburn and his friends might lament their dependence on political authorities based in Brussels over which they have no control. But the form of dependence that allegedly exists between the European Union and its member states pales into insignificance compared with the dependence that a sovereign and nominally independent Britain would face in a world dominated by the United States, China, Russia, and a politically integrated European superstate. The notion that "independence" could exist outside this European superstate is a mere pipe dream.

The more plausible claim of nationalist-inspired eurosceptics is that a state needs, as a condition of exercising both domestic control and international power, to be able to produce, sustain, and express a shared conception of nationality. People will accept commands from a "sovereign" that represents their national will but not from one that does not. From this perspective, Europe will never be able to act effectively in the world until it generates its own European nationalism. In response to this claim, it must, I think, be conceded that there will always be at least some people who will resonate more to the call and customs of their perceived ancestors. For such people, historical memories and generational continuities are more important than living well in the present or working together for a more prosperous future. But these people, present probably in all cultures at all times, have rarely been able to prevent new, more all-encompassing forms of political membership from emerging. Indeed, if local nationalists were always the decisive force in history, it would be impossible to explain how the great European nation-states ever came into existence. People in early modern Europe came, over a period of generations, to shift the horizon of their loyalties and attachments from the local to the national. There is no obvious reason why, *under the right combination of circumstances*, this could not happen again.

This book might be interpreted as an effort to identify the *right combination of circumstances*. To this end, I have tried to specify, first, the conditions of any adequate democratic justification for the European project and, second, a more specific security-based justification for this project. This security-based justification does not entail, as I have tried to show in this concluding chapter, that Europeans would be well advised to transfer immediately all responsibilities for foreign, security, and defense policy to a newly minted superstate. The sovereignist project of European political integration requires, no less importantly, an appropriate process of integration. This process must acknowledge the widely held and deeply felt skepticism of people like the "Metric Martyr." The process of European integration best suited for this new, more skeptical Europe is through the construction of parallel, nonduplicative political structures that can gain legitimacy only as they demonstrate efficacy.

✳ *Notes* ✳

INTRODUCTION

1. Joseph Weiler, *The Constitution of Europe* (Cambridge: Cambridge University Press, 1999), esp. ch. 1.

2. For an account of the background to the case involving Steven Thoburn—who sadly died in March 2004—see the website *www.metricmartyrs.co.uk*. The case of Thoburn and others was appealed at the Queen's Bench in February 2002. Lord Justice Laws's decision against Thoburn and the other appellants contains a very illuminating discussion of the current status of national and EU law; see *www.metricmartyrs.co.uk/page/appealjudge.htm*

3. Frederick Forsyth, "A Simple Question," *Salisbury Review* 19.4 (Summer 2001): 7.

4. Satan's lines from Milton's *Paradise Lost* (ch. 1, lines 257–63) read as follows:

> Here at least
> We shall be free; th' Almighty hath not built
> Here for his envy, will not drive us hence:
> Here we may reign secure; and, in my choice,
> To reign is worth ambition, though in Hell:
> Better to reign in Hell than serve in Heaven.

5. The failure of the intergovernmental council at Nice in December 2000 to resolve successfully the future balance of power between member states provided the initial impetus for the establishment of a European Convention. For useful discussions of the rationale and organization of the European Convention, see Koen Lenaerts and Marlies Desomer, "New Models of Constitution-Making in Europe: The Quest for Legitimacy," *Common Market Law Review* 39 (2002): 1217–53, and Peter Norman, *The Accidental Constitution: The Story of the European Convention* (London: Eurocomment, 2003).

6. European Convention website, *http://european-convention.eu.int/enjeux.asp?lang=EN*

7. Preamble, *Provisional Consolidated Version of the Draft Treaty Establishing a Constitution for Europe* (June 14, 2004). The full text of the treaty is available at *http://ue.eu.int/igcpdf/en/04/cg00/cg00086.en04.pdf*. All references to the Constitutional Treaty in this chapter refer to this document (CIG 86/04).

8. A further reason why the treaty is unlikely to settle the question of Europe's political future is that it reads, as Noel Malcolm rightly points out, more like a manifesto—a program for the future ("onwards and upwards," as he puts it)—than a document that merely defines the roles and responsibilities of the EU's

component political institutions. See Noel Malcolm, "A federal constitution with the heart of a manifesto," *Daily Telegraph*, August 27, 2003.

9. Joschka Fischer, "Vom Staatenverbund zur Föderation—Gedanken über die Finalität der europäischen Integration," in Christian Joerges, Yves Mény, and Joseph Weiler, eds., *What Kind of Constitution for What Kind of Polity? Responses to Joschka Fischer* (Florence and Cambridge, MA: European University Institute and Harvard Law School, 2000).

10. Lenaerts and Desomer, "New Models of Constitution-Making in Europe," 1223.

11. For an insightful critique of the convention from someone who was a participant, see Gisela Stuart, *The Making of Europe's Constitution* (London: Fabian Society, 2003).

12. See, for example, Kalypso Nicolaïdis and Robert Howse, eds., *The Federal Vision: Legitimacy and Levels of Governance in the United States and the European Union* (New York: Oxford University Press, 2001), especially the editors' introduction and conclusion; James Tully, *Strange Multiplicity* (Cambridge: Cambridge University Press, 1995); James Tully, "The Agonic Freedom of Citizens," *Economy and Society* 28 (1999): 161–82; and James Tully, "The Unfreedom of the Moderns in Comparison to Their Ideals of Constitutional Democracy," *Modern Law Review* 65 (2002).

13. The so-called Open Method of Coordination (OMC), which was introduced in the Lisbon Summit (March 2000), might be interpreted as the fourth aspect of this postsovereign conception of the European project. For the reasons explained in chapter 6, I conceptualize this form of governance as a component of "constitutional flexibility." For helpful discussions of OMC, see Dermot Hodson and Imelda Maher, "The Open Method as a New Mode of Governance," *Journal of Common Market Studies* 39 (2001): 719–46; and Sabrina Regent, "The Open Method of Coordination: A New Supranational Form of Governance," *European Law Journal* 9 (2003): 190–214.

14. Classic works include Ernst Haas, *The Uniting of Europe* (London: Stevens, 1958), and *Beyond the Nation-State* (Palo Alto, CA: Stanford University Press, 1964); Alan Milward, *The European Rescue of the Nation-State* (Berkeley and Los Angeles: University of California Press, 1992); Andrew Moravcsik, *The Choice for Europe: Social Purpose and State Power from Messina to Maastricht* (Ithaca, NY: Cornell University Press, 1998); and John Gillingham, *European Integration, 1950–2003: Superstate or New Market Economy?* (Cambridge: Cambridge University Press, 2003).

15. Consider here, for example, the eurosceptic critique of the EU put forward in Gillingham, *European Integration*. Gillingham criticizes, often to devastating effect, many of the EU's current policies and institutions. Yet while his book can be read solely as a critique of the existing European *product* of integration, this book also has a lot to say about various possible projects of European integration. Thus Gillingham advocates jettisoning the project of constructing a federal

European superstate in favor of a no less far-reaching alternative project: the construction of a European free trade area. Gillingham does not himself, however, provide anything close to a justification for this alternative project. I say more about the failings of eurosceptics to justify their own preferred projects in chapter 3.

16. For an example of this line of argument, see Joseph Weiler, "Europe's *Sonderweg*," in Nicolaïdis and Howse, *The Federal Vision*.

17. Consider here, for instance, Philippe Schmitter's description of the EU as "a postnational, unsovereign, polycentric, non-coterminous, neo-medieval institution." Philippe Schmitter, "Some Alternative Futures for the European Polity and Their Implications for European Public Policy," in Yves Meny et al., eds., *Adjusting to Europe: The Impact of the European Union on National Institutions and Policies* (London: Routledge, 1996), 26.

18. For an excellent discussion of the division of powers (or competences) in the EU, see Grainne de Burca and Bruno de Witte, "The Delimitation of Powers between the EU and Its Member States," in A. Arnull and Daniel Wincott, eds., *Accountability and Legitimacy in the European Union* (Oxford: Oxford University Press, 2002).

19. For more on the contrast between "a loosely intergovernmental system" and "tight supranationalism," see Helen Wallace, "Designing Institutions for an Enlarging European Union," in Bruno de Witte, ed., *Ten Perspectives on the European Constitutional Treaty* (Florence: RSCAS European University Institute, 2003), 86.

20. Margaret Thatcher's policies toward the European Union suggest, however, that this generalization about intergovernmentalists stands in need of some qualification. At one level, Margaret Thatcher was the quintessential intergovernmentalist and an implacable foe of supranationalism. Yet Thatcher supported the Single European Act (1986), which represented the first major break with national vetoes. Thatcher was led to support the Single European Act on the grounds that without some measure of majority voting an effective European level of government would be impossible. While Thatcher did not want a European level of government with expansive powers over a wide range of policy areas, she did want the European level of government to have the power to strike down those policies of national governments that were market restricting. For a helpful and balanced discussion of Thatcher's approach to the Single European Act, see Leon Brittan, *A Diet of Brussels* (London: Little, Brown, and Company 2000), 35–39.

21. For discussions of the EU that recognize that conflicts over these market-oriented issues are at least as important as conflicts over the division and distribution of powers, see Fritz W. Scharpf, *Governing in Europe: Effective and Democratic?* (Oxford: Oxford University Press, 1999); Simon Hix and Christopher Lord, *Political Parties in the European Union* (London: Macmillan, 1997); Liesbet Hooghe and Gary Marks, "The Making of a Polity: The Struggle over European

Integration," *European Integration Online Papers* 1, no. 004 *http://eiop.or.at/eiop/ texte/1997-004a.htm;* and Mark Pollack, "A Blairite Treaty: Neo-liberalism and Regulated Capitalism in the Treaty of Amsterdam," in Karlheinz Neunreither and Antje Wiener, eds., *European Integration after Amsterdam* (Oxford: Oxford University Press, 2000).

22. The Constitutional Treaty tries not to take sides on the nature and merits of market-regulating policies by including both neoliberal and social democratic provisions. Consider, for instance, the following:

> The Union shall offer its citizens an area of freedom, security, and justice without internal frontiers, and *a single market where competition is free and undistorted.* (Article 1–3:2, emphasis added) The Union shall work for a Europe of *just development based on balanced economic growth, a social market economy,* highly competitive and aiming at full employment and social progress. (Article 1–3:3, emphasis added)

23. Exemplary in this respect are the conflicts that emerged—roughly at the same time the convention was sitting—over the rules and regulations governing temporary workers and hostile takeovers. For a discussion, see "European Takeovers: Reform's Last Gasp," *Economist,* May 24, 2003, 64–65. For Blair's fears on harmonization of tax policy, see Juhan Parts and Tony Blair, "The enlarged EU must be free to compete," *Financial Times,* November 3, 2003.

24. Wolfgang Muchnau, "The kind of EU the French would vote for," *Financial Times,* September 27, 2004.

25. For useful discussions of these tensions, see the series "The Divided West" in the *Financial Times,* May 26–30, 2003; and Ivo H. Daalder and James M. Lindsay, *America Unbound: The Bush Revolution in Foreign Policy* (Washington, DC: Brookings Institution Press, 2003).

26. Nonetheless, the Constitutional Treaty of 2004, much like the Draft Treaty of 2003, was received by British eurosceptics as a victory for those who favored a European superstate. See, for instance, "Ignore the flannel—it's a surrender," *Daily Mail* (London), June 21, 2004.

27. Preamble, *Constitutional Treaty.*

28. Article 1–1:1, *Constitutional Treaty.*

29. For a general description of the European political system, see Helen and William Wallace eds., *Policy-Making in the European Union,* fourth edition (Oxford: Oxford University Press, 2000), 3–81.

30. The EU Commission currently (2005) consists of one commissioner per member state. From 2009, "the Commission shall consist of a number of Members, including its President and the Union Minister for Foreign Affairs, corresponding to 2/3 of the number of Member States . . . selected . . . on the basis of equal rotation between the Member States."

31. For an interesting discussion of the eventual size of the EU, see Timothy Garten Ash, "The European Orchestra," *New York Review of Books,* May 2001.

32. For a typical example of this point of view, see Andrew Sullivan, "The Euro Menace: The USE vs. the USA," *New Republic*, June 16, 2003.

33. "Blair: EU constitution rules out superstate," *Guardian*, June 23, 2003. Compare here also the comment of the British foreign minister, Jack Straw: "The current draft treaty shows that we are making progress towards our kind of Europe: a union of nations, not a superstate. It should help to settle the balance between the nations and the union where it should be, with the nations as the anchor of the union." *Daily Telegraph*, August 7, 2003. Blair made the same point about the Constitutional Treaty: "The treaty . . . makes it plain that the EU is not and will not be a federal Superstate. Rather it establishes clearly where the EU can and cannot act and confirms that the EU is a union of nation-states." *Guardian*, September 9, 2004. It is revealing that not all European leaders see it this way. Consider, for instance, the claim of the German chancellor, Gerhard Schroeder, who described the Constitutional Treaty as a "milestone on the way to further European integration." "Wir werden dieser weg weiter gehen," *Frankfurter Allgemeine Zeitung*, July 3, 2004.

34. Daniel J. Elazar, *Exploring Federalism* (Tuscaloosa: University of Alabama Press, 1987), 5–6.

35. Elazar, *Exploring Federalism*, 12.

36. For some of the intellectual background to federalism, see the essays in Daniel Elazar, ed., *Federalism as Grand Design: Political Philosophers and the Federal Principle* (Lanham, MD: University Press of America, 1987); and Stephen Woodard, "The Simple Guide to the Federal Idea," *http://jef-europe.net/federalism/archives/00934.html*.

37. See Istvan Hont, "The Permanent Crisis of a Divided Mankind," in John Dunn, ed., *The Crisis of the Nation-State* (Cambridge: Polity Press, 1994), now placed in a broader context by Istvan Hont, *The Jealousy of Trade* (Cambridge, MA: Belknap Press of Harvard University, forthcoming).

38. For a helpful discussion, see Richard Bellamy, "The Political Form of the Constitution: The Separation of Powers, Rights and Representative Democracy," in Richard Bellamy and Dario Castiglione, *Constitutionalism in Transformation: European and Theoretical Perspectives* (Oxford: Blackwell, 1996), 436–56.

39. "Citizens are directly represented at Union level in the European Parliament. Member States are represented in the European Council and Council of Ministers by their governments, themselves accountable to national parliaments, elected by their citizens." Article 1–45:2, *Constitutional Treaty*.

40. See here the description of federalism provided on the JEF website (*http://www.jef-europe.net/federalism/archives/000928.html*), *http://www.jefeurope.net/federalism/archives/000929.html*.

41. David McKay, *Designing Europe: Comparative Lessons from the Federal Experience* (Oxford: Oxford University Press, 2001), 24.

42. In describing the United States as resembling more closely a unitary state than a federal polity, it is important not to be misled by the example of France.

The centralized political system of France represents an extreme example of a unitary state. The conception of the unitary state defended in this section does not preclude a variety of forms of decentralization. Not all unitary states have followed the centralized French model. Some have managed to achieve a unifying, one-dimensional level of representation while pursuing various forms of decentralization and local autonomy.

43. Margaret Thatcher, "Bruges Speech," in Martin Holmes, ed., *The Eurosceptic Reader* (London: MacMillan, 1986).

44. This problem is present, for instance, in Gillingham, *European Integration.* Indeed, the subtitle of this provocative, historical work is "Superstate or New Market Economy?" Much of the book is devoted to an attack on the EU's market-restricting policies.

45. For a helpful survey of the contributions of political theorists to the study of European political integration, see Heidrun Friese and Peter Wagner, "Survey Article: The Nascent Political Philosophy of the European Polity," *Journal of Political Philosophy* 10 (2002): 342–64.

46. I use the term "European polity" inclusively to cover all possible political arrangements that possess a European level of government, including a unitary state and a *federal polity*.

47. On this point, see Yves Meny, "*De la democratie en Europe*: Old Concepts and New Challenges," *Journal of Common Market Studies* 41 (2003): 1–13; and Andrew Moravcsik, "In Defence of the Democratic Deficit: Reassessing Legitimacy in the European Union," *Journal of Common Market Studies* 40 (2002): 603–24.

48. Claus Offe, "The Democratic Welfare State in an Integrating Europe," in Michael Th. Greven and Louis W. Pauly, eds., *Democracy beyond the State: The European Dilemma and the Emerging Global Order* (Lanham, MD: Rowman and Littlefield, 2000), 77–83.

49. See especially John Rawls, *Political Liberalism* (New York: Columbia University Press, 1991). For helpful discussions of this aspect of Rawls's later work, see Burton Dreben, "Rawls's Later Work," and Charles Larmore, "Public Reason," both in Samuel Freeman, ed., *The Cambridge Companion to John Rawls* (Cambridge: Cambridge University Press, 2003).

50. See here the extremely provocative and stimulating works of Richard Bellamy and Dario Castiglione, especially Richard Bellamy, "The 'Right to Have Rights': Citizenship Practice and the Political Constitution of the EU," in Richard Bellamy and Alex Warleigh, eds., *Citizenship and Governance in the European Union* (London: Continuum, 2001); Richard Bellamy and Dario Castiglione, "Building the Union: The Nature of Sovereignty in the Political Architecture of Europe," *Law and Philosophy* 16 (1997): 421–45; Richard Bellamy and Dario Castiglione, "The Normative Challenge of a European Polity: Cosmopolitan and Communitarian Models Compared, Criticized and Combined," in Andreas Føllesdal and Peter Koslowski, eds., *Democracy and the EU* (Berlin:

Springer Verlag, 1998) 245–80; Richard Bellamy and Dario Castiglione, "Between Cosmopolis and Community: Three Models of Rights and Democracy within the EU," in Daniele Archibugi, David Held, and Martin Köhler, eds., *Reimagining Political Community: Studies in Cosmopolitan Democracy* (Cambridge: Polity Press, 1998); and Richard Bellamy and Dario Castiglione, Legitimising the Euro-'Polity' and Its 'Regime': The Normative Turn in EU Studies," *European Journal of Political Theory* 2 (2003), pp. 7–34; and Richard Bellamy, "Sovereignty, Post-sovereignty and Pre-sovereignty: Reconceptualizing the State, Rights and Democracy in the EU," in Neil Walker, ed., *Sovereignty in Transition* (Oxford: Hart, 2003), 167–90. The work of Bellamy and Castiglione blends "republican" themes present in the work of Philip Pettit and Quentin Skinner with the "agonistic" themes present in the work of James Tully. For a discussion of republican approaches to the EU, see Damien Chalmers, "The Reconstitution of European Public Spheres," *European Law Journal* 9 (2003): 127–89; and Friese and Wagner, "Survey Article," 353–61.

51. This problem undermines many of the federal and postsovereign recommendations put forward by the editors in Nicolaïdis and Howse, *The Federal Vision*. Their recommendations work only in a world where the organization of political communities does not need to be mindful of competitive power politics. For more discussion of this point, see chapter 7 below.

52. For an insightful overview, see Tony Judt, "The Way We Live Now" and "America and the World," *New York Review of Books*, March 27 and April 10, 2003.

53. For the standard expression of this point of view, see Lord Robertson, "A Global Dimension for a Renewed Transatlantic Partnership," *http://www.nato.int/docu/speech/2002/s020219a.htm*, February 19, 2002. See also Geoff Hoon, "Making European Defence Stronger," *www.britishembassy.at/speeches/0011hoon_european_defence.rtf*, November 14, 2000. For a skeptical assessment, see Anatol Lieven, "The End of the West," *Prospect*, September 2002.

54. For the classic statement of Europe as a civilian power, see Francois Duchene, "Europe in World Peace," in Richard Mayne ed., *Europe Tomorrow* (London: Fontana, 1972), and Francois Duchene, "The EC and the Uncertainities of Interdependence," in Max Kohnstamm and William Hager, eds., *A Nation Writ Large* (London: Macmillan, 1973). Recently this idea has been dusted off by (among others) Andrew Moravcsik, "The Quiet Superpower," *Newsweek International*, July 2002; and Jan Zielonka, *Explaining Euro-paralysis: Why Europe Is Unable to Act in International Politics* (New York: St. Martin's Press, 1998).

55. I owe this analogy to Gideon Rose, who actually likes the idea of playing "Batman."

56. For a useful overview of some of these efforts, see Anne Deighton, "The European Security and Defense Policy," *Journal of Common Market Studies* 40 (2002): 719–41.

57. See here, for example, David Beetham and Christopher Lord, *Legitimacy and the European Union* (London: Longman, 1998), and the essays gathered in the

following collected volumes: Bellamy and Castiglione, eds., *Constitutionalism in Transformation*; Bellamy and Warleigh, *Citizenship and Governance in the European Union*; Percy B. Lehning and Albert Weale, eds., *Citizenship, Democracy, and Justice in the New Europe* (London and New York: Routledge, 1997); Albert Weale and Michael Nentwich, eds., *Political Theory and the European Union: Legitimacy, Constitutional Choice, and Citizenship* (London and New York: Routledge, 1998); and Føllesdal and Koslowski, *Democracy and the European Union*.

58. See especially Beetham and Lord, *Legitimacy and the European Union*; Bellamy and Castiglione, "Legitimizing the Euro-'Polity'"; Neil Walker, "The White Paper in Constitutional Context," Jean Monnet Program Working Paper New York University Law School, June 1, 2001, and "Constitutionalizing Enlargement, Enlarging Constitutionalism," *European Law Journal* 9 (2003): 365–85.

59. Walker, "The White Paper," 5–13; Walker, "Constitutionalizing Enlargement," 368–70; these distinctions build, as he acknowledges, on Beetham and Lord's conception of "performative legitimacy" and Bellamy and Castiglione's distinction between "regime legitimacy" and "polity legitimacy."

60. See Walker, "Constitutionalizing Enlargement," 368–69.

Chapter 1
Justification

1. For the complaint, common among eurosceptics, that European political integration has never been adequately justified, see Noel Malcolm, "Sense on Sovereignty," in Holmes, *The Eurosceptic Reader*. I discuss Malcolm's argument in more detail in chapter 6 below.

2. Federico Mancini, *Democracy and Constitutionalism in the European Union: Collected Essays* (Oxford: Hart, 2000).

3. Such is, at least, the implication of Philippe Schmitter, *How to Democratize the European Union . . . and Why Bother?* (Lanham, MD: Rowman and Littlefield, 1999).

4. Neil MacCormick, *Questioning Sovereignty: Law, State, and Nation in the European Commonwealth* (Oxford: Oxford University Press, 1999); Nicolaïdis and Howse, *The Federal Vision*.

5. Bruce A. Ackerman, *The Future of the Liberal Revolution* (New Haven, CT: Yale University Press, 1992), 40. The term "federal Europe," as noted in the previous chapter, is ambiguous. It is not clear whether Ackerman is using the term to refer to what I have termed the sovereignist or postsovereignist variants of a politically integrated Europe.

6. Ackerman, *The Future of the Liberal Revolution*, 40.

7. Although Ackerman speaks of the "national welfare state," it would be more accurate to speak of welfare *states* in the plural. The welfare state, as a number of scholars have pointed, takes a different form in different European countries. See, on this topic, Gosta Esping Anderson, *Three Worlds of Welfare Capital-*

ism (Princeton, NJ: Princeton University Press, 1990); and Scharpf, *Governing in Europe*. In his more recent work, Ackerman has proposed a variety of utopian schemes that would substantially modify democratic, capitalist societies. See especially Bruce Ackerman and Anne Alstott, *The Stakeholder Society* (New Haven, CT: Yale University Press, 1998). It is not clear how these proposals bear on his case for a federal Europe.

8. Luc Boltanski and Laurent Thévenot, *De La Justification: Les Économies de la Grandeur* (Paris: Gallimard, 1991).

9. R. W. Burchfield et al. eds., *Oxford English Dictionary*, vol. 8 (Oxford: Clarendon Press, 1989).

10. For a brilliant exploration of the way that arguments about "fit" apply in debates about work, see J. Russell Muirhead, *Just Work* (Cambridge, MA: Harvard University Press, 2004).

11. Edmund Burke, *Reflections on the Revolution in France* (Indianapolis: Hacket, 1986 [1790]).

12. John Rawls, *Justice as Fairness: A Restatement* (Cambridge, MA: Belknap Press of Harvard University, 2001), 3.

13. Jürgen Habermas, *Between Facts and Norms* (Cambridge MA: MIT Press, 1996).

14. For what is involved in teasing out the background ideas and assumptions of daily politics of a particular period, see Don Herzog, *Poisoning the Mind of the Lower Orders* (Princeton, NJ: Princeton University Press, 1997).

15. I have adapted this distinction from Bellamy and Castiglione's concepts of regime legitimacy and policy legitimacy; see Bellamy and Castiglione, "Legitimizing the Euro-'Polity.'"

16. Bruce A. Ackerman, *We the People*, vol. 1 (Cambridge, MA: Belknap Press of Harvard University, 1991).

17. For an example of someone who thinks that the EU in its current form is already a federal state, see Stephen Haseler, "The Case for a Federal Future," in Ian Taylor et al., *Federal Britain in Federal Europe?* (London: Federal Trust for Education and Research, 2001), 51–96. For Haseler, "we in Europe have now reached the point where, in effect, we inhabit a new political structure which amounts to a state." In a later work, he argues that the European Union is already both a superstate and a superpower that is capable of challenging the United States. Stephen Haseler, *Super-state: The New Europe and Its Challenge to America* (London: I.B. Taurus, 2004). This line of argument has three weaknesses. One, the EU in its present form is clearly not a state nor anything close. In the current EU, the power lies with nation-states and their representatives in the European Council and Council of Ministers. Second, not only is the EU itself weak, but it weakens Europe's nation-states, whose scope for independent action it constrains. Third, Haseler's usage of the term "Super-state" is misleading, for it suggests that, insofar as the EU can and does project power abroad, then it qualifies ipso facto as a "Super-state." While the term "Super-state" clearly means

179

different things to different people—Thatcherite eurosceptics employ the term, for instance, to describe an interventionist market-constraining state—it would be better to use the term to describe a European polity that is either a unitary centralized sovereign state or a federal state like the United States that centralizes the most important governmental functions (such as income tax, foreign policy, and defense policy).

18. Here (and throughout this book) I am dating these treaties to the year they were signed rather than one year later when they took effect. Thus the Single European Act, for instance, was signed in 1986, but it did not enter into force until July 1987. Likewise the Treaty on European Union (Maastricht Treaty) was signed in 1992, but it did not enter into force until November 1993. For a simple but straightforward discussion of the treaties, see Timothy Bainbridge, *The Penguin Companion to European Union* (London: Penguin Books, 2000), 487–92.

19. Andrew Moravcsik, "Federalism in the European Union: Rhetoric and Reality," in Nicolaïdis and Howse, *The Federal Vision*, 163–64.

20. Moravcsik, "Federalism in the European Union," 164. Moravcsik does not always strike such a deflationary note when describing European integration. Consider the opening sentences of his own magisterial book on Europe: "The construction of the European Community (EC) ranks among the most extraordinary achievements in modern world politics. . . . EC rules influence most aspects of European political life, from the regulation of the habitat of wild birds to voting within the World Trade Organization." Moravcsik, *The Choice for Europe*, 1.

21. For useful discussions of the role of justification in contemporary political theory, see Fred d'Agostino, *Public Reason* (New York: Oxford University Press, 1996), and "Public Justification," *Stanford Online Encyclopedia of Philosophy*, 2003 (available at *http://plato.stanford.edu/entries/justification_public*); Mark Evans, "Is Public Justification Central to Liberalism?" *Journal of Political Ideologies* 4 (1999): 117–36; Rainer Forst, "The Basic Right to Justification: Towards a Constructivist Conception of Human Rights," *Constellations* 6 (1999): 35–60; Gerald Gaus, *Justificatory Liberalism: An Essay on Epistemology and Political Theory* (New York: Oxford University Press, 1996); and Stephen Macedo, *Liberal Virtues* (Oxford: Oxford University Press, 1991). For more specific discussions of Rawls's usage of justification, see Arthur Ripstein, "Foundationalism in Political Theory," *Philosophy and Public Affairs* 16 (1987): 115–37; Thomas M. Scanlon, "Justification," and Charles Larmore, "Public Reason," both in Freeman, *The Cambridge Companion to John Rawls*; and Rainer Forst, *Contexts of Justice* (Berkeley and Los Angeles: University of California Press, 2001).

22. For Hampshire's political theory, see especially Stuart Hampshire, *Innocence and Experience* (Cambridge, MA: Harvard University Press, 1989); and Stuart Hampshire, *Justice as Conflict* (Princeton, NJ: Princeton University Press, 1999). For Hampshire's differences with Rawls, see "Liberalism: The New Twist," *New York Review of Books*, August 12, 1993, 43–48.

23. For a revealing discussion of the pros and cons of the filtering and fun-

neling approaches to justice, see the exchange between John Rawls and Jürgen Habermas in *Journal of Philosophy* 92 (1995): 109–80. Habermas, like Hampshire more of a filterer than a funneler, thinks that Rawls overloads his theory of justice by incorporating a conception of the person and a list of primary goods. Rawls, a funneler, complains that Habermas's filtering approach yields indeterminate outcomes. For a helpful discussion of this debate, see Rainer Forst, "Die Rechtfertigung der Gerechtigkeit: Rawls' Politischer Liberalismus and Habermas' Diskurstheorie in der Diskussion," in Hauke Brunkhorst and Peter Niesen, eds., *Das Recht der Republik* (Frankfurt am Main: Suhrkamp, 1999).

24. John Rawls, *A Theory of Justice* (Cambridge, MA: Harvard University Press, 1971), and *Political Liberalism*.

25. Earlier I noted that justificatory arguments can be more or less restrictive; they can act, in other words, as a *funneling* mechanism (leaving a single determinate justified outcome), or they can act solely as a *filtering* mechanism (leaving a range of justified outcomes).

26. Rawls, *A Theory of Justice*, 21.

27. The status of these values as specified (rather than deduced from some more fundamental value or principle) and provisional (rather than final conclusions) is a feature of the "constructivism" that informs this approach. The acceptability of these values turns, at least in part, on the plausibility of the overall argument that takes these values as a premise. The overall plausibility of the argument thus provides an important element in the effort to make these values a plausible and persuasive point of departure.

28. For an example of a moral and political theory that claims to offer such a universal, apodictic justification, see Alan Gewirth, *Reason and Morality* (Chicago: University of Chicago Press, 1979).

29. For a helpful reminder of the importance of this process, see J. Donald Moon, *Constructing Community: Moral Pluralism and Tragic Conflicts* (Princeton, NJ: Princeton University Press, 1992).

30. Christopher Bertram, "Political Justification, Theoretical Complexity, and Democratic Community," *Ethics* 107 (1997): 563–64.

31. Rawls himself has something like this point in mind when he argues, "A conception of justice is to be the public basis of the terms of social cooperation. Since common understanding necessitates certain bounds on the complexity of the principles, there may likewise be limits on the use of theoretical knowledge in the original position." Rawls, *A Theory of Justice*, 142; cf. also Rawls, *Political Liberalism*, 182. See also, on the importance of "accessibility," Amy Gutman and Dennis Thompson, *Why Deliberative Democracy?* (Princeton, NJ: Princeton University Press, 2004), 144–47.

32. This criticism applies to much of the literature produced on Europe's alleged "democratic deficit."

33. This approach informs, for instance, Loukas Tsoukalis, *What Kind of Europe?* (Oxford: Oxford University Press, 2003).

34. Michael Burgess, *Federalism and European Union: The Building of Europe, 1950–2000* (London and New York: Routledge, 2000).

35. For the most intellectually sophisticated study of the role of ideas in the process of European integration, see Craig Parsons, *A Certain Idea of Europe* (Ithaca, NY: Cornell University Press, 2003).

36. Milward, *The European Rescue of the Nation State*, 436.

37. For examples of this practice, see, for example, Joshua Cohen, "Review Symposium on Robert Dahl's *Democracy and Its Critics*," *Journal of Politics* 53 (1991): 215–231; and Ronald Dworkin, *Freedom's Law: The Moral Reading of the American Constitution* (Cambridge, MA: Harvard University Press, 1996).

38. For the notion of a justification that no one could "reasonably reject," see T. M. Scanlon, *What We Owe to One Another* (Cambridge, MA: Harvard University Press, 1998).

Chapter 2
Nationalism

1. For representative examples of conservative, socialist, and liberal critiques of nationalism, compare, respectively: Elie Kedourie, *Nationalism* (London: Hutchinson, 1960); Eric Hobsbawm, *Nations and Nationalism since 1780* (Cambridge: Cambridge University Press, 1990); and Friedrich A. Hayek, *The Road to Serfdom* (Chicago: University of Chicago Press, 1944).

2. The claim that the initial steps along the process of European integration took place in the context of a broadly antinationalist intellectual climate is not to say, however, that "overcoming nationalism" was a central causal factor in this process. For a cold-eyed treatment of the early postwar European treaties, see Milward, *The European Rescue of the Nation-State*. It is important to recognize here, however, that "the rescue of the nation-state" is not the same as "the rescue of nationalism." The relationship between "nation-state" and "nationalism" is, as this chapter shows, a complex one.

3. For the idea that there now exists "an emerging consensus" on the merits of liberal nationalism, see Will Kymlicka, "Liberal Culturalism: An Emerging Consensus?" in *Politics in the Vernacular* (Oxford: Oxford University Press, 2000), 39–48.

4. Ernest Gellner, *Nations and Nationalism* (Ithaca, NY: Cornell University Press, 1983), 123. For a brief account of Gellner's personal attitude toward his inherited cultures, see Ernest Gellner, *Nationalism* (New York: New York University Press, 1997), vii–x. For an overview of Gellner's contribution to the study of nationalism, see the contributions to John Hall, ed., *The State of the Nation: Ernest Gellner's Theory of Nationalism* (Cambridge: Cambridge University Press, 1999).

5. "Nationalism is primarily a political principle which holds that the political and the national unit should be congruent." Gellner, *Nations and Nationalism*, 1. In a later work, he expands on this definition in the following way:

Nationalism is a political principle which maintains that similarity of culture is the basic social bond. Whatever principles of authority may exist between people depend for their legitimacy on the fact that members of the group concerned are of the same culture (or, in nationalist idiom, of the same "nation"). (Gellner, *Nationalism*, 4)

Despite the emphasis in these definitions on nationalism as a principle of political legitimacy—nationalism (2) in my typology—Gellner's sociological theory seems more directly oriented toward explaining what I have called nationalism (1). Oddly, Gellner never seems to notice the difference between nationalism (1) and (2).

6. "On one matter, practically all scholars agree. As an ideology and movement , nationalism is modern. It dates from the late eighteenth or very early nineteenth centuries, and it originated in Western and Central Europe, and the United States." Anthony D. Smith, *Nationalism and Modernism* (New York: Routledge, 1998), 97.

7. For some of the difficulties with the industrialization-based explanation of nationalism, see Brendan O'Leary, "What Is Living and What Is Dead in Gellner's Theory of Nationalism," in Hall, *The State of the Nation*.

8. For a useful overview of recent debates on nationalism, see Smith, *Nationalism and Modernism*. Smith himself is the leading exponent of the so-called ethno-symbolism school, which emphasizes the role of ethnic symbols in the construction of modern nations: see Anthony D. Smith, *The Ethnic Origin of Nations* (Oxford: Blackwell 1986); and Anthony D. Smith, *Myths and Memories of the Nation* (Oxford: Oxford University Press, 2000). For the criticism that Gellner has underestimated the role of the international state system in the rise of nationalism, see Michael Mann, *The Sources of Social Power, vol. 2, The Rise of Classes and Nation-States, 1760–1914* (Cambridge: Cambridge University Press, 1994), and Michael Mann, "Nation-States in Europe and Other Continents: Diversifying, Developing, Not Dying," *Daedalus* 122 (1993), 115–40. Gellner has replied to criticisms from Mann, Smith, and others in Gellner, "Reply to Critics," in John A. Hall and Ian C. Jarvie, eds., *The Social Philosophy of Ernest Gellner* (Amsterdam: Rodopi, 1996).

9. For an influential example of this position, see Yael Tamir, *Liberal Nationalism* (Princeton, NJ: Princeton University Press, 1993). I discuss this line of argument in more detail in chapter 6.

10. Margaret Canovan, *Nationhood and Political Theory* (Cheltenham, UK: Edward Elgar, 1996), 119.

11. For a useful historical assessment, see Paul A. Rahe, *Republics Ancient and Modern* (Chapel Hill and London: University of North Carolina Press, 1994).

12. The sovereign state that Hobbes invented in his writings in the seventeenth century did not actually appear on the world historical stage until much later. For various accounts of the rise of the modern sovereign state, see Martin

Van Creveld, *The Rise and Decline of the State* (New York: Cambridge University Press, 1999); Mann, *Sources of Social Power*; and Hendryk Spruyt, *The Sovereign State and Its Competitors* (Princeton, NJ: Princeton University Press, 1994).

13. Thomas Hobbes, *Leviathan* (Cambridge: Cambridge University Press, 1996), [1651] 114.

14. See, for example, the opening paragraphs of Thomas Hobbes, *De Cive* (Cambridge: Cambridge University Press, 1998 [1647]), ch. 6, and Hobbes, *Leviathan*, ch. 16. For the seminal account of Hobbes's theory of representation, see Hanna Fenichel Pitkin, *The Concept of Representation* (Berkeley and Los Angeles: University of California Press, 1967), ch. 4.

15. As David Runciman has, in this context, noticed, "States in the modern world are the things that governments represent, and it was the discovery of representation as a mechanism of government which emancipated states from the confines of geography." David Runciman, "Invented Communities," *London Review of Books*, July 19, 2001.

16. For the contrast between the "civic nation" and the "ethnic nation," see, among many other authorities, Roger Brubaker, *Citizenship and Nationhood in France and Germany* (Cambridge, MA: Harvard University Press, 1992); and Michael Ignatieff, *Blood and Belonging: Journeys into the New Nationalism* (London: Chatto and Windus, 1993). Something like this distinction is present, in the form of a distinction between "Western" and "Eastern" nationalism, in Hans Kohn, *The Idea of Nationalism* (New York: Collier-MacMillan, 1944). For some insightful criticisms of this distinction, see Will Kymlicka, "Misunderstanding Nationalism," Bernard Yack, "The Myth of the Civic Nation," and Kai Nielsen, "Cultural Nationalism, Neither Ethnic nor Civic," in Ronald Beiner, ed., *Theorizing Nationalism* (Albany, NY: State University of New York Press, 1999).

17. Thus Hobbes in *De Cive* writes, "What actually is a Crowd [Multitudo] of men (who unite by their own decision in a single commonwealth)? For they are not a single entity but a number of men, each of whom has his own will and his own judgement about every proposal." Hobbes, *De Cive*, 75.

18. Given this aspect of Hobbes's political theory, it is difficult to accept the line of argument put forward by Bernard Yack in his otherwise extremely perceptive article on this topic; see Bernard Yack, "Popular Sovereignty and Nationalism," *Political Theory* 29 (2001): 517–36. For Yack,

> the new doctrine of popular sovereignty. . . . introduces a distinction between, what we might call, "the people's two bodies." Alongside an image of people who actually participate in political institutions, it constitutes another image of the people as a prepolitical community that establishes these institutions and has the final say on their legitimacy. (519)

Yack sees this latter conception of people as "a community from which the state derives its legitimate authority" and as providing "a bridge over the chasm that separates individuals from each other in their efforts to shape and control the authority of the state" (521). Yet Hobbes, who shares this new doctrine of popular sovereignty, clearly does not think that it gives rise to the idea of a people as a prepolitical community. Indeed, such an idea is, for Hobbes, both nonsensical and dangerous. It is nonsensical because it assumes that a people can exist prior to its embodiment in "a Civill Person." It is dangerous because it might lead to the thought that this prepolitical community provides a standard to measure the legitimacy of the artificially constituted "Civill Person." In short, there is, contrary to Yack's argument, no necessary link between popular sovereignty and the idea of a prepolitical community, whether conceived as a "People" or a "Nation."

19. For some extremely insightful remarks on this topic (and many others, to do with a European nation-state), see Canovan, *Nationhood and Political Theory*, esp. 118–19 and 138–39.

20. "Before 1750 or so, the idea of imposing the same language and "the same uniform ideas" (Rabaut's phrase) on Basque shepherds and Breton fishermen, Picard farm laborers and Lyonnais servants, Parisian lawyers and Marseilles merchants, to say nothing of Versailles courtiers, would have struck observers as self-evidently absurd. It was only in the later eighteenth century that it became thinkable." David Bell, *The Cult of the French Nation: Inventing Nationalism, 1680–1800* (Cambridge, MA: Harvard University Press, 2001), p 198–99. For Bell, the rise of nationalism in France was a reaction to the demise of a theocentric worldview and the recognition that a new basis of social and political order were necessary. My own view is that these religious changes were significant for the rise of the nation-state primarily because they led to what I have called "democratization."

21. For a general overview, see Gwyn A. Williams, *When Was Wales?* (London: Penguin Books, 1982).

22. This view informs the writings of many contemporary multiculturalists, including Charles Taylor and Will Kymlicka.

CHAPTER 3
EUROSCEPTICISM

1. For a useful compendium of such criticisms, see the website of the Bruges Group (*www.brugesgroup.com*).

2. This "softly, softly" method of proceeding was the intended design of Jean Monnet and the early architects of European integration and was worked up into a theory of European integration by, most famously, Ernst Haas. For a characteristic eurosceptic critique of the "secrecy" and "deception" involved in such an approach, see Christopher Booker and Richard North, *The Great Deception: The Secret History of the EU* (London: Continuum, 2003).

3. For a seminal social scientific approach to nationalism, see Karl Deutsch, *Nationalism and Social Communication* (New York: John Wiley and Company,

1953). Some sociological theorists favor a more expansive definition that sees nationalism as a "discursive formation" on and about nations, states, and collective identities; for an example of such an approach, see Craig Calhoun, *Nationalism* (Minneapolis: University of Minnesota Press, 1997).

4. The distinctions between sociological and ideological nationalism, on the one hand, and conservatism and liberalism, on the other, cut across the seven different types of nationalism identified in the previous chapter.

5. Although Burke was a "Whig," the features of "conservative" thought described in this paragraph are nowhere more eloquently defended than in Burke, *Reflections on the Revolution in France*. For an illuminating discussion of Burke as a progenitor of modern conservatism, see Herzog, *Poisoning the Mind of the Lower Orders*.

6. The precise form of the disengagement that the Conservatives seek is somewhat unclear. Much depends on whether other EU member states would permit Britain to reject the Constitutional Treaty and the euro while nonetheless remaining a full member. In the likely event that the EU refuses to allow Britain to reject the European Constitutional Treaty, the Conservative policy implies seeking either some form of associate membership or even complete withdrawal from EU institutions. The official position of the Conservative Party on Europe tends to change in line with the personal views of the leadership. For a recent expression of the leader's position, see Michael Howard, "A New Deal for Europe," speech at Berlin, February, 12, 2004: *http://www.conservatives.com/ news/article.cfm?obj_id=88336*.

7. Enoch Powell, *The Common Market: The Case Against* (Kingswood, UK: Elliot, 1971), 55.

8. Enoch Powell, *Reflections of a Statesman: The Writings and Speeches of Enoch Powell* (London: Bellew Publishing, 1991), 34–35.

9. Powell, *Reflections of a Statesman*, 167–72.

10. Powell, *Reflections of a Statesman*, 60.

11. Powell on England/Britain: "The relevant fact about the history of *the British Isles and above all England* is its separateness in a political sense from the history of continental Europe. The English have never belonged and have always known that they did not belong to it." Powell, *Reflections of a Statesman*, 34 (emphasis added). Powell then cites Henry VIII's assertion that "this realm of England is an imperium of itself." For Powell, the Reformation was primarily a political event: "The whole subsequent history of Britain and the political character of the British people have taken their color and trace their quality from that moment and that assertion."

12. Powell, *Common Market*, 67.

13. Powell, *Common Market*, 120.

14. More recent examples of this strand of conservative euroscepticism include John Redwood, *The Death of Britain* (New York: St. Martin's Press, 1999),

and Peter Hitchens, *The Abolition of Britain: From Winston Churchill to Princess Diana* (San Francisco: Encounter Books, 2002).

15. For a useful overview of these changes, see David Butler, Vernon Bogdanor, and Robert Summers, eds., *The Law, Politics and the Constitution* (Oxford: Oxford University Press, 1999).

16. Consider, for instance, Powell's discussion of Europe's capacity for an independent foreign and defense policy. Powell, *Common Market*, 43, 76.

17. The use of the plural "European societies" is important. It would simply beg the question against the nationalist eurosceptics if the "public values " were tied more closely to the practices and institutions of a common European society.

18. Britain's de facto national anthem—"Rule Britannia"—was, for example, composed only in 1740. There is an extensive literature on the English/British question. See, for example, Linda Colley, *Britons: Forging the Nation, 1707–1837* (New Haven, CT: Yale University Press, 1990); Norman Davies, *The Isles: A History* (Basingstoke, UK: Papermac, 1999); and Jeremy Black, *A New History of England* (Stroud, UK: Sutton Publishing, 2000).

19. Offe, "The Democratic Welfare State in an Integrating Europe," 85.

20. See David Miller, "The Nation-State: A Modest Defence," in Chris Brown, ed., *Political Restructuring in Europe: Ethical Perspectives* (London: Routledge, 1994); and David Miller, *On Nationality* (Oxford: Clarendon Press, 1995).

21. David Miller, "The Left, the Nation-State, and European Citizenship," *Dissent* (Summer 1998): 47–53.

22. Miller, "The Nation-State," 137.

23. Miller, "The Nation-State," 141.

24. Miller, *On Nationality*, 111.

25. Miller, *On Nationality*, 67.

26. Miller, *On Nationality*, 70.

CHAPTER 4

WELFARE

1. Karl Polanyi, *The Great Transformation* (Boston: Beacon Press, 2001 [1944]).

2. I have resorted to the contrasting terms *Rechtstaat* and *Sozialstaat* partly out of pretentiousness and partly because English lacks a contrasting term to welfare state. Neither the terms "nightwatchman state" nor "liberal state" capture what people (including Hayek and Habermas) have in mind when speaking of a *Rechtstaat*.

3. For an example of this perspective, see Gillingham, *European Integration*.

4. For a discussion, see Scharpf, *Governing in Europe*.

5. This is what Margaret Thatcher had in mind when she complained, in her Bruges speech: "We have not rolled back the frontiers of the state in Britain only to see them re-imposed at the European level, with a European Superstate,

exercising a new dominance from Brussels." In contrast to Thatcher's usage of the term "superstate"—a usage that Gillingham (*European Integration*), also adopts—I take the term to signify a unitary centralized state (like France) or a relatively centralized federal state (like the United States). For me, the term "European superstate" does not signify any type of economic policies, whether market conforming or market constraining.

6. For one of the few discussions that acknowledge that the economic policies of any future Europe ought to be a matter of choice, see the excellent book by Loukas Tsoukalis, *What Kind of Europe?*

7. Tony Judt, *A Grand Illusion* (New York: Hill and Wang, 1996), 97.

8. For descriptions and typologies of these differences, see Anderson, *Three Worlds of Welfare Capitalism*.

9. Consider, for instance, Adam Smith, *An Inquiry into the Nature and Causes of the Wealth of Nations* (Indianapolis: Liberty Press, 1976 [1776]).

10. Friedrich A. Hayek, "The Economic Conditions of Interstate Federalism," in *Individualism and Economic Order* (London: Routledge, 1948).

11. Hayek, "Economic Conditions of Interstate Federalism," 258.

12. Hayek, "Economic Conditions of Interstate Federalism," 260.

13. Hayek, "Economic Conditions of Interstate Federalism," 262.

14. Hayek, "Economic Conditions of Interstate Federalism," 263.

15. Hayek, "Economic Conditions of Interstate Federalism," 264.

16. Hayek, "Economic Conditions of Interstate Federalism," 266.

17. Miller, "The Left, the Nation-State, and European Citizenship," 47–53.

18. Margaret Thatcher, *The Downing Street Years* (New York: HarperCollins, 1993).

19. Smith, *Wealth of Nations*, 266–67.

20. As Adam Smith put the point in a letter to La Rochefoucauld in 1785: "In a Country where clamour always intimidates and faction often oppresses the Government, the regulations of Commerce are commonly dictated by those who are most interested to deceive and impose upon the Public." E. C.Mossner and I. S. Ross, eds., *The Correspondence of Adam Smith* (Indianapolis: Liberty Press, 1987).

21. Friedrich A. Hayek, *Law, Legislation and Liberty: The Mirage of Social Justice* (Chicago: University of Chicago Press, 1976).

22. Scharpf, *Governing in Europe*, 121.

23. Hayek, *Law, Legislation and Liberty*, ch. 9.

24. Scharpf, *Governing in Europe*, 30.

25. Jürgen Habermas, *The Inclusion of the Other* (Cambridge, MA: MIT Press, 1998); *The Postnational Constellation* (Cambridge, MA: MIT Press, 2001); "Why Does Europe Need a Constitution?" trans. Michele Everson, European Union Institute, 2001; "Der 15. Februar-oder: Was die Europäer verbindet," in *Der gespaltene Westen* (Frankfurt am Main: Suhrkamp, 2004).

26. Habermas, "Why Does Europe Need a Constitution?" 8.

27. Habermas, "Why Does Europe Need a Constitution?" 7.

28. Habermas, *The Inclusion of the Other*.

29. Habermas, *The Inclusion of the Other*, 116–17.

30. For critiques of Habermas's argument concerning the adequacy of a thin constitutional patriotism, compare Charles Larmore, *The Morals of Modernity* (Cambridge: Cambridge University Press, 1996), 205–21; Miller, *On Nationality*, 163–65; and, for a more extended discussion on the very idea of constitutional patriotism, Jan Werner Muller, *On Constitutional Patriotism* (Princeton, NJ: Princeton University Press, 2005).

31. "In view of the subversive forces and imperatives of the world market and of the increasing density of worldwide networks of communication and commerce, the external sovereignty of states . . . is by now . . . an anachronism." Habermas, *The Inclusion of the Other*, 150.

32. Habermas, *The Inclusion of the Other*, 106.

33. Habermas, "Why Does Europe Need a Constitution?" 8.

34. In "Der 15. Februar," Habermas extends this point to include a further set of distinctively European attributes. I say more about this text in the concluding section.

35. Göran Therborn, *European Modernity and Beyond* (London: Sage, 1995); compare also the document produced by the EU Commission.

36. Will Hutton, *The World We're In* (London: Little, Brown, 2002).

37. There is a vast literature on the topic of Europe's democratic deficit. See, for a representative sampling of different positions, Weiler, *The Constitution of Europe*; Dieter Grimm, "Does Europe Need a Constitution?" *European Law Journal* 3: 282–302; Moravcsik, "In Defence of Europe's Democratic Deficit"; and Larry Siedentop, *Democracy in Europe* (London: Penguin, 1999).

38. Hayek, *Law, Legislation and Liberty*.

39. Hayek, *Law, Legislation and Liberty*.

40. Hayek, *Law, Legislation and Liberty*, 70–71.

41. Hayek, *Law, Legislation and Liberty*, 68–69.

42. Isaiah Berlin, *Four Essays on Liberty* (London: Oxford University Press, 1969), 130.

43. John Gray, *Hayek on Liberty* (London: Routledge, 1998).

44. Hayek, *The Road to Serfdom*.

45. For an important discussion of this point, see Van Creveld, *Rise and Decline of the State*.

46. Habermas, *The Inclusion of the Other*, 157.

47. Habermas, *The Postnational Constellation*, 77.

48. These figures refer to unemployment levels as of December 2003.

49. The idea of a monocausal theory of unemployment is itself a profoundly misguided enterprise. Unemployment always has a variety of causes. See, for a more sophisticated account, Richard Layard et al., *The Unemployment Crisis* (Oxford: Oxford University Press, 1994).

50. To cite two of many possible examples: in the summer of 2004, Levi Strauss closed all its remaining manufacturing facilities in western Europe, including two factories in Spain, one in Scotland, and one in Belgium. As a company spokesman explained: "The costs of production of our two plants in Spain are double those of other factories that we have in Poland, Hungary, and Turkey." "Levi's culmina su repliegue en Europa occidental con el abandono de Espana," *El Pais* (Madrid) June 4, 2004, 75. In the very same week, Mainetti, the world's leading manufacturer of clothes hangers, closed all its production facilities in France and Spain in favor of new factories in Tunisia, Bangladesh, Hong Kong, Romania, Turkey, and Morrocco. "La crisis en el sector textile llega al mayor fabricante de perchas," *El Pais* (Madrid), June 7, 2004, 82.

51. Van Creveld, *Rise and Decline of the State*, 336–414.

52. *Lochner v. New York*, 198 U.S. 45, 75–76 (1905) (Holmes, O., dissenting).

53. For a description of the "Conservative Welfare Regime"—an ideal type that captures key features of the German and French welfare systems—and its principal differences from the "liberal welfare regime" and the "social democratic welfare regime," see Gosta Esping Anderson, *Social Foundations of Postindustrial Economies* (Oxford: Oxford University Press, 1999), 73–94.

54. Habermas, "Why Does Europe Need a Constitution?"

55. Habermas, "Der 15. Februar," 46.

56. Habermas, "Der 15. Februar," 48.

57. For more on this point, see Margarita Estevez Abe and Glyn Morgan, "Varieties of Capitalism: Varieties of Social Justice," Working Paper (2005), Minda da Ginzburg Center for European Studies, Harvard University. For some insightful criticisms of the EU thinking on economic matters, see Alberto Alesina and Roberti Perotti, "The European Union: A Politically Incorrect View," NBER Working Paper 10342 (available at *www.nber.org/papers/w10342*.)

CHAPTER 5
SECURITY

1. Noel Malcolm, "Sense on Sovereignty."

2. For very helpful overviews of the realist approach to international relations, see Jack Donnelly, *Realism and International Relations* (New York: Cambridge University Press, 2000); and Michael W. Doyle, *Ways of War and Peace: Realism, Liberalism,and Socialism* (New York: Norton, 2002).

3. Hans J. Morgenthau, *Politics among Nations* (New York: A. A. Knopf, 1948); compare also the same author's *The Purpose of American Politics* (New York: Knopf, 1960), and *Scientific Man vs. Power Politics* (Chicago: University of Chicago Press, 1974).

4. Kenneth Waltz's most important writings include *Man, the State, and War: A Theoretical Analysis* (New York: Columbia University Press, 1964), *A Theory of International Politics* (Reading, MA: Addison-Wesley, 1979), "The Emerging

Structure of International Politics," *International Security* 18 (1993): 50–78, "Globalization and Governance," *PS* 32 (1999): 693–700, and "Structural Realism after the Cold War," *International Security* 25 (2000): 5–41.

5. For a useful collection of representative views, see David A. Baldwin, ed., *Neorealism and and Neoliberalism: The Contemporary Debate* (New York: Columbia University Press, 1993).

6. Waltz, "Emerging Structure of International Politics," 74.

7. Waltz, "Structural Realism after the Cold War," 27.

8. Waltz, A *Theory of International Politics*, 126; Waltz, "Emerging Structure of International Politics," 38.

9. See here, for example, Robert J. Art, "Why Western Europe Needs the United States and NATO," *Political Science Quarterly* 111 (1996): 1–39.

10. Following the end of the Cold War, a number of structural realists, including Waltz, speculated on the likely response to US "unipolarity." Important statements of the structural realist position include Christopher Layne, "The Unipolar Illusion: Why New Great Powers Will Rise," *International Security* 17 (1993): 5–51; John J. Mearsheimer, "Back to the Future: Instability in Europe after the Cold War," *International Security* 15 (1990): 5–56; Waltz "Emerging Structure of International Politics." Waltz's more recent contributions to this debate include "Globalization and Governance" and "Structural Realism after the Cold War." For a useful overview of this debate, see the contributions to G. John Ikenberry, ed., *America Unrivaled: The Future of the Balance of Power* (Ithaca, NY: Cornell University Press, 2002).

11. Waltz, "Structural Realism after the Cold War," 28.

12. Waltz, "Structural Realism after the Cold War," 32.

13. Andrew Moravcsik, "Taking Preferences Seriously: A Liberal Theory of International Politics," *International Organization* 51 (1997): 513–24.

14. Moravcsik, "Taking Preferences Seriously," 519.

15. Moravcsik, *The Choice for Europe*.

16. Moravcsik, "In Defence of the Democratic Deficit."

17. See Chalmers Johnson, *Blowback: The Costs and Consequences of American Empire* (New York: Metropolitan Books, 2000), 175–192.

18. Robert Kagan, "Power and Weakness," *Policy Review* 113 (2002): 6.

19. John Stuart Mill, *On Liberty* (Cambridge: Cambridge University Press, 1993 [1851]), 81.

20. David A. Baldwin, "The Concept of Security," *Review of International Studies* 23 (1997): 5–26.

21. See, for example, Barry Buzan, *People, States, and Fear: An Agenda for International Security Studies in the Post–Cold War Era*, second edition (Hemel Hempstead, UK: Harvester Wheatsheaf, 1991); Bary Buzan, Ole Waever, and Jaap de Wilde, *Security: A New Framework for Analysis* (Boulder, CO: Lynne Rienner, 1998); and Ole Waever, "Securitization and Desecuritization," in Ronnie D. Lipshutz, ed., *On Security* (New York: Columbia University Press, 1995). For

criticisms of these broader conceptions of security, see Baldwin, "The Concept of Security"; Stephen M. Walt, "The Renaissance of Security Studies," *International Studies Quarterly* 35 (1991): 211–39; and Bill McSweeney, *Security, Identity and Interests: A Sociology of International Relations* (Cambridge: Cambridge University Press, 1999). For a useful overview of this debate, see Olav F. Knudsen, "Post-Copenhagen Security Studies: Desecuritizing Securitization," *Security Dialogue* 32 (2001): 355–68.

22. My account of the place of the concept of "security" in the history of western political thought relies heavily on Emma Rothschild, "What Is Security?" *Daedalus* 124 (1995): 53–98. I am also indebted to a number of important unpublished writings by Melissa Lane and Jeremy Waldron on the concept of security.

23. Hobbes, *Leviathan*, 231.

24. Smith, *Wealth of Nations*, vol. 1, book III, 376–427.

25. John Stuart Mill, *Principles of Political Economy* (London: Longmans, Green and Co., 1909), book 4, ch. 1, 697

26. John Stuart Mill, "Utilitarianism," in *On Liberty and Other Essays* (Oxford: Oxford University Press, 1991), 190.

27. Rothschild, "What Is Security," 59.

28. Rothschild, "What Is Security," 61.

29. Jean Jacques Rousseau, "On the Social Contract," in *Basic Political Writings of Jean Jacques Rousseau* (Indianapolis: Hacket, 1987), 144.

30. For a related argument concerning "natural rights," see Richard Tuck, "The Dangers of Natural Rights," *Harvard Journal of Law and Public Policy* 20 (1997): 683–93.

31. The term "basic societal values" includes but is broader than "political legitimacy." For more on this issue, see Glyn Morgan, "Security and Political Legitimacy," in Melissa Lane and Glyn Morgan, eds., *Security: Political and Philosophical Perspectives* (Cambridge University Press, forthcoming).

32. John Locke, *Two Treatises of Government* (Indianapolis: Hacket, 1987), 50.

33. Cited from an interview in *Nation* (Bangkok), March 8, 1999, A5.

34. Jeremy Waldron, "Security and Liberty," *Journal of Political Philosophy* 11 (2003): 191–210.

35. For the concept of "pluralistic security communities," see Karl W. Deutsch, *Political Community and the North Atlantic Area: International Organization in the Light of Historical Experience* (Princeton, NJ: Princeton University Press, 1957). More recent discussions include the contributions to Emanuel Adler and Michael Barnett, eds., *Security Communities* (Cambridge: Cambridge University Press, 1998).

36. Baldwin, "The Concept of Security."

37. Van Creveld, *Rise and Decline of the State*.

38. Hedley Bull, *The Anarchical Society: A Study of Order in World Politics* (New York: Columbia University Press, 1995).

39. While the approach to "world order" adopted here is indebted to Bull's writings, the distinction between "world order," "international state system," and "international society" is not faithful to Bull's own usage of these terms; nor is it meant as either an interpretation or a corrective of Bull's international relations theory. I merely claim that this tripartite distinction is useful for conceptualizing and evaluating arguments that claim that European political integration would bolster security.

40. Bull, *Anarchical Society*, 4.

CHAPTER 6
A POSTSOVEREIGN EUROPE

1. Weiler, "Europe's *Sonderweg*."

2. MacCormick, *Questioning Sovereignty*.

3. Among the many contemporary political philosophers who have written favorably about this postsovereign polity, compare William Connolly, *Identity/ Difference: Democratic Negotiations of Political Paradox* (Minneapolis: University of Minnesota Press, 2002; Bhikhu Parekh, *Rethinking Multiculturalism: Cultural Diversity and Political Theory* (Cambridge, MA: Harvard University Press, 2000); and—perhaps most influentially—Tully, *Strange Multiplicity*; "The Agonic Freedom of Citizens"; and "The Unfreedom of the Moderns."

4. Jo Shaw, "Post-national Constitutionalism in the European Union," *Journal of European Public Policy* 6 (1999): 479–597, and "Flexibility in a Reorganized and Simplified Treaty," *Common Market Law Review*, 40 (2002): 279–311.

5. MacCormick, *Questioning Sovereignty*.

6. MacCormick, *Questioning Sovereignty*, 128.

7. Neil MacCormick, "A Comment on the Governance Paper," *Jean Monnet Working Papers* 06/01 (available at *http://www.jeanmonnetprogram.org/papers/01/012501.html*).

8. For a comprehensive discussion of the concept of "subsidiarity," see Andreas Føllesdal, "Subsidiarity," *Journal of Political Philosophy* 6 (1998): 231–59.

9. MacCormick, *Questioning Sovereignty*, ch. 12.

10. Weiler, *The Constitution of Europe*, 200; and Weiler, "Europe's *Sonderweg*."

11. Weiler, *The Constitution of Europe*, 343.

12. Weiler, *The Constitution of Europe*, ch 2.

13. Weiler, "Europe's Sonderweg," 70.

14. Weiler, "Europe's *Sonderweg*," 68.

15. The Draft Constitutional Treaty still falls short of providing for an unambiguous *pouvoir constituant* (or "we the people"). The treaty speaks of European citizens and Europe's member states as cofounders.

16. Weiler, "Europe's *Sonderweg*," 68.

17. Weiler, *The Constitution of Europe*, 301.

18. Weiler, "Europe's *Sonderweg*," 66.

19. Weiler, *The Constitution of Europe*, 336.

20. For an insightful discussion of these issues, see Scharpf, *Governing in Europe*.

21. For the impact that the EU stability pact has had on Portugal, the poorest country in the EU-15, see Peter Wise, "What has the European Union ever done for us?" *Financial Times*, July 29, 2002, 3.

22. *Johann Gottfried Herder: Another Philosophy of History and Selected Political Writings*, Ioannis D. Evrigenis and Daniel Pellerin, eds. (Indianapolis: Hackett, 2004).

23. Weiler, *The Constitution of Europe*, 338ff.

24. Weiler, *The Constitution of Europe*, 342.

25. Weiler, *The Constitution of Europe*, 342.

26. MacCormick, *Questioning Sovereignty*, 183.

27. MacCormick, *Questioning Sovereignty*, 183.

28. Jeremy Waldron, "Multiculturalism and the Cosmopolitan Alternative," in Will Kymlicka, ed., *The Rights of Minority Cultures* (Oxford: Oxford University Press, 1996).

29. For an example of a Scottish nationalist who remains enamored of sovereignty, see Tom Nairn, *Scotland and Britain* (London: Verso Books, 2000).

30. Schmitter, *How to Democratize the European Union*.

31. Schmitter, *How to Democratize the European Union*, 18.

32. Philippe C. Schmiter, "What Is There to Legitimize in the European Union . . . and How Might This Be Accomplished?" *Jean Monnet Working Papers* 06/01 (available at *http://www.jeanmonnetprogram.org/papers/01/011401.html*), 7.

33. Tully, *Strange Multiplicity*; and Tully, "The Unfreedom of the Moderns."

34. Tully, *Strange Multiplicity*, 30.

35. Tully, "The Unfreedom of the Moderns," 4.

36. Philip Pettit, *Republicanism: A Theory of Freedom and Government* (Oxford: Clarendon Press, 1997); Philip Pettit, *A Theory of Freedom* (Oxford: Polity Press, 2003); and Bellamy, "Sovereignty."

37. Pettit, *A Theory of Freedom*, 139.

38. Pettit, *A Theory of Freedom*, 139.

39. Bellamy, "Sovereignty," and Bellamy, 'The Right to Have Rights.'"

40. Bellamy, "Sovereignty," 184.

41. Bellamy, "Sovereignty," 188.

42. Alexis de Tocqueville, *Democracy in America*, J. P. Mayer, ed., George Laurence, trans. (Garden City, NY: Doubleday, 1969), 170.

43. Robert Keohane, "Ironies of Sovereignty": the European Union and the United States, *Journal of Common Market Studies* 40 (2002): 743–65.

44. MacCormick, *Questioning Sovereignty*, 142.

45. Schmitter, *How to Democratize the European Union*, 19.

46. Duchene, "Europe in World Peace," and Duchene, "The EC and the

Uncertainities of Interdependence." I have more to say about the concept of "civilian-power Europe" in the next chapter.

47. For a more recent exploration of these ideas, see Therborn, *European Modernity and Beyond*, and Göran Therborn, "Europe—Superpower or a Scandinavia of the World?" in Mario Tèlo, ed., *European Union and New Regionalism: Regional Actors and Global Governance in a Post-hegemonic Era* (Aldershot: Ashgate, 2001).

48. Jan Zielonka, *Explaining Euro-paralysis: Why Europe Is Unable to Act in International Politics* (New York: St. Martin's Press, 1998).

49. Zielonka, *Explaining Euro-paralysis*, 229.

50. Hedley Bull, "Civilian Power Europe: A Contradiction in Terms," in Loukas Tsoukalis, ed., *The European Community: Past, Present and Future* (Oxford: Basil Blackwell, 1983).

51. Zielonka, *Explaining Euro-paralysis*, 228; compare here also Robert Cooper, *The Post-modern State and the World Order*, second edition (London: The Foreign Policy Centre, 2000), and *The Breaking of Nations: Order and Chaos in the Twenty-First Century* (London: Atlantic Books, 2003).

52. For a trenchant discussion, see Brendan Simms, *Unfinest Hour: Britain and the Destruction of Bosnia* (London: Allen Lane, 2001).

53. For a more skeptical view of "civilian-power Europe," see Stelios Stavridis, "'Militarising' the EU: The Concept of Civilian Power Europe Revisited," *International Spectator* 36: 43–50.

54. See here Waltz, "Emerging Structure of International Politics," Waltz, "Structural Realism after the Cold War;" and John J. Mearsheimer, *The Tragedy of Great Power Politics* (New York: Norton, 2001).

CHAPTER 7

A SOVEREIGN EUROPE

1. Stanley Benn, "The Uses of Sovereignty," in Anthony Quinton, ed., *Political Philosophy* (Oxford: Oxford University Press, 1967), 82.

2. Malcolm, "Sense on Sovereignty."

3. Malcolm, "Sense on Sovereignty," 352.

4. Malcolm, "Sense on Sovereignty," 352.

5. Malcolm, "Sense on Sovereignty," 352.

6. Malcolm, "Sense on Sovereignty," 360.

7. Malcolm, "Sense on Sovereignty," 361.

8. Malcolm, "Sense on Sovereignty," 362.

9. Neil MacCormick, as we saw in the previous chapter, makes precisely this argument. See MacCormick, *Questioning Sovereignty*, ch. 12.

10. Malcolm, "Sense on Sovereignty," 364.

11. Malcolm, "Sense on Sovereignty," 364.

12. For useful discussions of this aspect of sovereignty, see Stephen Krasner, *Sovereignty: Organized Hypocrisy* (Princeton, NJ: Princeton University Press, 1999); and MacCormick, *Questioning Sovereignty*.

13. For the insight that there is an important conventionalist aspect to sovereignty, I am indebted to Krasner, *Sovereignty*, and W. G. Werner and J. H. de Wilde, "The Endurance of Sovereignty," *European Journal of International Relations* 7 (2001): 283–313.

14. For a useful discussion of this and other aspects of sovereignty, see Raymond Geuss, *History and Illusion in Politics* (Cambridge: Cambridge University Press, 2000).

15. Robert Jackson, *Quasi-States* (Cambridge: Cambridge University Press, 1996).

16. Werner and de Wilde, The Endurance of Sovereignty."

17. Waltz, *Theory of International Politics*.

18. Krasner, *Sovereignty*.

19. To recall the distinctions made in the introductory chapter: The term "federal" has two diametrically opposed meanings. I use "federal" here—much in the same way Eurosceptics do—to refer to a relatively unitary and centralized European polity. This usage is a perversion of the original term *federal*, which referred to a decentralized polity that parceled out powers to different regionally or functionally organized groups.

20. Waltz, "Structural Realism after the Cold War, 915.

21. For a more detailed assessment of the divergences in values between the United States, "Old Europe," and "New Europe," see Glyn Morgan, ed., *The Ideas in Anti-Americanism* (Princeton University Press, forthcoming).

22. For a discussion of the innovations in Bush's foreign policy, see Daalder and Lindsay, *America Unbound.*

23. Prodi quoted in *Economist*, April 24, 2003.

24. "Blair calls for Euro 'superpower,'" *Guardian*, October 7, 2000.

25. For useful discussions of this aspect of America's history, see Samuel H. Beer, *To Make a Nation: The Rediscovery of American Federalism* (Cambridge, MA: Harvard University Press, 1993); Keohane, "Ironies of Sovereignty"; and Fareed Zakaria, *From Wealth to Power: The Unusual Origins of America's World Role* (Princeton, NJ: Princeton University Press, 1998).

26. James Madison, *Vices of the Political System of the United States*, in William T. Hutchinson et al., eds., *The Papers of James Madison* (Chicago and London: University of Chicago Press, 1962–77), vol. 9, 348–57.

27. For a useful range of arguments on this topic, see Charles Tilly, *Coercion, Capital and European States, AD 990–1990* (Oxford: Blackwell, 1990); Mann, *Sources of Social Power*; and Spruyt, *The Sovereign State and Its Competitors*.

28. Spruyt, *The Sovereign State and Its Competitors*.

29. In order for the argument to be decisive, it would be necessary to weigh more carefully the relative gravity of the threats that Europeans face from re-

taining the current intergovernmental status quo and shifting to a unitary federal Europe. Even if one were to think—as I do—that Europeans could enhance their security in a federal European polity, this does not mean that Europeans ought to immediately set up such a polity. There are more prudent and less prudent ways of planning the process of European political integration. I say more about the process of European integration in the following chapter.

30. For helpful discussions of recent developments, see Deighton, "The European Security and Defense Policy"; and Mette Eilstrup Sangiovanni, "Why a Common Military and Defense Policy Is Bad for Europe," *Survival* 45 (2003): 193–206. I discuss Sangiovanni's argument in detail in the following chapter.

31. For an optimistic assessment of Europe's current strengths, see Moravcsik, "The Quiet Superpower."

32. Moravcsik, "The Quiet Superpower."

33. For a useful popular summary, see Joseph Nye, *The Paradox of American Power: Why the World's Only Superpower Can't Go It Alone* (New York: Oxford University Press, 2002).

34. Keohane, "Ironies of Sovereignty," 748.

35. For provocative arguments to this effect, see Robert Kagan, *Paradise and Power* (New York: Knopf, 2003).

36. Keohane, "Ironies of Sovereignty," 762.

37. For a useful overview, see Tony Judt, "America and the World," *New York Review of Books*, April 10, 2003.

38. These differences are apparent from the regular Pew surveys. For a more general assessment of these divergences, see Glyn Morgan, "The Ideas in Anti-Americanism." (Princeton University Press, forthcoming).

39. As Rumsfeld put it, "I said last year [2001] that the mission defines the coalition, and I think that this was not only a correct statement, but it has been an enormously helpful concept in this war on terror." Quoted in Ivo H. Daalder, "The End of Atlanticism," *Survival* 45 (2003): 156.

40. For a scathing assessment, see Simms, *Unfinest Hour*.

41. Malcolm, "Sense on Sovereignty," 352.

42. Hobbes, *Leviathan*, ch. 30, p. 376.

43. Rousseau, "On War," cited from Richard Tuck, *The Rights of War and Peace* (Cambridge: Cambridge University Press, 1999), 203.

Conclusion

1. For a useful account, see Samuel Huntington, *American Politics: The Promise of Disharmony* (Cambridge, MA: Belknap Press of Harvard University, 1981).

2. Sangiovanni, "Why a Common Security and Defense Policy Is Bad for Europe."

3. This document is available at *http://www.whitehouse.gov/nsc/nss.pdf*.

* Index *

abortion, 44

accessibility requirement, 18, 25, 33, 36–38, 41, 181n31

accountability, 38

Ackerman, Bruce, 24–25, 28, 178n5, 179n7

active citizenship, 103, 124. *See also* civic republicanism

Adler, Emmanuel, 192n35

Afghanistan, 138, 158

Africa, 138

Alesina, Alberto, 190n57

Al Qaeda, 158

Alstott, Anne, 179n7

Andersen, Gosta Esping, 178n7, 188n8, 190n53

anti-Americanism, 21

Archibugi, Daniele, 177n50

Arendt, Hannah, 123

Arnull, Anthony, 173n18

Art, Robert, 191n9

Ash, Timothy Garton, 174n31

assimilation, 53, 54

Atlantic Alliance, 20, 166, 167. *See also* NATO

Austin, John, 112

Austria, 6, 83

Baldwin, David, 191n5, 192n21

bare citizen, 34–36, 43, 62, 86–87, 103–4, 110

Basques, 119

Beer, Samuel, 196n25

Beetham, David, 177n57, 178n58

Beiner, Ronald, 184n16

Belgium, 68, 83, 190n50

Bell, David, 185n20

Bellamy, Richard, 125–26, 175n38, 176n50, 178n58, 179n15, 194n39

Benelux countries, 6

Benn, Stanley, 195n1

Bentham, Jeremy, 112

Berlin, Isaiah, 82

Bertram, Christopher, 36, 181n30

Black, Jeremy, 187n18

Blair, Tony, 9, 12, 147, 174n23, 175n33, 196n24

Bogdanor, Vernon, 187n15

Boltanski, Luc, 179n8

Booker, Christopher, 185n2

Bosnia, 130, 154

Britain, 1, 6, 8, 9–11, 21, 127, 82–83, 122, 134, 136–39, 148, 150; eurosceptics and, 1, 20, 58–64, 136, 154; parliamentary sovereignty and, 61–62, 148

Brittan, Leon, 173n20

Brittany, Bretons, 119

Brown, Chris, 187n20

Brubaker, Rogers, 184n16

Bulgaria, 6

Bull, Hedley 107, 129, 131, 150, 192n38, 193n39, 195n50

Burca, Grainne de, 173n18

Burgess, Michael, 182n34

Burke, Edmund, 26, 179n11, 186n5

Bush, George, W., 146

Butler, David, 187n15

Buzan, Barry, 191n21

Calhoun, Craig, 186n3

California, 15

Canada, 115, 122

Canavan, Margaret, 43, 185n19

Castiglioni, Dario, 175n38, 176n50, 178n58, 179n15

Catalonia, Catalans, 113, 119

Central America, 140

Chalmers, Damien, 177n50

China, 128, 144, 158

Christianity, 36

Cicero, 100